"Gerhard Lohfink offers yet another new text that is fully biblical, theological, liturgical, and practical in his presentation of Christian theology for our time. *Between Heaven and Earth* ranges across the Scriptures and the liturgical life of the church with insights that are thoroughly traditional and startlingly new. Radiantly translated by his student Dr. Linda Maloney, every page challenges the reader to reconsider, to pray again scriptural texts that have too soon been filed under 'been there, studied that' in our minds. Lohfink's paragraphs sharpen knowledge and faith with a 'both/and' dialectic that is harder to put down than a favorite novel."

— Dr. Eileen C. Burke-Sullivan
Vice President for Mission and Ministry
Heaney Chair in Pastoral, Liturgical Theology
Creighton University

Gerhard Lohfink

Between Heaven
and Earth

New Explorations of Great Biblical Texts

Translated by

Linda M. Maloney

LITURGICAL PRESS
Collegeville, Minnesota

www.litpress.org

1	2	3	4	5	6	7	8	9

Library of Congress Cataloging-in-Publication Data

Names: Lohfink, Gerhard, 1934– author. | Maloney, Linda M., translator.
Title: Between heaven and earth : new explorations of great Biblical texts / Gerhard Lohfink ; translated by Linda M. Maloney.
Other titles: Ausgespannt zwischen Himmel und Erde. English
Description: Collegeville, Minnesota : Liturgical Press, [2022] | "Gerhard Lohfink, Ausgespannt zwischen Himmel und Erde. Grosse Bibeltexte neu erkundet, 2021 Verlag Herder GmbH, Freiburg im Breisgau." | Summary: "In this book Gerhard Lohfink interprets a spectrum of biblical texts, some familiar, others not. He explores them in a spirit of curiosity, questions them insistently, and confronts them with the realities of our present day, from COVID-19 to the inner loneliness experienced by so many"— Provided by publisher.
Identifiers: LCCN 2021057396 (print) | LCCN 2021057397 (ebook) | ISBN 9780814667323 (hardcover) | ISBN 9780814667330 (epub) | ISBN 9780814667330 (pdf)
Subjects: LCSH: Bible—Meditations
Classification: LCC BS491.5 .L6413 2022 (print) | LCC BS491.5 (ebook) | DDC 242/.5—dc23/eng/20220126
LC record available at https://lccn.loc.gov/2021057396
LC ebook record available at https://lccn.loc.gov/2021057397

For Linda Maloney
in gratitude

Contents

Part III: In the Joy of Faith

Foreword

Believers stand before an infinite horizon. They look up to heaven and yet they are firmly fixed on earth. They wonder at the immeasurability of the universe and stare in amazement at a tiny flower. They know the depths of the human heart and they are consoled by an infant's smile.

They focus on individuals and yet they have understood that God needs a people in the world. They have recognized that they have to do everything themselves and they constantly realize that all is grace. They live wholly in the moment and yet they reach out toward "the one who is to come." They know they are dust and at the same time are infinitely beloved of their Creator. They believe in judgment but equally in the endless depths of God's mercy. They have countless mothers and fathers in faith—but what is decisive is their life in Christ.

Everything experienced since Abraham in the unceasing experiment of faith stands in the one, unique Book—and yet their faith is not a religion of the book; it is rejoicing in the Holy Spirit. Again and again they are fascinated by the way the church's faith is profoundly rational and they are happy that, at the same time, this faith transcends all reason in the mystery of the triune God.

Those who believe in Jesus Christ are earth-rooted but not earthbound: they are also stretching toward heaven. Even children and youth can sense the wingspan of faith, but they cannot measure it yet. For that we need a whole life. We need sisters and brothers who join us in the journey toward God, and we need a living relationship with Sacred Scripture so that we can understand it better and better and dare to live it.

Accordingly, the following texts are addressed not only to those far off who are interested in getting a better idea of Jesus Christ and his message. They are directed equally, and even more, to Christians who long to understand the Bible better and more deeply. I wish my readers much excitement and joy as they make their journey through Scripture on the paths traveled in this book.

I dedicate the book in gratitude to my former student in Tübingen, the Reverend Doctor Linda Maloney. She has been back in the United States for a long time and is a tireless worker like those named in Romans 16:12. Alongside all her professional duties she eloquently and skillfully translates my books into English.

6 January 2021   Gerhard Lohfink

Part I

Basics

Meaningless Existence in the Universe?

The well-known British author Ian McEwan, in a novel simply entitled *Saturday*, describes a single day—a dramatic Saturday in the life of the neurosurgeon Henry Perowne. It is part of his job to open skulls and probe deeply into the greyish-white substance of the brain; he does this routinely. Perowne considers himself a materialist. In the very first pages of the novel he begins to reflect on people who believe in God, but he does not call them "believers in God." His expression is "the supernaturally inclined." He tries to locate them in psychiatric terms, thus:

All these "supernaturally inclined" people (in the context the reader can only picture Muslims and Christians) suffer from an "excess of the subjective," ordering the world "in line with [their] needs." They are sick, and their sickness consists in a refusal to contemplate their own "unimportance." So they create a bombastic system of relationships involving such things as God, creation, ascension, eternal life.

This system of relationships, which is really a delusion, enables them to regard themselves as infinitely important and meaningful. In reality the human being is an utterly insignificant speck of dust in a cold and empty universe, but the "supernaturally inclined" refuse to accept that. Hence the insane system they have created, which is supposed to comfort them! Hence the striving to create metaphysical mountains out of humanity's absolute insignificance—carried to the point that it becomes a sickness! At the extreme end of their system, and of all religious systems, "rearing like an abandoned temple, lies psychosis."[1]

---

[1] Ian McEwan, *Saturday* (New York: Random House, 2005), 16–17.

Certainly our brain surgeon does not formulate his thoughts with such sharp definition. He is not an aggressive atheist but a genteel and sympathetic scientist. Still, there can be no doubt of his profound skepticism. Our future is not determined by "an all-knowing supernatural force." There is no "kindly childloving God," and "appetites" are "sated in this world, not the next." Therefore: "Rather shop than pray."[2]

All these associations run through Henry Perowne's mind in the very first hours of that Saturday on which the novel takes place. The day will then develop dramatically.

A Delusion?

If we were thrown together with that neurosurgeon, how could we engage him in conversation? Should we tell him that it is not believers in God who live in a world of delusion but possibly he himself? Could it be that precisely those who deny God are suffering from a short-sightedness that prevents clear thinking? To take just one example: Don't determined atheists avoid the question of why the universe, or the world, exists at all?—why there is something and not nothing? Christians have a reasonable answer to this fundamental question. Atheists have to constantly repress it or give inane answers such as: the universe has simply existed forever, or: it came about accidentally, all by itself.

Could it be that there are people who deny God only because they cannot bear not to be God themselves? To put it a little differently: They themselves want to be in charge, to have power, to be their own law. That in itself means living a delusion. When Raymond Kurzweil, Director of Engineering at Google, was once asked whether there is a God, he responded: "Not yet!" His answer reveals humans' burning desire to play God and to make everything—really everything—that is technologically possible, no matter the consequences.

There does not seem to be much sense to such arguments. We would only be throwing back the stone tossed at us, and we could argue forever about which side is really living in an unreal paradigm that refuses to recognize the reality of the world or even perverts it.

---

[2] McEwan, *Saturday*, 32, 73, 127.

The Power of Jesus

When I have to deal with such questions I ultimately turn to a relatively simple procedure: I consider, one by one, the great figures in world history—those the philosopher Karl Jaspers called the "paradigmatic individuals." At the end I have nobody left but Jesus, the one who says of himself in the last chapter of Matthew's gospel: "All authority in heaven and on earth has been given to me" (Matt 28:18). What is this hidden power by which Jesus has continually been at work in history for nearly two thousand years?

It is not political power. It is not the power of armaments, atomic weapons, or swifter research. It is most certainly not the power of capital, nor is it that of the masses who protest in the great city squares. It is definitely not the power of propaganda and potent words, skillful indoctrination and seduction.

Jesus' power is of a different kind. It is simply that he is the "truth" (John 14:6). Jesus is the truth in the sense that he alone has the solution to human suffering and the dire distress of society. His solution lies in communities in which people freely join their lives with those of others and live according to the Sermon on the Mount. There is no other solution for the world's misery. Everything else has long since been tried: egoism that makes the self the center of the world and only asks: "What is good *for me*?"; hedonism that seeks human happiness in momentary thrills, in acquisition and consumption; individualism that says "Everyone for him- or herself! Don't trust anybody!"; communism and fascism, which turn people into a collective and try to force them to enjoy it.

The nineteenth and twentieth centuries were a chain of unending experiments in what is best for humanity—and all of them had dreadful consequences: the death or anonymous suffering of many millions. The only way for people to be able to live together in peace and freedom is Jesus' Sermon on the Mount, lived out in communities that follow his path. Jesus really brought the solution: that is his "power."

Free from Oneself

On a deeper level Jesus' power consists in his wanting nothing for himself. All and everything he wanted was for God's plan to succeed:

he lived entirely for the gathering and renewal of the people of God in which every individual as such is precious and irreplaceable—and still is truly a people. Because Jesus was free *from* himself, he was free *for* God, and so God was able to act through him and in him to become Presence for the world.

This is a gentle, even meek power that lifts human beings into their own freedom—quite the opposite of the power wielded by the authorities of this world. This kind of "power" cannot be seized, cannot be achieved by conquest, cannot be finagled. It can only be "given." That is why, in that powerful scene at the end of Matthew's gospel, speaking as the Crucified One whom God has raised up to heaven, Jesus can say: "All authority in heaven and on earth has been given to me."

When I let the paradigmatic individuals of this world pass before my eyes I behold admirable men and women from whom I can learn, but none who has such power, such truth, such clarity, such knowledge of human beings and the world—and at the same time exudes such a fascination, one that does not seduce but bestows ultimate freedom.

The Christian Paradigm

Thus faith in the God of Jesus Christ is not some paradigm that we Christians thought up in order to be able to see ourselves as important within the infinity of the universe. Our paradigm is uniquely Jesus of Nazareth—and those who came before him, since Abraham. We are following not a projection but, rather, an experience that has been a thousand times tested, proved, suffered through in the world and its history, and has found its summit and goal in this Jesus.

What, then, of the accusation that we refuse to accept the insignificance of humanity within the universe? That charge reveals the absence of any notion of what the biblical tradition really says. We Christians admit with the utmost seriousness that we really are altogether meaningless. We are leaves on the breeze, dust in the cosmos, ultimately nothing but a handful of earth. On Ash Wednesday we receive a cross of ashes drawn on our foreheads and hear

"Remember that you are dust and to dust you shall return."

Yet at the same time we believe that we are beloved of God and, with Christ, are already "seated with him in the heavenly places" (Eph 2:6). That is precisely what we celebrate on the feast of the Ascension. This book will be about recognizing and appreciating this state of being unbound between heaven and earth.

From Adam's Rib

Genesis 2:4-25 tells how God forms the human being out of the soil of the field, breathes the breath of life into its nostrils, and gives it the Garden of Eden as its dwelling. A little later God creates a woman by placing the human creature in a deep sleep, removing one of its ribs, and shaping the woman from it.

When I was ten years old I thought it funny that God would have acted like a surgeon and snipped out Adam's rib. Today I am in awe of the text. I no longer hear it naïvely, and most certainly not in fundamentalist fashion.

Fundamentalists have to read the story in Genesis 2:4-25 as an historical account and imagine God as anesthetist and surgeon, but we have the marvelous freedom to appreciate the story of the creation of the man and the woman at the beginning of the Bible critically and appropriately. That means the images can really remain *pictures* for us, and that is precisely how we can understand their theological intent. This is what gives the images their power and truth.

Sacred Scripture begins with *two* creation narratives that are completely different. That is how they show us that they are meant to be read rightly. The first narrative is in Genesis 1:1–2:4a, the second in Genesis 2:4b-25. Anyone who reads these two texts as documentary reports falls into an irresolvable conflict with the fact of evolution. Supposedly, when the wife of a nineteenth-century Anglican Bishop of Worcester was told about Charles Darwin and his theory of evolution she cried out: "Dear me, let us hope it is not true, but if it is true, let us hope it does not become widely known!"

We need not have such naïve anxiety. If we let the images in the creation stories remain *images* we will have no difficulty with evolution, and what is much more important, we will really grasp something about the human mystery.

Humans and Animals

Let us consider one of the magnificent images in Genesis 2: God forms "every animal of the field and every bird of the air" out of the ground in order to create a "helper" for the human being—a helper as "partner," or "counterpart," one who is its "equal" and will put an end to its loneliness. Then God presents all the beasts to the human creature, one by one. But the attempt fails; it does not achieve its goal. It is true that the human gives each animal a name, that is, puts the world in order around it and by naming that world creates it anew. The human being "conceives" the world, orders it in terms of concepts, and so understands it. But there is no being to be found that corresponds to the human.

What an image—so long as we understand it as an *image*! The all-knowing and all-powerful God makes an effort, experiments, and attempts solutions that fail. Here the text is very close to the phenomenon of evolution, which aims toward a goal but makes its way by means of "trial and error."

Certainly the image reveals something more: if the human creature cannot find the deeply desired partner in any animal, the chief aim of the text is to say that the human being is different, is more than all the animals. Geneticists are right to say that 98 percent of our genetic material is the same as that of chimpanzees, but natural scientists are not talking about the Spirit of God, who encompassed the yet-unformed world from the beginning and whom God the creator (again in pictorial terms) breathed into the human as "the breath of life." Natural scientists do not talk about that Spirit, and they cannot because of the limitations of their methods. That is: as soon as they assert that the "whole of reality" can be described and explained in every detail by the methods of natural science they are making a basic choice that remains nothing more than a postulate.

But our text continues: what God intended with the animals— a being "equal" to the human—was not achieved. In terms of our current way of viewing the world it means that the human being is not yet a social creature. Socio-biologically speaking it already lives in herds, howls with the pack, hunts with the pride, hurls itself at the beast that has been slain and shares the spoils—but what constitutes personal communion is not yet reality, or is so only in its rudimentary beginnings.

"Male and Female"

So God takes a rib from the human being and builds it into a woman and brings her to the *ādām*, the man, who breaks into a jubilant cry. His prosaic words are shaped in Hebrew into a poetic text. The man cries:

> *This at last is bone of my bones*
> *and flesh of my flesh!* (Gen 2:23)

Feminists of both genders are deeply unsatisfied with this picture. They scent male lust for domination and the worst kind of patriarchal pretensions. To say that the man was there first and the woman was created from the man's rib appears to reveal the arrogant sense of male superiority that clings to such texts.

But we can understand the text differently by reading it within the whole of the Bible. Previously, in Genesis 1:1–2:4, there was a first, comprehensive story of creation that envisioned no kind of male priority; instead, it simply says:

> *So God created humankind in his image,*
> *in the image of God he created them;*
> *male and female he created them.* (Gen 1:27)

Besides: do we have to instantly imagine a battle of the sexes when it is said that the woman was taken from the man's side? A Jewish commentary comes much closer to the point:

> *God did not create the woman from the man's head, so that she would rule over him, and not from his feet, so that she would be his slave, but from his side, so that she would be close to his heart.*

Moreover, later in the second creation account it does not say "therefore a woman shall leave her father and mother and cling to her husband," but instead, and completely contrary to the institutions and social structures of the time:

> *Therefore a man leaves his father and his mother and clings to his wife, and they become one flesh.* (Gen 2:24)

Because at that time it was the *woman* who had to leave father and mother, not the *man*, this is a revolutionary text. Contrary to the social conventions of the ancient Near East, it proposes a contrast-world that rests entirely on the elementary power of love between man and woman.

Indeed, it is not only this conclusion to the second creation account but the whole narrative that possesses an inexhaustible depth. How unfathomable the very beginning:

> The LORD God formed the human being from the dust of the ground, and breathed into its nostrils the breath of life; and the human became a living being. (Gen 2:7)

Today we can use more abstract and sophisticated terms and still we cannot attain the power of the ancient images. We can say that God gave such power to matter that it was able to develop to the stature of a human being, even though that took an unimaginably long time. It was God's intention that it should do so on its own. God allowed matter all the time it needed so that ultimately, in the human being, it might become conscious of itself.

The Human Needs Help

But let us return to our text. It says not only that God made the human a living being (Gen 2:7). It says: the human is more than merely a living being. Otherwise the animals would have sufficed as partners. The human is a being that comes fully to itself only in community with another "thou." That is depicted in the creation of the woman from the human's side and God's presentation of the woman to the man. It is also heard in the man's exclamation, which is not the roaring of a ruler but a cry of joy. These images are meant to tell us that being human is being-with—being together in trust and in the joy of mutual help.

That all sounds lovely. But when we look at the world we have to acknowledge that life is *not* a "being together in trust." The bird searching the meadow for worms repeatedly lifts its little head and looks around, for safety's sake. That unceasing watchfulness is an image of pure mistrust. Indeed, trust is not a natural condition; it has to be created. Trust has to be achieved in pain and sacrifice.

Thus it is clear that the two creation stories at the beginning of the Bible were by no means intended, in the first place, to tell about a past primal beginning. Instead, they tell us how God envisioned human beings and for what purpose. It took a very long time for human beings to become human, and that process only reached its goal in liberation and redemption through Jesus Christ.

Hence the Bible pushes us to read the text about the creation of the woman also in terms of God's new creation, namely, the church. Then, in its more profound, overall biblical sense, this text depicts how the church, as the "new Eve," came forth from the side of Christ, the "new Adam." The theologians of the early church located that procession of the church from Christ's side in the event of the Cross. That is how much it cost to create genuine community. It is only in an expanded view reaching to the cross of Christ that the terrible truth of Genesis 2 becomes visible: the human being is created toward and for a "thou," certainly, but for that relationship with the Other to succeed is something impossible in terms of pure nature, of simple biology.

Certainly there are rare cases of marriages that succeed because of a lucky constellation or an almost natural gift, but the church cannot count on that. It is very realistic. It knows that human beings need help, and that help is the church itself, coming from the crucified body of Christ. That help is the bondedness of the Christian community.

In such a community it is possible for the unmarried also to live a fulfilled life. In it marriages can succeed. In it married couples can rediscover one another. In it there is even the possibility that married people can separate and yet not be alone. In it there are marriages for the sake of the reign of God and unmarried people who live for the sake of the reign of God—because there is a "new family," namely, the church.

The Vitality of Christianity

None of that is because the church is an assembly of heroes and heroines. The British-German journalist Alan Posener wrote in 2002:

> *The enormous power of Christianity rests not least on the fact that it makes its protagonists so weak. There are no "action heroes" at work here. Betrayal and denial, venality and the fear of death exist even in the innermost circle. No other world religion has comparable courage. No other world religion looks people so fixedly and unflinchingly in the eye. All that, indeed, is a heritage from Judaism . . . . No people has so implacably criticized itself in its holy*

books, so consistently demeaned its kings, showed its heroes so humanly fallible as the chosen one . . . . It is a history in which even perfidy and betrayal become instruments of salvation.[1]

"Becoming instruments of salvation." May we not apply this text from Alan Posener even to the married and the unmarried in our congregations? There is so much brokenness, so much weakness. There are so many failures and so many lovely dreams that were not fulfilled! Yet all that can become a tool for the one thing that is so much greater than our dreams—namely, for the one thing that God always regards as the goal: a world transformed by the living witness of the people of God. As soon as Christians turn to that goal with their whole strength, the goal that the Bible calls the "reign of God" or the "kingdom of God," something astonishing happens: marriages are healed. Partners who had become estranged find one another anew. Children's hearts turn back to their parents. At the very least the lonely are consoled, letting their separation become an "easy yoke and a light burden" (Matt 11:30) so that the dignity of husband and wife is restored.

I sometimes think that what Genesis 1–2 describes is still not finished: God is still working on the rib—that is, the relationship between husband and wife—and on the new family of the church that comes forth from the crucified body of Christ. The church is still on the road. Through it God is still working on the world, undeterred. And God invites us to be coworkers.

[1] From the author's private notes.

COVID-19

Plagues, epidemics, and pandemics have long marked the history of humankind. I think of the time of the Black Death, when whole districts in Europe were depopulated. Scholars estimate that in the years 1331–1353 the plague took some 140 million lives. But the Black Death is no longer a living memory for us. Much closer in time is the "Spanish Flu" that raged in 1918–1920. It cost some 25 to 50 million human lives worldwide. But that, too, is in the distant past.

Despite the breathtaking numbers of victims of those "historic plagues," we can say that no pandemic has yet struck the world population with such fury as COVID-19 (= coronavirus disease 2019), and none has previously led to a comparable worldwide destruction in all parts of society. The reason is, of course, the reality of the twenty-first century with its social mobility and vacation travel, its thick traffic, and an economic interwovenness never known before.

COVID-19 is experienced nearly everywhere in the world as a profound rupture because the virus rules our lives. It affects everyone in one way or another, and no one can escape the new situation—not even those who act as if they can ignore the pandemic or even deny it. This plague will change the society in which we live. Obviously it likewise presents probing questions to theology and the church.

What does it mean that the church, which by its very nature is "assembly," suddenly can no longer gather together in person—or can only do so if all participants wear masks, follow peculiar guidelines fixed to the floors of their churches, then sit far apart, no longer singing together, not offering each other the peace-greeting, and practically not speaking to one another after the service? Don't get me wrong! I am very much in favor of following public regulations for church gatherings—if, that is, we are talking about a government of laws. But what would it mean if a crisis of this kind, with corresponding restrictions, should last for years?

14

Besides, what does COVID-19 mean for "theodicy," the question of God's omnipotence and the purpose of creation? Can Christian faith still speak of an omnipotent and benevolent God when, because of the mercilessness of this pandemic, countless old and sick people are snatched away, the economy is on its last legs, the poor in Brazil, India, and elsewhere have nothing to eat, and social interaction is profoundly destroyed?

The theodicy question arose acutely in Europe for the first time when an earthquake destroyed nearly the whole city of Lisbon on All Saints' Day in 1755. People who survived the raging fires by escaping to the sea were drowned by a gigantic tsunami. Nearly every church in Lisbon was a heap of ruins. Nothing remained intact but the red-light district. After the news of this catastrophe many European intellectuals hesitated to believe any longer in the providence and parental kindness of God.

Since then the theodicy problem has raged again and again, especially in light of the murder of millions of Europe's Jews by the Nazi regime. Now the whole question arises anew, for many, in the context of the coronavirus pandemic.

Some theologians attempt to resolve the problem of theodicy by reducing God's creative power, or they go still further and say that, in light of the global misery, God can never again be called "almighty." We can no longer consider God the "lord of history," they say. God seems helpless in face of the endless suffering; in fact, God in Christ submitted to that same suffering in order to be in solidarity with the world.

The idea of God's suffering with the world is correct. But can God's omnipotence be curtailed? The notion of a helpless, powerless God is a self-contradiction, but still weightier is the fact that it is absolutely unbiblical. Not even the book of Job reduces God's omnipotence and creative wisdom one iota. Quite the contrary! The great divine speeches in Job 38–41 are designed precisely to demonstrate God's sovereignty. Still, they also emphasize the inaccessibility of God and the mystery of divine creative wisdom.

Thus the problem of theodicy cannot be resolved by theology's questioning God's omnipotence. It has to be approached differently— namely, first of all with the aid of a rational theology of creation that takes seriously what the whole of evolution really means.

I have said quite deliberately ". . . *first of all with the aid of a rational theology of creation,*" which means that creation theology by no means has the last word in the question of theodicy. The last word belongs to the death of Jesus and the raising of Jesus from the dead—and that "last word" (in this chapter, at least) can remain unspoken. No one can speak "last words" all the time. We are dealing here with "next-to-last words." They are what is at issue here, because unless we have understood what "creation" is, we cannot understand what "resurrection" means as the goal of creation.

A Snippet of Creation Theology

Let me begin with the phenomenon of human love—in particular, a love that has been purified in common life and is capable of genuine dedication. Obviously one of the foundations of the love between man and woman is the sexual realm, something we have in common with our animal ancestors: attraction, longing, desire, and the fulfill-ment of desire are simply animal in nature. Certainly they can be such if the human being behaves like an animal or is more animalistic than any beast. But longing and desire can also be *humanly* shaped; indeed, they must be. Love achieves its specifically human ripeness only at the moment in which it no longer seeks merely its own plea-sure but, above all, the happiness of the other—when it says "thou" in the fullest sense: "You, with all that you are," "Only you," "You always," "Being with you for the sake of others." It is precisely in that moment that love presumes freedom.

True human love cannot attempt to instrumentalize the other for one's own pleasure or to shape and model the other according to one's own image. True love cannot mean, either, that one is surren-dered to another; then it would be the worst kind of prison. Real love has chosen the other in freedom and it presumes that in return it will be granted the dignity proper to every human being. Genuine love is therefore inseparably bound up with freedom. Love that is not mutually given in full assent remains fragmentary. The greatest, most beautiful, and most human thing in the world thus presumes free-dom—free, total acceptance of the other.

And let us go a step further! Freedom, too, has its preconditions: namely, it presumes history. That should be obvious, because freedom did not fall from heaven one day and simply exist thereafter. It needed a long "history of freedom" in order, little by little, to become what it can be. Freedom had to be desired, achieved, and often bitterly fought for. It was not a matter of course. We all live in the spaces of freedom that others have opened for us in the course of history. At some point, in the dawn of humanity, there must have been individuals who did not simply follow their instincts like the animals but who instead *chose* something they thought was good and proper—or better and more proper than something else. That was the beginning of the history of human freedom. It is more than "natural history." It began to grow slowly, like a plant that is still very tender and constantly in danger.

The mighty field of history in which historians labor is a constantly confused but ultimately unstoppable story of enlightenment, emancipation, and the quest for freedom. Each individual's story of freedom is rooted in and lives out of this larger history and gives its own new impulses to it, again and again.

The history of emancipation and freedom thus extends far beyond mere natural history; it transcends and transforms it. *But obviously it presupposes it.* The history of human freedom is based on and embedded in the history of Nature, of the universe, of evolution. My central point here is that we must acknowledge this. We can clarify this crucial fact in terms of the phenomenon of "successive generations."

The history of freedom develops in epochs. To take one example, there was the epoch of the European Enlightenment, with all its one-sidedness but also with all its insights. It is true that the First World War and all its consequences finally destroyed the naïve optimism about "progress" that reigned in the eighteenth and nineteenth centuries, but it by no means wrecked the fundamental insights of the Enlightenment. Something similar happened long ago in Greece, and in Israel. A genuine history of freedom presumes the succession of generations and requires newer and newer generations that build on the insights of their predecessors while modifying, improving, or even revolutionizing them. Precisely because the human history of freedom and enlightenment is unthinkable without the succession and dialogue of many generations it also presumes the end and demise of those who have preceded and fought the battles before them.

That puts us right in the middle of the immense event of evolution, which lives precisely from ending, disruption, and death—simply because space is required for the testing of new things and advancing those that are successful. Evolution presupposes constant mutation, the continued life of successful mutants, but also the collapse and end of obsolete forms.

At precisely this point it is good to look into a book published in 1895. Its author was Herbert George Wells and its title is *The Time Machine*. It was the precursor and pathbreaker for famous dystopian novels such as Aldous Huxley's *Brave New World* (1932) and George Orwell's *1984* (1949). The "time traveler" who is the principal figure in Wells's book has invented a time machine that takes him into the Fourth Dimension, so that he can speed through millennia. On his first journey the machine brings him to the year 802,702. As he exits the machine he finds himself at the place where his house used to be, but in a new, radically changed world. When at last, after terrible experiences, he returns to the day of his departure he tries to describe to his friends the altered world that had confronted him. They listen very skeptically. This is how it goes:

> *Some day [the whole world] will be intelligent, educated, and cooperating; things will move faster and faster toward the subjugation of Nature. In the end, wisely and carefully we shall readjust the balance of animal and vegetable life to suit our human needs.*
>
> *This adjustment, I say, must have been done, and done well: done indeed for all time, in the space of Time across which my machine had leaped. The air was free from gnats, the earth from weeds or fungi; everywhere were fruits and sweet and delightful flowers; brilliant butterflies flew hither and thither. The ideal of preventive medicine was attained. Diseases had been stamped out. I saw no evidence of any contagious diseases during all my stay. And I shall have to tell you later that even the processes of putrefaction and decay had been profoundly affected by these changes.*[1]

In this part of his story the time traveler presents a utopian human dream: that of a world in which there are no more weeds but only cultivated plants; no more annoying gnats or mosquitoes but only beautiful butterflies; no dangerous microbes, no illnesses, and nothing of a threatening nature. The earth has been altered, down to the microscopic world, by an international science.

It speaks for the intelligence of H. G. Wells, of course, that the time traveler's interpretation just quoted proves in the course of the book to be an extremely dangerous deception. The apparently redemptive alteration of the world had been accompanied by the rise of a beastly and abysmal anti-world producing constant fear, horrors, and death.

---

[1] H. G. Wells, *The Time Machine: An Invention* (New York: Henry Holt, 1895), 71–72.

For the moment, though, let us consider the quoted section! No more weeds, no mosquitoes, no microbes, no decay? Bitter experience has shown us in the meantime how to correct such mistakes. We no longer speak of "weeds" but of "wild plants." We deliberately let "weeds" grow on the edges of fields and roads because, little by little, even the slowest among us begin to grasp that otherwise there will soon be no insects left, and without insects any number of birds will vanish—and, because our world is so interconnected, unimaginably more will cease to exist.

We also know that without microbes and decay our planet would very rapidly become a gigantic garbage heap. After all, microbes are Nature's cleanup crews, and decay steadily cleanses our planet. All the same, we continue to pursue the illusion of a world without illnesses, and that is because we fail to recognize that sicknesses have something to do with evolution, and that a completely sterile and eternally restyled world cannot exist—and must not.

Therefore we must keep in view the whole vastness and utterly radical nature of the phenomenon of evolution: from the rise of the initial organic compounds through the development of macromolecules and the first one-celled animals to the rise of *homo sapiens sapiens*—and throughout it all, the appearance and disappearance of countless biological forms and beings. We cannot escape the insight that the birth and death of the individual and, clearly, deformation and illness as well, are all essential parts of evolution.

Yes, obviously illnesses too! Life on our planet would be unthinkable without microbes, without mutating bacteria and viruses. For example, viruses create many highly dangerous sicknesses in plants, animals, and humans. But as they repeatedly creep into cells they bring new DNA material into the inherited substance, and in this way they have driven and accelerated evolution to an extraordinary degree.

To take another example: without the multitudes of bacterial (and viral!) flora in our gut we would die very quickly. The human being is a highly complicated ecosystem in which bacteria play a vital role. However, a disturbance of the intestinal flora can make one sick, and cells can mutate, causing cancer. Of course, if they could not mutate there would have been no evolution, no mammals, and never any human beings.

Let me summarize: real love presupposes freedom, and freedom can only develop within a history of freedom. But a genuine history of freedom presupposes the succession of generations in natural history and evolution—and evolution is unimaginable without constant change: not without catastrophes, not without sicknesses, and not without death. I can envision no possibility of interrupting this chain of causation at any point and thus conceiving creation in another way.

However, if love is the goal of all creation, and if love requires evolution, with all its shadows of innovation and decay, as the condition of its freedom, then creation is good. That brings us, finally, to Sacred Scripture, for it, too, says clearly, unmistakably, and with the utmost emphasis: everything God has created is good. Creation lives out of God's eternal caring and reflects it as well.

The Play of Creation Wisdom

Israel's wisdom literature speaks especially, and repeatedly, of the beauty, order, and appropriateness of creation. A particularly important figure in this context is "Wisdom," a *personification* of God's creative wisdom. In the eighth chapter of Proverbs, "Wisdom" seems to appear in the figure of a "child at play." I say "seems to" because the interpretation of the corresponding Hebrew words in Proverbs 8:30 allows for other possibilities, namely "master worker" or simply "constant."

> *The LORD created me at the beginning of his work,*
> *the first of his acts of long ago.*
> *Ages ago I was set up,*
> *at the first, before the beginning of the earth.*
> *When there were no depths I was brought forth,*
> *when there were no springs abounding with water.*
> *Before the mountains had been shaped,*
> *before the hills, I was brought forth—*
> *when he had not yet made earth and fields,*
> *or the world's first bits of soil.*
> *When he established the heavens, I was there,*
> *when he drew a circle on the face of the deep,*
> *when he made firm the skies above,*
> *when he established the fountains of the deep,*
> *when he assigned to the sea its limit,*
> *so that the waters might not transgress his command,*

when he marked out the foundations of the earth,
then I was beside him, like a beloved child;[2]
and I was daily his delight,
rejoicing before him always,
rejoicing in his inhabited world
and delighting in the human race. (Prov 8:22-31)

In this glorious poem, then, "Wisdom" is God's companion in creation. She herself was created, certainly—but then she was present in a mysterious way through the whole process of creation. That process is described in images drawn from ancient Near Eastern knowledge of the world. What is crucial is that God, the Creator, works sovereignly, thoughtfully, and planfully, step by step, masterfully and meaningfully. Evidently God has a plan in mind for creation, and there is a suggestion that "Wisdom" herself is that architectural plan. That is precisely why it is so firmly emphasized that she is there *from the beginning*. But even if she is not depicted here as a kind of architectural plan, her unceasing presence in any case reveals to her the planned nature of Creation and thus its wisdom. And because she was there from the beginning she can also convey the order of the universe to human beings.

If the translation of Proverbs 8:30 quoted here is correct, it could be an especially touching feature of the poem that Wisdom plays on the globe like a child. But she plays not only on the whole earth; in the same moment she plays *before God*. She is God's joy, God's "beloved child," and she herself has joy and pleasure in what God creates.

The lightness, the playfulness, the beauty, and the utter perfection of creation could scarcely be better expressed than in the image of joyful, unbounded play. Naturally, the metaphor of "creative wisdom's play" is also used to say that *God* rejoices in creation. It was not a painful birth, most certainly not a miscarriage, but an easy and glorious game—and it could remain so forever if people would pay attention to creation's wisdom and play along with it. Thus personified Wisdom also has to say, immediately after this poem:

---

[2] NRSV "master worker."

And now, my children, listen to me:
    happy are those who keep my ways.
Hear instruction and be wise,
    and do not neglect it.
Happy is the one who listens to me,
    watching daily at my gates,
    waiting beside my doors.
For whoever finds me finds life
    and obtains favor from the LORD;
but those who miss me injure themselves;
    all who hate me love death. (Prov 8:32-36)

In other words: those who do not respect the structures of creation, those who distort Nature's blueprint and thus God's creation do themselves the utmost damage. It is not God who "punishes" them; they punish, fall short of, and even destroy themselves. And it is not only individuals who destroy themselves. Today we may add: world society could destroy itself. The nuclear weapons on alert today would be sufficient to destroy all humanity many times over.

A Growing History of Evil

The creation account of the so-called "Priestly document" in Genesis 1:1–2:4a ultimately says the same as the quoted text from the book of Proverbs, though in a completely different form. At the beginning of Genesis we also have a description of the world's creation; in part it uses the same inventory of the created world as is found in Proverbs 8:22-31. But above all, the direction and goal are identical: the creation account in Genesis means to say that God's creation was good. The text emphasizes it, like a refrain, no fewer than six times: "God saw that it was good" (Gen 1:4, 10, 12, 18, 21, 25). Finally, on the sixth day, the formula is expanded:

God saw everything that he had made, and indeed, it was very good.
(Gen 1:31)

With those words this text also shows what is at stake when it speaks of creation: it is successful, it is good, it is in fact "very good." God's creation is something God can survey with pleasure.

However: when we read the subsequent chapters in Genesis we quickly see that we are only told, and must be told, about God's *good* creation because a terrifying history of evil begins right away: The very first human beings let themselves be tempted, distrust God, and violate God's commandment (Gen 3:1-24).

The results of their sin appear almost immediately, in the next generation. There is rivalry between two brothers: in the end, out of pure jealousy, Cain kills his brother Abel (Gen 4:1-16). Obviously this is not an historical account of an incident at the beginning of human history. Rather, what is told here is first and above all what happens over and over again in history after Evil has broken into the world: rivalry between brothers such that one wants to kill the other.

Then, in the generations after Cain, there emerges a man named Lamech. He does not hold to the law of blood-vengeance, intended to control major incidents of violence: he boasts to his wives that he will revenge himself not seven times but seventy times seven (Gen 4:15, 23-24). That, too, happens over and over in history: individuals' lust for domination, their pride, and their thirst for power create unspeakable misery and plunge the world into chaos.

As the number of people on earth increases more and more, the Bible goes on to say, evil grows along with them. The narrator asserts: "The LORD saw that the wickedness of humankind was great in the earth, and that every inclination of the thoughts of their hearts was only evil continually" (Gen 6:5). As the story goes on, this evil inclination is described more precisely as a lust for slaughter: "the earth is filled with violence" (Gen 6:13).

Thus the creation account in Genesis 1:1–2:4a intends to show that the world was initially good when it was created by God, but sin breaks into that good creation and a history of evil begins, a history that consists primarily of an ever-more-rampant violence. Thus the narrative in the first chapters of Genesis makes a clear distinction between *creation* and *history*. Evil does not lurk in God's creation; it develops in history, which rapidly becomes a history of evil. Still, God does not leave it that way: in Genesis 12 God begins a "counter-history" by calling Abraham. The whole Bible tells the story of that counter-history.

Certainly one could object that if the first humans sinned right away, if criminal violence in the form of fratricide existed at the very beginning of human history, if "the thoughts of human hearts were only evil continually" so that God had to set a "counter-history" in motion—doesn't that all go to prove that God's creation was not at all good? Isn't it true that what God made was a fundamental failure?

But here again we have to think of creation as evolution. The human being comes from the animal world, and that world includes violence, eating and being eaten, the intricate and interwoven networks of nourishment. But not only those! It is by no means so that animals favor their own kind. Woe to the rat that wanders by accident into the nest of another tribe of rats. The minute the "native" rats scent the alien rat its fate is sealed: it will be torn to pieces.

Clearly such structures of aggression persisted within the human species for a long time. Our tribe against their tribe! Our clan against that other clan! Whoever doesn't smell like us is our enemy! Whoever's skin is a different color from ours is inferior! It is no exaggeration to say that behavioral patterns of that kind still lurk within us.

But at some point in the long history of human becoming, for the first time the possibility of freedom and reason appeared. From then on people, if they followed these new possibilities, no longer engaged in brutal violence against their fellow humans. Since then it is no longer necessary to give free rein to group-egoism. But those who rejected that newly opening possibility became "more beastly than any beast," because they now had infinitely more opportunities, thanks to their intelligence, to destroy the members of their own species.

Thus the unbroken chain of violence that Genesis relates also presumes—to use a modern term—deliberate refusal in the face of new opportunities that have been achieved in the course of a long history of culture and freedom. It was only this *deliberate refusal in light of new possibilities for human sympathy and community* that created evil. And because evil (just as much as good) is imitated and so begets more evil, a history of self-perpetuating evil began. Potentials for evil arose into which humans were born without any personal fault, and what happened was precisely what church dogmatics speaks of—using a concept that is regrettably easy to misunderstand—as "original sin."

The consequences of this chain of evil, this self-accumulating potential for iniquity, were and are enormous. The new possibilities for freedom and goodness that entered human life could have sharpened the sense of the meaningfulness of creation. But where iniquity spread, there the view was obscured, goodness became unrecognizable, and meaningful structures were perceived as futility.

For example: The beginning of a serious illness must not necessarily produce profound fear, naked misery, feelings of isolation and loneliness. Sickness could also be an experience of human care and concern, even a sense, drawn from faith, of being sheltered in God. The same is true for death. It can be a breaking-off and nevertheless a surrender and a hope-filled trust in God. Experience of the world could have been an increasing sense of meaning. But it turned out differently. A gigantic potential for self-created misery clouds our view of the meaningful structures of creation.

It must be clear by now that those who continually complain that God created mosquitoes, decay, mutating viruses, dangerous bacteria, and faulty cells and, besides, allowed evil to enter history have not understood what evolution is. Ultimately they want a complete, sterile, glass house of a world, a lotusland in which happiness is prefabricated and honey drips into people's mouths.

In such a world there would be no freedom and therefore no real love. In such a world we would be mere marionettes: infantile, contented bio-machines programmed to feel happy, as Aldous Huxley so masterfully caricatured them in *Brave New World*. In the sterile, artificially propagated society conditioned to unceasing pleasure that Huxley describes there is no failure, no sickness, and no sort of misery any more. There is death, of course, at some point, but it happens in a drugged half-sleep and zombie-like bliss in a death center erected for the purpose.

God wanted a different world—a world in which there is love, which comes from freedom; in which there is suffering that allows people to mature; in which there is misfortune that tests them. Still more: God wanted a world that is not yet finished, a world where humans can join in, full of longing to heal the wounds of history and to become human in the fullest sense—rooted in earth, reaching toward heaven.

How a History of Sin and Guilt Happens Today

All this we can now apply to COVID-19. As we have seen, the world in which we live is not God's pure creation. It already has a long history behind it; in fact, it *is* history by its very nature. But that history can be clouded and darkened by the accumulation of human guilt; it can even be ruined. Then it becomes a history of disaster.

Let us simply assume that the new virus SARS-CoV-2 (= severe acute respiratory syndrome coronavirus 2) did not happen through human planning, as in a laboratory commissioned by a government to create biological weapons. Had that been the case, the action itself would have been profoundly criminal.

However, the virologists tell us that in this case SARS-CoV-2 was constructed differently. The virus is not of human making, but in all probability arose through an accidental transfer from animal to human—possibly by way of the gigantic market for wild animals in the Chinese metropolis of Wuhan, where one may find not only meat from domesticated animals for sale but also that of snakes, rats, salamanders, frogs, and a variety of birds as well as ground bones and the dried dung of bats—probably not as a delicacy but for medicinal purposes. Certainly one may ask whether in the twenty-first century that kind of pseudo-medical magic is not an evil in itself.

In any case, afterward human evil immediately and in a positively terrifying way joined hands with the story of the new virus: the existence of the highly dangerous corona variant was kept in the dark within the People's Republic of China for a brief period—a time, however, that was enormously important for the spread of the virus; such are the ancient silent tactics of dictatorships. Along the same lines, a number of Western politicians at first minimized, downplayed, and instrumentalized the virus for their own ends in the game of power politics, as has become fairly obvious. Some of them are still doing it.

The corona crisis not only uncovered the irresponsibility of certain politicians and revealed their true faces, however. Sadly, it also showed that research into the possibility of corona mutants was not sufficiently advanced, even though the severe effects of the respiratory syndrome caused by SARS-CoV (since 2002) and MERS-CoV (since 2012) should have sent a warning signal. Precisely here it was fairly clear that the so-called coronaviruses came from a reservoir of animal pathogens.

In many countries emergency services were even less prepared. The crisis revealed with brutal clarity the deficient healthcare systems, the lack of breathing apparatus and intensive-care beds, the shortage of expert personnel, and the inability of public procurers to maintain a supply of breathing masks for catastrophic situations.

It was not only politicians and power-brokers who failed. As the first wave of the pandemic was fading and some relaxation of lockdowns began, it was precisely in the free Western countries that more and more people refused to listen to reason and protested against the regulations set by their governments in regard to corona. They came from all cracks and crannies, pouring into the streets: mask-refusers, immunization skeptics and rejecters, corona minimizers, pandemic deniers, conspiracy theorists, esoterics, and contrarians. They wanted to demonstrate their contempt for government restrictions such as social distancing, wearing masks, and restricting contacts. Care for others, especially the old and sick, was of no concern to them. Police supervision and even the exercise of force is hard put to cope with such ignorance and even recklessness.

But the real problem—at least in the free societies of the European type—was not these social-critical demonstrations. The true problem was the many who simply could not understand that the highly dangerous pandemic of COVID-19 can only be encountered with focused attention and the most extreme discipline. In the stores and where it was required, they dutifully wore their masks, but as soon as they were outside—and this is something that could be observed in every street and on every corner—it did not enter their heads to keep their distance. It was no different at home. Many people never even considered doing without the usual visits and gatherings. That kind of undisciplined behavior was the real cause of the so-called second wave of the pandemic in the late fall and winter of 2020 (and the surge in mid-2021 due to the Delta variant).

There was no malice behind that lack of insight; rather, it was due to the complete inability to grasp a wholly new situation, to see the broader connections (such as the threatened collapse of the healthcare system), and to change one's own way of life—at least for a little while. In the face of such inability to empathize, to begin to feel comfortable in such an unaccustomed social situation, a free state is helpless. Here it has reached its limits. It can only warn, admonish, appeal, plead—but it cannot compel understanding.

So it was not malice that underlay the inability of many as we have described it, and yet the question arises: must we not speak of guilt here also? I am talking about the guilt, the fault that consists of an acquired or self-created inability to abandon one's own habits, rituals, and convenience, to leave one's comfort zone, and even to think about other people and about larger contexts at all. Such an individual and likewise collective torpor can certainly involve guilt.

This whole list could easily be expanded and deepened. It shows us that an event that at first is purely biological in nature but then sets profound social processes in motion can, because of human failure, inertia, ignorance, attitudes of "I know better," arrogance, and criminal manipulation intertwined with evil, set in motion a history of guilt and malice and thus create genuine misery.

Signs of a Counter-History

Everyone who has endured the pandemic with open eyes, and is still doing so, certainly has very different things to report. Such reports come from numerous research institutions that work day and night analyzing the virus, the way it is spread, and the ways to counter it: we learn of the admirable dedication of physicians, hospital workers, and many others who assist them—of countless people who offer themselves spontaneously to help older people—of teachers who have given profound attention to preparing digital lessons—in short, of a wave of willingness to help, of solidarity, and of community effort. Here we should also mention worldwide cooperative medical projects that have arisen in response to the COVID-crisis. The history of this great, immediate human effort has yet to be written.

Certainly this raises another theological question that to me seems as if it may be the most important: What is the relationship of this positive aspect of the history of the virus's effects, this wave of solidarity and human cooperation, to the idea of the "reign of God"? Jesus himself, after all, worked against sickness, need, the isolation of individuals—against human suffering in every form—and he saw that campaign as signaling the arrival of God's reign (Luke 11:20). May we place the unbelievable devotion of so many helpers in the time of the coronavirus in this context and associate it with the coming of the reign of God? I would have no difficulty in doing so.

I say this because the reign of God that Jesus proclaims reveals itself not only in Jesus' actions and those of his disciples and is not located only in Israel; its desire is to encompass the whole world through Jesus and his disciples. It calls for as many sympathizers as possible, and it even needs people who are totally unaware that they are acting as Jesus did and yet do so—often, in fact, shaming Christians who not only do not do their duty but have even forgotten it altogether.

Therefore I dare to say that the selfless devotion of many women and men in the time of this pandemic certainly has something to do with the coming of the reign of God. The battle against the illness and the coming of the reign of God cannot be separated. They belong together.

Obviously all I have just said is not yet the "last word" about the reign of God. The last word on the coming of the reign of God is Jesus' surrender of his life, his representative death, his resurrection from the dead. But the reign of God also has its "next-to-last words," its "forecourt," a broad field in which the obstacles to the coming of the reign of God need to be eliminated.

Outlook

In all probability the COVID crisis will keep us on our toes for a long time. At the moment the whole world is counting on the new vaccines—and rightly so! Yet coronaviruses mutate, just as do all viruses and bacteria. Some virologists say that, like the flu, this illness will recur repeatedly in new waves. COVID-19 could become an enduring crisis that weakens only very slowly. If that should happen, what would such an ongoing crisis do? Will it deepen the already-simmering conflicts throughout the world and bring forth new power struggles? Will it dig the existing trenches in society even deeper? Will the chaos that SARS-CoV-2 sets loose in the human immune system develop into a chaos that encompasses the whole of world society?

Or will the profound interruption of our stupid habits by the virus become the occasion for strengthened *meaningful* medical research, something that cannot occur except through international coopera-tion? And will that interruption give the impulse, at last, to the insight that in our world national egoisms and power games are not only highly dangerous but have become positively childish and laugh-able—because the world has become so networked and the balance of our blue planet so endangered that only a profound reversal can save us?

So will the global corona crisis ultimately become another part of the history of evil, or will it instead become something like salvation history or at least a distancing from things that stand in the way of the coming of the reign of God? The virus SARS-CoV-2 allows for both. Everything depends on us—on what we do with this biological phenomenon. The virus, viewed through the electron microscope, looks temptingly beautiful, almost like a flower—and yet its shape is also reminiscent of the highly explosive naval mines in both world wars. It could be a sign of destruction, or it could be a sign of our repentance.

Does God Have a Name?

Exodus 2–15, the departure of Israel from "the house of slavery in Egypt," is one of the longest narratives in the Old Testament. It is a stunning tale of liberation, filled with revolutionary theology. But this great narrative is not only about the liberation of Israel from a theocracy based on profound structures of injustice. Alongside the theme of liberation from misery there is a broader one: we could call it the "self-disclosure of the true God." The two themes are firmly linked together.

God Conceals the Divine Name

God's self-disclosure begins with the sending of Moses to Pharaoh, the overlord of Egypt. The purpose of that sending: Pharaoh is to release Israel to depart into freedom. But Moses resists. He does not see himself in a position to appear before Pharaoh, still less to lead Israel out of Egypt. Moses simply does not want to, and he has a whole series of reasons for his refusal—just as *we* produce every conceivable reason for trying to evade God's will.

Although Moses says he cannot speak and has never been able to do so eloquently, because he is "slow of speech and slow of tongue" (Exod 4:10), suddenly he is capable of arguing with God to an astonishing degree and presents a whole series of reasons for his resistance. For example, he says the Israelites would reject him and refuse to believe that God has sent him. They would say to him: "What is the name of this God who you say has spoken to you and sent you? Anybody can come and say he has talked with God. What is his name? What kind of God is he?" If they ask me that, says Moses, what could I possibly answer? (Exod 3:13).

So Moses asks for God's name, and he receives a very unusual response from God. It is so unconventional and peculiar that interpreters are wrestling with it to this day—because God does not give

Moses a name, but instead says: "I will be who I will be!" and adds: "Thus you shall say to the Israelites: '[The] I-will-be' has sent me to you" (Exod 3:14).

This "I will be who I will be" is often given in modern Bible translations or interpretations as "I am the *I-am.*" That is not entirely wrong, and yet it is not really true to the intent of the statement, because God's response to Moses' question about God's name is a definite refusal to give a name. It means nothing other than: I will not tell you a name. I do not permit anyone to speak to me of such a thing. You have no need for a divine name to know who I am. You need do only one thing: pay close attention to what will happen. What is about to happen to you and to the Egyptians will show you who I am. *Who I truly am will thus be shown.* History, and not a name, will reveal it. Therefore: "I will be who I will be"—namely, in my actions. But you will not be given a name.

That is more or less how we should describe God's response, and it makes clear that the name "Yнwн" is interpreted here in such a way that it becomes a non-name.

God Is Revealed in Actions

Thus the Exodus narrative makes fundamental statements about Israel's God. First of all: unlike the gods of the nations, each of whom has a name, Israel's God does not. The pagan gods were called Amun or Isis, Ishtar or Marduk, Zeus or Hera. In the ancient world there were endless divine names and even dynasties of gods. There was a special god or goddess for every aspect of life. Religious scholars call them "portfolio gods."

In Egypt, for example, Ra was the god of the sun. Then there was Khons, the god of the moon. Hapi, the god of fertility, was responsible for the life-sustaining Nile floods, but there was also Hathor, the goddess of love, dance, and beauty. There was Ma'at, the goddess of justice and truth, and Neith, the hideous goddess of war. Bastet was the goddess who protected against demons. Then there were Tefnut, the goddess of fire, and Set, the god of storms, evil, and destruction.

We could go on and on with the list, and it would become utterly clear that every striking and important natural reality and aspect of life in Egypt became a divine reality personalized as a god or a goddess. Ultimately the conclusion was that the gods come from the world's matter—and the world is divine. Israel's understanding of

God was fundamentally different from such an idea. The God of Israel is *not* a part of the world, and the world is most certainly not divine. It is creation. Anyone who wants to understand the faith of Israel and the church must not only perceive but almost stand aghast, horrified at this radical difference between the God of Israel and the gods of the nations.

The world-of-many-gods obviously had consequences for religion: because within it all gods were essentially specialized, it was necessary to call each by her or his correct name; otherwise they would not listen, and they would remain dumb. It was also unconditionally necessary to know the right name. Only then could one reach the god or goddess *responsible* for the particular occasion. Only then would the appropriate divinity realize that she or he was being personally addressed. In certain circles there were even secret names for gods, like our personal telephone numbers, available only to a small circle. Knowing such a secret name guaranteed access to the deity in question.

This whole system of gods could no longer apply to the God of Israel—at least not at the level of theology represented by the books of the Bible. It was no longer necessary to know a name for the God of Israel, most certainly not a special or secret name.

Still, there was another reason why God refused to reveal a personal name, something we have already spoken about and that is much more important for us. Who God is appears in God's saving acts. God's innermost being is revealed when God can no longer endure the misery of God's people. When God saves. When God liberates. When God leads this people out of oppression into freedom, and out of the land of oppression into a "good and broad land, a land flowing with milk and honey" (Exod 3:8).

Thus God's nature is shown in God's saving acts. If we want to define God, we can only say, "This is the one who led us out of Egypt," and later, "This is the one who gathers us from among the nations," and still later, "This is the one who raised Jesus from the dead." Those are the biblical definitions of God.

Therefore the great Exodus narrative also begins with the sound of a trumpet. It is not only about the delivery of Israel from oppression; at the same time it is about God's self-revelation. God is self-revealed in actions. What God will do—God's mighty, untiring, merciful action in and for Israel—that, and nothing other, is God's name.

May We Make Images of God?

In terms of that understanding it is altogether correct, theologically, that the Jews and the church with them have from ancient times refused to speak the word YHWH. We never say "Yahweh" or "Jehovah," but "the Lord." This is because if we utter the Tetragrammaton (the four letters YHWH) as a *word* we would make it a *name*, a divine name like Zeus or Jupiter. But according to Exodus 3:14 it is precisely *not* a divine name.

From that point of view it also seems to me to be wrong to represent God in pictures or statues. As magnificently as Michelangelo painted God in the Sistine Chapel (with a shapely nose, sleek grey beard, and well-defined arm muscles), the medieval book illustrators who showed only the hand of God on the upper edge of the picture did better. As God has no name like those of the pagan gods, so God also has no form and cannot be pictured.

Of course I am not speaking of Jesus: I mean God the Father. We can only chronicle God the Father: what God has done and still does. For the same reason theologians may not try to say who God is.

God should *not* be pictured. Whenever Christian art has done so, it has gone astray. Here again the Jews had the right intuition. It is not for nothing that Sacred Scripture tells us: "It is [God] who dwells in unapproachable light, whom no one has ever seen or can see" (1 Tim 6:16).

In John's Gospel, Sacred Scripture also invites us to consider a saying of Jesus: "Whoever has seen me has seen the Father" (John 14:9). That is: if we want to make an image of God for ourselves we must look to Jesus. *He* is the image of the true God. *He* is the icon of God. *In him* we see God's own self, and in and through him we may call upon God.

The Two Sides of Faith

"Faith" is a word foreign to most religions. It is not in their vocabulary, or if it is, that is because it has been introduced into their inventory of concepts through an encounter with the Jewish and Christian traditions. It is only in the Old and New Testaments that the idea of "faith" is completely at home—and there it is, in fact, central.

Faith Has Content

But what is "faith," anyway? When we Christians speak of "faith" today we usually think of the *content of faith*, such as the statements in the Creed. We say, for example, "such and such is our faith." So faith has concrete content. It is not something vague, fleeting, and fuzzy.

How did that happen? It is connected with the fact that we believe in *truths from tradition*, and that is because we believe primarily in things that have taken place in the world, in the course of *history*. We believe:

- that God called Abraham, our father in faith;

- that God led Israel out of Egypt;

- that God chose Israel as God's own people;

- that God has spoken through the prophets;

- that God is fully and forever communicated to us in Jesus;

- that Jesus proclaimed the reign of God;

- that Jesus celebrated the Last Supper with his twelve disciples;

- that he died on the cross for us;

- that he has risen from the dead;

- that he sent the Holy Spirit upon his disciples. . . .

Facts underlie all these statements. Of course, we do not simply believe in facts. The facts have to be interpreted. If we were to say simply, "Jesus was executed on the cross," that would not yet be a statement of faith. We have to add: he was executed because he witnessed to the truth and his opponents did not want to hear the truth. Thus he also died for our sake—because we, too, avoid the truth. But still more: Jesus interpreted his death as dying for the people of God, and accordingly we have to say a great deal more about the depth dimension of that death.

This is only one example. We could say the same about many, many more faith-statements. We do not believe simply in naked facts: we believe in facts that are understood in the light of faith and whose meaning is thus revealed.

Nevertheless, it remains true that our faith is centered on facts, events, happenings. We do not believe in some kind of mythology invented by human beings in order to grasp the meaning of the world and deal with the burdens of life. We most certainly do not believe in some ideology invented by fanatics in order to force their own ideas on humanity. Instead, we believe that God created the world, acted in the world, and is still at work among us. Even when we confess: "I believe in the Holy Spirit," that has to do with facts. What we confess then is that God is at work among us even today—as once on Pentecost—through the divine Spirit, and that we can experience this action of God in us when we open ourselves to the Spirit of God.

Faith Is Fidelity

There is yet another side to Christian faith. It is not only about *adhering to* particular propositions, *holding* certain facts to be true— even when those facts are interpreted. I would like to shed light on this other side that is essential to faith by quoting a line from the prophet Habakkuk. In the book with that name we find: "The righteous live by fidelity" (Hab 2:4). Biblical scholars are always a little uncertain about how to translate the Hebrew text at this point. Some read "the one who is righteous shall live by *faith*." Paul, too, for whom this statement was extremely important (see Rom 1:17; Gal 3:11; cf. Hab 2:4 NRSV), translates "faith" here. Other scholars translate: "the righteous live by their *fidelity*." Which is correct?

Both translations are right, because in Hebrew "faith" and "fidelity" can be the same word, *emunāh*, and that word means, above all, holding fast to God, that is, being faithful to God. We often forget that faith also means that: not merely believing particular principles but surrender to God, refusing to let go of God's hand, profound fidelity to God.

Still: something precedes this holding-fast-to-God, namely, God's bending toward humanity. God not only created us but turned toward us, communicated the divine self to us, reached out a hand to us, revealed to us God's inmost self. We can hold fast to God because God holds fast to us. We can be faithful to God because God is faithful.

So we not only believe the statements of the creed; we bind ourselves to God's fidelity. In truth, that is the real act of faith. Certainly we know of God's fidelity only through God's actions with us and our ancestors in faith. But that involves every faith-statement, all the content of faith, and all creeds, for they speak of the concrete, historical fidelity God has shown to God's people.

Jesus also understood faith in this twofold sense: for him, too, faith has concrete content that can be shaped into statements. These involve the great deeds of God in creation and history in which God's fidelity has been demonstrated. And God's greatest deed in history is that now the reign of God is coming, the reign of justice and nonviolence.

Therefore "faith" meant for Jesus, first of all, that one believes in the coming of the reign of God: that God acts *now*, works continually as the master of history, establishes a rule in the world that is altogether different from human rule. Obviously, this faith in the coming of the reign of God also includes faith in the one who proclaims that royal rule.

Thus for Jesus, too, faith is about concrete content, about statements. "The time is fulfilled, and the reign of God has come near" (Mark 1:15). That is an event, history happening, and it is even a statement Jesus challenges us to believe: "Repent and believe in this good news" (Mark 1:15).

And yet—for Jesus faith also has that other aspect I have named: faith as anchoring, faith as holding fast to God, unconditional trust, remaining in God's love, a fidelity shown in the service assigned to believers. Faith is, then, precisely this: fidelity and reliability in small things. Jesus illustrated this second side of faith in the parable recorded in Luke 17:7-10.

A Parable about Fidelity

Here we have a farmer with a relatively small plot; he can only afford one slave. That slave lives with him and works for him—from early morning till late at night. Because he is the only slave, he has to do everything: prepare and tend the field, herd the cattle, and, when he comes home dead tired in the evening, serve the master at table also. He cannot sit down at a laden table; he has to prepare the meal himself, tie up his long robe (literally "gird himself"; the NRSV writes "put on an apron"), and serve his master's dinner. Only when the owner has eaten and drunk, when the tableware has been removed and washed—only then can the slave think of his own needs (Luke 17:7-10). His master doesn't even thank him; he regards his slave's daily service as the most normal thing in the world, and the slave sees his work the same way: simply a matter of course.

This master is by no means depicted as a cruel slaveholder or the slave as an oppressed human being crying for liberation. The parable takes the hard social conditions of ancient society as they are, quite unsentimentally, and makes them an image of faith.

Thus the parable's intention is not simply to depict God or Christ in the figure of the slave's master. It is not meant to say: "This is how God is! You have to work for him without a break, until your tongue is hanging out. Human beings are God's miserable, oppressed workhorses and they have no right to protest." That would be more like the religions' image of God. In their tales human beings are quite often the laboring slaves, with no rights, serving the gods who celebrate their lavish feasts at golden tables. But that kind of image of God such as we find, for example, in the *Atrahasis* epic, is precisely *not* Jesus' image for God. For him the human being is not God's slave, created merely to perform the dirty work God doesn't want to have to do.

No, here the Son of God becomes a slave to humans. "I am among you as one who serves [at table]," Jesus says (Luke 22:27). Thus we may not simply see the master in the parable at Luke 17:7-10, who has his weary slave serve him in the evening, as an image for God or Jesus.[1]

The evangelist Luke uses the preceding verses, 17:5-6, to make it clear to us what this parable is about. The subject is "faith." The parable is meant to show us what faith is in concrete terms. Faith is pure service that makes no demands, no claims, does not seek recognition, does not insist on its rights: instead, it surrenders its rights to another.

Faith is pictured here as a complete reorientation from oneself to God's cause, a change so profound that believers no longer claim the right to determine their own lives but instead allow another to do so. They hand themselves over to another's will, like those who are enslaved: that is, they do the exact opposite of what modern humanism praises as "self-determination" and "self-realization."

It must be clear to everyone how risky and dangerous faith is when it is understood in that way: it can be hideously misused. That is precisely what we fear: that we will be exploited by someone else, lose our freedom and, with it, ourselves. For that reason the radical faith Jesus demands cannot be the choice of an individual within a society in which every individual fights for her or his own advantage. Anyone who lived that way would be brutally and unscrupulously exploited.

The faith that is service, what the gospel calls for, requires for its basis a space of common faith in which there are many other people who choose not themselves but God's cause. It requires the backing of people who regard one another as called by God. To put it another way: gospel faith needs a background in communities in which people care for one another in love and act as servants for the sake of the same thing: God's plan.

Where there is the mutual support without which faith cannot radiate, there the world is turned upside down: mountains will be moved, people can walk on water (Matt 14:29), huge trees take root in the sea (Luke 17:6). There a profound freedom arises, one in which each individual finds and realizes himself or herself—not in the

---

[1] Language usage reflects the biblical text. Clearly, the parable is not an endorsement of slavery, but an illustration of the point that faith is pure service, just as Jesus' saying that his disciples have to take up the cross is not an approbation of the Roman practice of crucifixion.—Tr.

prison that they are, in and of themselves, but in the broad banqueting hall of God's new world.

There the parable of the useless slave is overturned, for those who make Jesus' cause their own are ultimately no longer slaves, but friends. "I do not call you servants any longer," says Jesus, "for the servant does not know what the master is doing; but I have called you friends" (John 15:15).

A World Transformed

"If you had faith the size of a mustard seed, you could say to this mulberry tree, 'Be uprooted and planted in the sea,' and it would obey you."

(Luke 17:6)

A Tantalizing Word

This Jesus saying was important to the early church: the authors of the gospels quote it often (Matt 17:20; 21:21; Mark 11:23; Luke 17:6). Even Paul knew it (1 Cor 13:2). The saying must have clarified something crucial.

When Jesus' sayings were used frequently in the early church, there often came to be several versions of them. Such was the case with this one. In Matthew's and Mark's version it is a mountain that throws itself into the sea (meaning Lake Gennesareth, the "Sea" of Galilee). For Luke it is a tree. Variants of that sort show how alive the Jesus tradition was in the earliest church.

Luke put the free-floating Jesus saying into a new context, building a little scene around it. Here the Twelve suddenly appear from among the many disciples and ask Jesus: "Increase our faith!" In answer to that plea Jesus speaks the words about the faith that moves trees. What is the relationship between Jesus' answer and the apostles' petition? Does Jesus grant their request and increase their faith?

Evidently not! Instead, he shows the apostles that their plea is useless. It is by no means as good as it seems at first. It sounds pious; after all, it says "our faith is small; it needs to be greater." But the petition presupposes: "we already have a certain amount of faith, a basis for more. Our faith just has to be greater." Hence: "Increase our faith!"

As I have said: that sounds pious and appealing. In reality, Luke sees the apostles' plea as having nothing to recommend it. He immediately exposes it; in substance he has Jesus answer: "Your premise is false. You say your faith is still too little and it needs to be increased. That is precisely the illusion in which you are living. Your faith is not too small; it does not even exist yet. If it were present even to the least degree, it would already be enough. Even if your faith were as tiny as a mustard seed you could use it to change the world and make the impossible a reality."

That, in fact, is what the image of the replanting of a mulberry tree in the "Sea of Galilee" means (Mark 1:16; Matt 15:29; John 6:1, and frequently). Mulberry trees have especially large, deep-growing root systems. Displacing such a tree into Lake Gennesareth is utterly impossible. It is contrary to nature. It flies in the face of the laws of physics and biology; it is outside any human experience.

That is precisely the point Jesus seizes upon. "If you really had faith," he says, "even the tiniest bit, you could make the impossible possible and turn the world and its laws upside down. But since you can't do that, you must conclude that you have no faith at all. So leave off your pious talk and don't ask me to increase your faith."

I think that is the logic of the text in Luke's version. Faith is radicalized here to a positively terrifying degree. Faith is such a fundamental reorientation of life that there is no more or less. There is only the alternative: faith or no faith.

Reorientation of Life

That says something essential about faith. It is not an additional story on top of one's life-structure, such as: First we build our lives, as does everyone in our society—and then we add faith as something extra special. Then faith would be a kind of ornament and refinement of our own self-created life project.

But faith is by no means such an addition. It is a completely new orientation of the human person. It demands an either-or. Either one believes or not. Either one orients one's life entirely to the reign of God or one remains fixated on the old world. If we remain standing where we are and only turn our head slightly toward the new thing, we do not yet believe at all.

Obviously, that is not all that can be said about faith—not by a long shot. There remains, for example, the question: what is it really about?

Ask a Christian who knows her catechism what she, as a Christian, believes. She will probably answer: "I believe in God." That answer would be correct. Another might say: "I believe that Jesus is the Son of God," and that, obviously, would be correct also. What is so astonishing is that Jesus' saying about the mustard seed gives a different answer. Through their faith the disciples are to move mountains or trees into the sea, that is, turn the old world upside down and make the impossible possible. *Here* the goal of biblical faith is evidently a transformed world.

Luke uses the context to show more precisely what this means. That is, before the apostles ask for an increase of faith Jesus has said, in the Lukan composition:

> If another disciple[1] sins, you must rebuke the offender, and if there is repentance, you must forgive. And if the same person sins against you seven times a day, and turns back to you seven times and says, "I repent," you must forgive. (Luke 17:3-4)

Forgiveness without End

It is clear what this text is about: the new community of God built on constant forgiveness. Its essence *is* forgiveness. In the Christian community one must not forgive one's sister or brother once a day, but seven times a day—that is, constantly. That is the immediate context that precedes the saying about faith that moves mulberry trees. Jesus requires of his disciples a forgiveness that is constantly given anew.

The twelve apostles are realists. They rightly think: that doesn't happen. We can never manage that. We're not built that way! So they ask Jesus: "Increase our faith!"

We have to understand Jesus' answer this way: "You are quite right. Living on the basis of a forgiveness that the other accepts over and over again, that doesn't bear a grudge, that constantly views him or her with the kind eyes of God—that is truly impossible for human beings. It is as impossible as it would be for you to replant this mighty tree in the Sea of Gennesareth.

[1] Greek: your brother.

"But if you had faith, it would be possible. Then there would be community, then there could be fellowship without rivalries, without classes, and without the sublime mechanisms of oppression. Then a togetherness in which each one does not go her own way would be possible. If you had faith there would be a reconciled society that does not drift apart, that does not wear itself out in power struggles with one another, but that joins together in seeking the will of God. And so the old society would be turned on its head. Then the laws of the old world that seem to be as unchangeable as the laws of nature would be opened up to something entirely new. But all that can only happen out of faith."

Thus by bringing together the saying about continual forgiveness and the one about faith that moves mighty trees Luke makes clear: the goal of faith is not primarily the world beyond; it is not first and foremost the invisible. It is the concretely social, the visible, the here and now. Jesus did not preach heaven but the reign of God, and that reign desires a new society and with it a reconciled world that never again sinks down into hatred and war.

Continual forgiveness and reconciliation are thus only possible on the basis of faith, only out of a complete reorientation toward God's cause. Where such faith exists, mountains will be moved and trees will be replanted in the ocean: that is, there the laws of the old world will be crushed to give access to God's new world.

Walking on Water

The gospels do not just tell stories about the past that happened nearly two thousand years ago. They also tell us about ourselves, because the old stories keep happening anew. They suddenly take on life, bloom again, give believers consolation and help. After all, the present often proves burdensome and painful, and our faith is constantly threatened: by our doubt in God's power and by our fear that we would miss something if we surrendered ourselves entirely to God.

But our faith is not threatened only by ourselves; danger comes from outside as well. It is threatened by people who hate Christian belief, and still more by the superior laughter of those "in the know," for whom faith is simply superfluous and even an enemy of life itself.

Night on the Lake

The gospels tell about these constant threats against our faithfulness to God by raising up images that are more real than external facts ever can be. That doesn't exclude memory of historical events; not at all. Still, we do not do justice to the stories in the gospels if we continually ask whether what they tell about happened back then just as it is told and not some other way. We must not ask only what actually happened then but, above all, what the old stories want to tell us, today's hearers and readers. That is when they can happen for us too. Then they come to life in our midst.

Let us look at the story about walking on water in Matthew 14:22-33 from this point of view. The disciples are on Lake Gennesareth. It has grown late. It is night. Beneath them there is nothing but water. It is deep, apparently bottomless, and they cannot reach the shore

45

they are aiming at because a worrisome adverse wind has risen. Everyone who follows Jesus has to reckon with such situations: adverse winds and unfathomable depths.

This gospel really speaks quite graphically about the dangers to faith. It tells about our fear, the darkness in us, and the things that threaten faith from without: the adverse wind of the society in which we live.

Jesus' Presence

But Matthew 14:22-33 also says something quite different: that we are not alone. Jesus did not send out his disciples all alone, as individuals; they are together in a boat, and that boat is more than just a symbol of common work or friendship, for those are in short supply. Our reserves of sympathy and simply working toward a common goal are exhausted all too soon. Our egoism is usually stronger than our solidarity. The theologians of the early church already saw that boat as an image of the church.

What really protects that boat during the night—we could also say "what makes the church to be church"—is the presence of Jesus, who is mysteriously with his disciples. True, he is praying on a mountain far away, but precisely because he is with his Father he is entirely with his disciples. He comes from his "being with the father" to those disciples "in the fourth watch of the night," that is, in the first grey light of morning, as their protector.

He walks on the water. Nothing can threaten him. The deep has no power over him. He is held up because he trusts his heavenly Father and is completely one with the will of God. We, too, can be assured that Jesus comes to us, rescues us over and over again. He also shows himself to us, appears to us: namely, in the enduring form of his body, the church, in the assembly of believers, in the reception of the sacraments.

The bad part is just that we are normally so blind that we do not even recognize him when he comes to us. We don't understand his coming. We see ghosts instead. We are overcome with "great terror . . . terror such as has not been" (Ps 53:5):

> *When the disciples saw him walking on the lake, they were terrified, saying, "It is a ghost!" And they cried out in fear.* (Matt 14:26)

That is precisely our reaction. God wants to bring us help through people who speak to us in God's name. God comes to meet us through human messengers—and we pay no attention to God's offer of help. On the contrary: in our fear and anxiety we make the other into a threatening ghost. We see our independence, our freedom, our self-worth endangered. We become fearful for our sacred "I"—and then reality warps and we see phantoms.

The disciples would not have escaped their fear unless Jesus had spoken to them. Only his words: "Take heart, it is I; do not be afraid" (Matt 14:27) overcome their mistrust. Those words snatch the blindfold from their eyes and they suddenly know that they are seeing Jesus and not a chimera.

Peter's Courage and Peter's Fear

Matthew inserted another episode into the narrative he had received; this is not found in Mark or the corresponding parallel in John (cf. Mark 6:45-52 and John 6:16-21). In Matthew's version it is not only Jesus who walks on the water but Peter as well. When he sees Jesus approaching the boat, he says:

> *"Lord, if it is you, command me to come to you on the water."* (Matt 14:28-29)

Why is Peter so eager to walk on the water? We could interpret his wish in terms of depth psychology: it is the impulse to freedom, the wish to be able to move freely—the same longing that makes us dream at night that we can fly like a bird. Sweeping over the trees or walking on the water—those are the same thing. This is the longing to be able to do everything and to go wherever we want.

Still, that interpretation does not really fit the text. It is no accident that the episode is told about Simon Peter. In other places Peter also takes the initiative, fails, and yet is held fast by Jesus. This episode inserted into Matthew's story reflects the whole history of Peter's calling. The one who wants to build the eschatological Israel on Jesus (Matt 16:17-19) and yet denies him (Matt 26:69-75), and still finds forgiveness (John 21:15-19)—this Peter wants to be entirely where Jesus is. He wants to connect with him; he wants to shelter by him and do the same things that Jesus does. Simon's walking across the water to Jesus expresses the fact that he wants to live entirely with Jesus. His walking on the water is an image for his following Jesus.

This tells us that whoever follows Jesus in faith can even walk on water and be held up when one really should sink. Such a one will not be swallowed up by the world's chaos and the depth of meaninglessness. She or he will walk as if on solid ground.

But the episode with Simon Peter also shows that discipleship is not a game. It presumes trust and faith. If faith flees away and we surrender to fear, the water will not hold us any longer and we will begin to sink, as Peter did (Matt 14:30). But if our faith remains solid despite all challenges, it will lead us into freedom. Then the believer can fly like a bird and even walk on water—but it is a different flight and a different way of walking from what our all-too-human wishes desire. It is made possible by freedom from oneself, obedience to another will, listening to God's promises.

The Confession

The story continues: Jesus reaches out his hand and grasps Peter, and both climb into the boat.

> *When they got into the boat, the wind ceased. The disciples in the boat fell on their knees before Jesus, saying, "Truly you are the Son of God."* (Matt 14:32-33)[1]

Ultimately this confession shows that two levels of narrative are interleaved in our story: first there is the experience of the disciples with the *earthly Jesus*, experience that took place before Easter. That had already shown them that Jesus was the saving presence of God.

In Matthew's story, however, and elsewhere in the gospels, we also find the concentrated experience of the *church*, in which the pre-Easter history of redemption is continued in a new way and is necessarily expressed in some first statements of faith. Experience that sustains our whole life has to be expressed concretely, in *statements*.

We latecomers can enter into these experiences. It is not just ourselves and our private lives that Jesus repeatedly rescues from chaos; it is also our congregations and just as much the whole church. Therefore we, too, can confess before Jesus: "Truly, you are the Son of God."

---

[1] From the author's translation.

Compliment and Return Compliment

The eleventh chapter of Luke offers us a little scene that reveals something of Jesus' wit and also of his graciousness. One day, while he is talking to a crowd, a woman interrupts him. She shouts at him:

> *"Blessed is the womb that bore you*
> *and the breasts that nursed you!"* (Luke 11:27)

The Compliment

Older translations and commentaries often called this shout a "benediction of the mother of Jesus." But that does not really capture what the woman was saying. After all, the person being called blessed here is, of course, Jesus himself, but he is blessed by having his mother exalted. That is good Middle Eastern style (and by no means unknown in ancient Greek culture either). In the Middle East it is possible to praise someone by praising his or her mother, and similarly to insult someone by insulting that person's mother.

Obviously this little statement is also a basis for the church's later praise of Mary. It is good and right to praise Mary and call her blessed. But we only arrive at a true praise of Mary when that praise is inextricably bound up with looking at Jesus and listening to him. That is precisely what the church must conclude from this little scene.

The Return Compliment

So the woman in the crowd, by praising Jesus' mother, compliments Jesus himself. It just bursts out of her. She simply can no longer listen silently. She has to "raise her voice," as the text says literally. And how does Jesus respond to her enthusiastic shout? He answers promptly and just as succinctly:

"Blessed rather are those who hear the word of God and keep it!" (Luke 11:28)

What is that? Just a correction of what the woman said? Not at all! The woman gave Jesus a compliment. Jesus, as a polite Middle Easterner, offers her a compliment in return. After all, the woman has been listening to him; therefore she in turn is called blessed: "Blessed are those who hear the word of God and keep it."

Of course, Jesus' answer is not simply a return compliment. His response also contains a tactful clarification. We see that already in the way Jesus' answer is introduced: with a countering statement that bears a special emphasis in Greek: "*But he* said . . ." Add this as well: Jesus does not call the woman blessed all by herself. He wants to include all his listeners in the return compliment. Of course, he cannot say: "More than that: Blessed are you who hear the word of God and keep it" because Jesus has to leave open the question whether everyone in the crowd is keeping the word of God (see Luke 11:15-17). Thus the indirect "blessed are those who hear the word of God and keep it" is altogether appropriate (quite apart from the fact that benedictions in the Bible are usually in the third person).

Still, that by no means says everything that is contained in Jesus' answer. He not only opens the return compliment to a larger group of people—ultimately to the "new family" now coming to life in Israel (see Luke 8:19-21). No, he also indicates that "hearing" alone is not enough. It must be accompanied by a "keeping" of his words.

Hearing, Keeping, Doing

At this point something must necessarily be said about the word "keep." The NRSV, for example, does not read "Blessed rather are those who hear the word of God and keep it," but "Blessed rather are those who hear the word of God and obey it!" The translation of the underlying Greek verb *phylassein* with "obey" and not "keep" is very common and at first glance seems much more appropriate,[1] and yet translating "obey" loses something highly important.

---

[1] The RSV and the AV (King James) still read ". . . and keep it." NABRE has ". . . and observe it." The author's text uses "befolgen" for "obey." The word can also mean "follow," "act on," "abide by," or "keep [a rule]."—Tr.

In the background of "keep" lies a fixed usage from the Old Testament law texts, with which Jesus was very familiar—and that is simply because, like every devout Jew, he had learned them by heart from childhood. We can see this formulaic usage, for example, in Deuteronomy 7:12:

> If you [the addressee is Israel] [*hear*] these ordinances, and *keep* and *follow* them, the LORD your God will *keep* with you the covenant and the steadfast love which he swore to your [ancestors] to keep.[2]

Here, and at many other places in the Torah (for examples see Exod 15:26 and Deut 6:3; 13:19), we encounter this same threefold formula, or at least a version of it. Behind the formula lies a real process, that is, a very particular method for learning.

How does a child learn Torah? First the teacher (often the mother or father) recites it repeatedly: the child *hears* the Torah. Once having heard the texts often enough, the child knows them by heart. Now everything depends on not forgetting the texts thus learned by rote: the student must also *keep* them. She or he must protect and watch over them as a shepherd watches a flock. That is precisely what lies behind the Hebrew *shamar*, which appears regularly in these texts. Its basic meaning is "protect" and "watch over." The text must be "protected"—that is, nothing in it may be changed, and therefore one must know it by heart.

Certainly that is not all that is involved in the learning process. A student of Torah must not only *hear* and *memorize* the texts but also *do* them, live them. Only then can one fully understand the texts.

That was exactly how Jesus, too, "learned" the texts of Sacred Scripture as a child and youth. He *heard* them from his parents, over and over again; he *kept* them in his heart and mind (that is, he memorized them), and he *did* them.

For Jesus, as for every devout Jew, such a learning method was a matter of course. Consequently he had no need to explain the whole three-step process of learning Torah when he gave his brief and clearly stated answer to the woman. All he had to do was speak of "hearing" and "keeping." In another scene, the one in which Jesus

[2] RSV, modified.

separates from his family because they want to drag him back home, he speaks of "hearing" and "doing," here dropping the *middle part*:

> "*My mother and my brothers are those*
> *who <u>hear</u> the word of God and <u>do</u> it.*" (Luke 8:21)

In short: we must conclude that Jesus, in offering his return compliment to the woman from the crowd, first agrees with her. We can paraphrase: "Yes, your benediction was correct; it was not wrong. But something else is much more important: not only hearing the word of God (just as you are doing at this moment) but taking it so much to heart that you 'know it by heart,' can never forget it, and because of that never-forgetting you also *do* it, *keep* it, *follow* it."

Almost as an afterthought Jesus also makes it clear that what is important is not admiring him as a person but hearing, keeping, and doing the word of God. Jesus thus corrects what the woman said, but he does so with deliberate graciousness, in such a way that in the "return compliment" nothing of his correction is lost.

God's Own Word

Look at how many words I have used—and had to use—to interpret Luke 11:27-28. Jesus was better. He said it all in one brief sentence; it could scarcely have been more concise. He makes the woman a return compliment in a familiar form and with great kindness while still offering a tactful correction.

And yet that is by no means all there is to say, and Jesus' return compliment has not been adequately interpreted—because what was really happening there? Jesus calls blessed those who hear, keep, and do the word of God. That is not an instruction divorced from the concrete situation. It is a blessing on all those who were then gathered around Jesus and listening to him—assuming that they take in and keep the word of God. It is by no means a general, abstract statement about just anyone anywhere; it is concretely about those crowding in and listening to Jesus. These real listeners gathered around Jesus are blessed because *now* they are hearing the word of God. So in his three-part formula Jesus is not talking about the Torah in general; he is speaking about the teaching that HE and no other is presently speaking. *The word of God his listeners are to hear, keep, and do is his own word.*

That is outrageous. What Jesus speaks is the word of God—and not in the sense that he has received it as a prophet and now proclaims it, as he is commissioned to do, but because he himself directly and *immediately* speaks the word of God as the one who *is* himself the Word of God. Jesus' return compliment has a christological implication. That is: it contains within itself the christology that would later develop.

So we see that the little scene reported to us in Luke 11:27-28 is multidimensional: first there is the spontaneous and enthusiastic compliment of the woman shouting from the crowd; then an immediate return compliment from Jesus that affirms what the woman says and at the same time politely corrects her; and finally a Jesus who knows himself as the direct speaker of the word of God and who demands, with regard to his own word, precisely what God demands in regard to the Torah from Sinai: hearing, keeping the word, and doing it.

All that is immensely important for Christian faith: first our text speaks of the necessity to really "hear" the words of Scripture, to consider them again and again—sometimes contrary to our habits of hearing and reading, against internal reworkings of texts that have embedded themselves in us and that each of us carries around with us. In community worship and in our personal study of Scripture we must take in every text of Sacred Scripture as if we were hearing it for the first time.

Then it would be good if we would "keep" as many words of Scripture as possible, that is, learn them by heart. Then we would constantly carry them with us, so that we repeat them to ourselves and thus are able to take them deeper and deeper into our hearts.

Furthermore, we are to "do" them, because only when we do them can we really understand what these texts mean to say to us.

Finally, what is crucial is that we hear the Torah itself in the words of Jesus—not a *new* Torah, not even an *expansion* of Torah, but the clarification, the explanation, the fulfillment of the one Torah from Sinai—because Jesus, in his own person, is himself the living, eschatological Torah.

Apparently Contrary to All Reason

John's gospel contains a strange story. It takes place in Jerusalem and it is about "Greeks" who want to speak with Jesus. Most likely these are God-fearing Gentiles who have traveled to Jerusalem for the feast of Passover—that is, they are Israel-sympathizers who want to worship the true God in the temple. They seek a dialogue with Jesus, and so they approach Philip, who consults Andrew (these two are, significantly, the only two among the Twelve who have Greek names). Philip and Andrew then speak to Jesus and present him with the Greeks' request.

Now something strange happens in the story: nothing is said about any actual meeting between Jesus and the Greeks. Instead Jesus begins, without any preliminaries, to speak about his death. He seems to give Philip and Andrew no answer to what they have told him—and the Greeks disappear from the story (John 12:20-36).

Against All Logical Reasons?

I read not long ago that the Christian faith is the most rational one there is. Is that true? What is told here in John's gospel seems to fly in the face of every logic. At this point reason would say: "Take care that you have as many friends as possible, because in the course of your life you can quickly fall into a situation in which you have urgent need of others' help!" And every experienced business leader would say: "Create a network of connections for your firm and take every opportunity that arises to make international contacts—especially if your company intends to expand worldwide."

What happens in John 12:20-36? Jesus is offered new friends and contacts from abroad—and he doesn't even react. What an opportunity for Jesus to introduce his message into the Greek cultural sphere! Still more: what a chance for him to create new possibilities for his great task! After all, he knows that the air in Jerusalem is poisonous for him. He has to expect that they will make an end of him there. Why not preach among sympathizers and friends abroad what he is not allowed to say in his homeland, and thus strategically outflank his opponents in Jerusalem? That is precisely where the Greeks could be a help to him. But Jesus does not even speak with them. Is that rational?

Or can it be that the text does address them? Jesus suddenly speaks about his death—not with the Greeks, but possibly with their contacts, Andrew and Philip. Evidently, then, Jesus does not seek an escape route. Instead, he says:

> *"Those who love their life lose it, and those who hate their life in this world will keep it for eternal life."* (John 12:25)

But doesn't that make the whole thing even less rational? Is Jesus flirting with death? Is he living some sort of death-mysticism? In the end, is he even deliberately intent on dying? If that were the case we would have to turn away, somewhat put out, and whisper: "That seems sick!"

How God Changes the World

So is Christianity rational? Is the text we are discussing really reasonable? First we need to clarify the basis of Jesus' "operations." Could he have gone to another country?

The answer: No! He could not and would not. The fact that he could not is connected to a basic and highly rational rule of salvation history. Jesus knew that fundamental rule and took it to heart as none other ever did. We could say it this way:

The world cannot be changed by spreading messages worldwide. God introduced another way to overcome the potential for evil in human history. God began at a very particular place in the world, and with a single individual: namely, Abraham.

It went on from there. Beginning with Abraham, God gathered a people, a clearly-defined people taking its definition from the instruction at Sinai—a people to whom God made a promise—a people with prophets who again and again confronted Israel with God's truth, whether it was convenient or inconvenient—a people who had a center on which the promise depended, namely, the holy city Jerusalem. This people was to be a blessing for all peoples simply by remaining true to its calling and keeping its covenant with God. Jesus was born into that people; he was sent to that people. He was to gather it, sanctify it, and make it once and for all a hope for the nations.

That is one of the basic laws of salvation history, and it is absolutely rational. No inflated speeches, airy global strategies, diffuse world ethos, compacts only on paper—and most certainly not religious esotericism—can advance God's cause. In order to change the world, God needs a real community. Faith must be visible, socially comprehensible, its effects illuminating. It must be tangible in a concrete people; otherwise it is mere ideology or fantasy.

That is precisely why Jesus had to proclaim his message about the new and definitive gathering of the people of God in Israel and nowhere else—and not just in Israel but, in the end, in Jerusalem, that elect city that was again and again unfaithful. He had to appear before Israel's leaders, confront them with his mission for the people of God. Anything else would have been avoidance, flight, and lazy compromise.

Did Jesus Want to Die?

Now for the question of the death-wish! When Jesus said that he had to die in Jerusalem, that was no longing for death and most certainly not death-mysticism. It was sober clarity of vision and fidelity to his duty. Jesus had to fight for that fidelity, even in the depths of his own heart, because he, like all of us, loved his life. That is clear from a text in the Letter to the Hebrews, which says that Jesus implored God "with loud cries and tears" to save him from death (Heb 5:7). So Jesus had an elementary fear of death, just as we all do. No, Jesus was not driven by a sick death-wish. He was driven by fidelity to his duty and by love for the people of God.

We must also firmly reject the idea that God wanted a sacrifice, and a bloody one. No, God willed something altogether different: believing people who open themselves to God's actions. When the responsible authorities in Israel rejected Jesus and brought him to the cross, that was *not* what God willed. God did not want blood, but faith and repentance. That Jesus' bloody death shook many of God's people and led them to repent is an altogether different matter. It illustrates a reality we must speak about with the greatest care. I will call it "crucified love." In the end that crucified love is stronger than all unbelief and every evil.

A Heart That Is Pure Love

There is an unusual explanation for this rejected and crucified love that enters into death for Israel's sake: a text in the book of the prophet Jeremiah that speaks of an unimaginable hope. The text says that days will come in which God will place instruction, that is, the Torah from Sinai, no longer carved on stone tablets but in the hearts of the people of Israel (Jer 31:31-34). This names one of the greatest problems faced by every human being.

In one way or another we all want what is good, and yet we must again and again acknowledge, with horror, that we want it and at the same time we don't. Our will remains superficial. We will something out of routine or because nothing else seems possible, from a feeling of obligation, or even because others want it.

But we cannot command ourselves to will from our inmost being, from our hearts, from the ultimate depths of our existence. In and of ourselves we really do not will God and God's cause. On our own we really want only ourselves. We are afraid of God and secretly suspect that God's intentions for us are not good. In that way we constantly destroy our communion with God—just as Israel repeatedly broke its covenant with God.

Then the miracle happened: there was one person who did not have a heart of stone, who willed not himself but only God, his Father, and wanted only what God wanted: namely, that *through Israel* all the peoples of the earth might find peace. Here was a heart that was pure love and that blessed even those who pierced it.

Scripture tells us that if there is such a heart something will happen that exceeds all reason. It is not that the heart would be irrational; rather, it stands above all reason. That is: if there is such a heart, then the world will make sense again; at least in *one* place creation is as God wanted it to be—and then the covenant with Israel is renewed and God's wedlock with the people of God is healed again.

And then, *then* the moment has come in which others in Israel can follow and their hardened hearts can live again; then there can also be proclamation beyond Israel and even the Greeks can see and understand, and with the Greeks the many from all the nations. Not before! That is why Jesus says in the course of our text, in which only a superficial reading ignores the Greeks: "unless a grain of wheat falls into the earth and dies, it remains just a single grain; but if it dies, it bears much fruit" (John 12:24).

So it is clear: the text takes the Gentiles who have come to speak with Jesus seriously: radically so. But for that very reason he comes to the point immediately and points to the precondition for all outreach to the Gentiles: the repentance of God's own people. And that repentance cannot happen unless the grain of wheat dies. How true this parable is! There are things in this world that can be altered only by death.

I have said that if there is this *One,* this *one* heart, all others can follow. Then the miracle of relying totally on God can happen for them, too. We can experience that in ourselves. When we renew our baptismal covenant at the Easter Vigil, this blessed experience is offered to us: something we ourselves cannot do, for what we bring with us is only our sinfulness. But we are incorporated into the love of the Crucified, and in that love we can bear rich fruit for God's great plan with the world.

Where Is the Land?

The promise of land is fundamental for the Old Testament. The patriarch Abraham, who is called by God so that in him "all the families of the earth shall be blessed," hears from God in Genesis 12:1:

> *"Go from your country and your kindred and your father's house to the land that I will show you."*

From that point on, the keyword "land" runs throughout nearly every book of the Bible. The last book of the Hebrew Bible, 2 Chronicles, ends with the command of Cyrus of Persia that all those in his kingdom who belong to the people of the God of Israel should return from exile to the land of their ancestors—meaning the real ground of Israel.

How did Jesus see it? Unquestionably, the promise of the land appears in his words, too: "Blessed are the meek, *for they will inherit the land*," says Jesus in the third Beatitude (Matt 5:5). Is that only an image, in contrast to the Old Testament?[1] Is it only figurative? Purely spiritual? Does it point to a country of souls, a land of interiority? In the end, does "land" here really mean heaven?

Houses and Fields

The key to understanding this question, which is so fundamental for Christian faith, is found in Mark 10:29-30, where Jesus says:

> *". . . there is no one who has left house or brothers or sisters or mother or father or children or fields, for my sake and for the sake of the good news, who*

---

[1] The usual English translation, "for they will inherit the earth," shifts the Beatitude to the metaphorical level.—Tr.

> *will not receive a hundredfold now in this age—houses, brothers and sisters,*
> *mothers and children, and fields, with persecutions—and in the age to come*
> *eternal life."*

This text contrasts the families whom Jesus' disciples have left behind and the new family they find in following Jesus. A simple contrast would have sufficed: brothers and sisters, fathers, mothers, children. But that list is framed by the naming of houses and fields. That must have been deliberate. This is not just about the *persons* in the new family. It is also about the share of Jesus' disciples in the "land."

A brief but pregnant notice in the Acts of the Apostles shows us what we should understand by that. The author of Acts reports that Barnabas, a native of Cyprus, had bought a field (Acts 4:36-37). Probably Barnabas, like many Diaspora Jews, had moved to Jerusalem and acquired a piece of land near the city in order to cement his belonging to the land of Israel and his share in the blessings of the messianic era. He sold that field—according to Acts—for the sake of the Jesus community, because its upbuilding was more important to him than possession of the field.

This illustrates what Mark 10:29-30 means: the houses and fields abandoned by Jesus' disciples were their share in the Holy Land. Those are lost to them, and yet their share in the Land of Promise is not lost (any more than it was lost to Barnabas). Their "land" will be the new family that Jesus gathers around himself. There they find everything again, a hundredfold; there they truly enter into "the Land." The promise of land to Israel is fulfilled on the ground of the new family.

The gift of the land, a central blessing in the Old Testament, is thus by no means shifted to pure interiority in the New Testament. It is fulfilled in the post-Easter communities that quickly spread like a net across the land, for in those communities there are not only brothers and sisters with whom one joins one's life. There are also houses in which the people gather. Establishing a room for the assembly or having rooms and houses made available was essential, as is clear from the frequent mention of "houses" in early Christianity. The reference is not only to particular families but also to their houses, where the people assembled.

The Land Remains a Reality

We should therefore guard against reading the promise of new houses and fields in Mark 10:29-30 as something purely symbolic. Jesus was thinking of the houses in which his disciples were received at evening when he sent them out through the land of Israel (Matt 10:11-15; Mark 6:10; Luke 9:4; 10:5-12). Those were a necessary background to his gathering of the people of God. There were not only disciples who traveled with him; there were also many friends and sympathizers throughout the land. Later their houses often formed the basis for Christian communities.

Thus the "land" in the New Testament is not dissolved into something purely spiritual. It is protected from that kind of hasty spiritualizing. It has something movingly visible about it. It remains real—just as real as the "hundred brothers and sisters, mothers and children" Jesus promises his disciples.

At least since Jesus, though, it is also clear that "land" cannot mean "state." Such an interpretation would be questionable even in light of the Old Testament. Abraham was not promised a state, but a land, and when Israel escaped from the theocracy of Egypt it received at Sinai not a constitution but a new order of society. Thus the "land" is not a "state" or "nation-state." The question remains: will this "land" remain forever tied to a particular territory?

The Expansion of the Promise of Land

In Romans 4:13, Paul speaks of ancestral Abraham no longer as "heir of the land" but instead of the "world." He is writing very much within the frame of the classic biblical tradition of the land promise, but now the original promise is expanded to include the whole world.

That by no means signifies that it is suddenly spiritualized. This is still very concretely about houses and assembly rooms, about communities within which everyday reality is formed and transformed within the ordering of the reign of God. But now the possession of land for Jesus Messiah applies to the whole world.

This "expansion of the promise of land" does not begin in the New Testament. It is attested in early Judaism: in the book of Jubilees (ca. 150 BCE) Abraham is promised all the land that lies under the heavens as his heritage (see esp. Jub. 32:17-19). No doubt the background here is a positive interpretation of the Jewish Diaspora and the expansion of Jewish synagogues throughout the whole of the ancient world.

If we keep all these distinctions in mind we can ultimately hold fast, with much less effort, to the exceptional meaning of the land of Israel for every Jew and, to a lesser degree, for every Christian as well.

Once God led our father Abraham into this real land; here God gathered a people; here the temple stood; here Jesus lived. God desires the saving transformation of the whole world, but that had to begin in a concrete, definable place. Salvation is neither timeless nor placeless. Therefore the profound symbolism of the land of Israel cannot be abandoned. Still, it should now be clear that "land" in the sense we have described has nothing to do with a theocracy or a state religion.

What about the State of Israel?

Certainly, all that being said, the question of the present state of Israel arises: can it be biblically justified? Regarding this question Christians, at least European Christians and especially Germans, have to be extremely careful. After all, it was the duty of Christians to point their Jewish sisters and brothers to the "land" in the New Testament sense: an open land, one in which there was room for synagogues and for all the children of Israel.

Historically, Jews lived among Christians but were continually robbed by them, driven out of their homes, excluded, or killed—despite the fact that the Christians in particular were obligated to protect and console their Jewish sisters and brothers. After World War II the European Jews had to build a state for themselves in order to be able to live in some kind of security.

As long as that history has not been dealt with, and in a time when European anti-Judaism is again virulent, Christians must refuse to offer Jews any advice about the right way to think about the "land." We Christians can only seek to realize our own understanding of the "land"—that is, an international network of communities living according to the Sermon on the Mount. That is so because, since the New Testament, a "state" interpretation of the land can no longer exist—not, at least, for us Christians. Most certainly, "state churches" and a "church state" in the sense that was familiar in past centuries (such as the Papal States that once covered nearly half of central Italy) have nothing—absolutely nothing—to do with the New Testament.

The "Poor" in the Sermon on the Mount

The Sermon on the Mount has an entryway, namely, the Beatitudes. No one can get inside without going through the entry. Like the Sermon itself, the Beatitudes have retained their fascination—but their absoluteness has frightened many.

On first hearing, of course, the Beatitudes sound pleasant, even encouraging. Who does not rejoice when the nonviolent and those who create peace are called happy, when the sorrowful are promised consolation and the hungry that they will be filled? There are too many poor in the world, too many who have been ensnared and their lives betrayed for us not to listen when someone tells us: it will not always be that way; everything will change, especially for the poor and the hungry.

But if we read the Beatitudes more closely and pay attention to their form as we find it in Matthew (Matt 5:3-12), we begin to have doubts about our usual understanding of them—about what we have too hastily read in them.

Are they really talking about the deprived and oppressed, the starving and miserable people on earth? The very first beatitude (Matt 5:3) is irritating. It is not the poor who are called blessed, but literally the "poor in spirit."[1] According to the fourth (Matt 5:6), it is not the hungry who will be filled but those "who hunger and thirst for righteousness."

Those Matthean additions all by themselves (cf. the different version in Luke 6:20-23) provoke the question: who are these beatitudes about, anyway? Today we mainly think in a social context (they are about eliminating poverty), and we unavoidably think globally (they

---

[1] The German *Einheitsübersetzung* paraphrases: "those who are poor in the sight of God." The English "poor in spirit" goes all the way back to the Authorized (King James) Version, as does "hunger and thirst after righteousness."—Tr.

are about the world as a whole). Hence we can no longer imagine Jesus other than as someone who has the poor of this world in view and wants to make their cause his own. We will see that this idea is altogether correct. But at first reading it seems that the text says the opposite—and we have to take this awkwardness in the Beatitudes seriously, or else we will miss the whole point.

So Who Is Called Blessed?

For the moment let us consider the "poor in spirit." That expression has been ridiculed so often that we can scarcely speak it any more, but in Jesus' time it had a different melody from what it has for us. If we want to know what "poor in spirit" might have meant, we are best advised to read the book of the prophet Zephaniah.

That prophet baldly describes the crisis in Judah that had ballooned during the royal period. Jerusalem is a city that is "soiled, defiled, and oppressive," governed by a powerful upper class. Israel's princes and judges are as violent as "lions" and "wolves," its prophets are "reckless," "faithless" persons, its priests "have profaned what is sacred" and "do violence to the Torah" (Zeph 3:1-4). Hence, from a human point of view, there is no future for the people of God. It is destroying itself.

Even so, God wants to rescue this people—and that is because of the task God has planned for it. The book of Zephaniah describes with the greatest precision how that plan will succeed. The crucial text reads:

> On that day you shall not be put to shame
>> because of all the deeds by which you have rebelled against me;
>> for then I will remove from your midst
>> your proudly exultant ones,
>> and you shall no longer be haughty
>> in my holy mountain.
> For I will leave in the midst of you
>> a people humble and poor.[2]
>> They shall seek refuge in the name of the LORD—

[2] NRSV "lowly."

> *the remnant of Israel;*
> > *they shall do no wrong*
> > *and utter no lies,*
> > *nor shall a deceitful tongue*
> > *be found in their mouths.* (Zeph 3:11-13)

This text is the biblical background for the "poor" in Matthew 5:3. They are the believing "remnant" of the people of God who, despite being persecuted and humiliated, still try to live according to God's social order and place their hope in God alone. These "little ones," these powerless people, physically poor as well, are promised a new, secure, and fulfilled life in the land. The concepts contrary to "poor" in this text should be noted. They are "proudly exultant," "haughty," and "deceitful." "Poor" thus relates here to "humble," but above all, these "poor" are not all the suffering people on earth: they are the poor among the people of God who do not give up hope in the promises and await everything from God.

Accordingly, the "sorrowful" in Matthew are, first of all, not everyone who suffers in this world; they are those who get into trouble for God's sake. They sorrow over the condition of the people of God— over their own unbelief and that of others, which obstruct the revelation of God's glory. The sorrowing are "those who mourn in Zion" (see Isa 61:3). And the hungry and thirsty in Matthew are those who thirst and hunger "for righteousness." That touches on one of Israel's greatest themes: this is about the Torah, the social order given at Sinai, by means of which God wants to create a just society living peacefully in the midst of the world.

So the Sermon on the Mount is not interested in declaring that the social order from Sinai is outdated. Instead, it draws it into the brilliant, clarifying, and discerning light of Jesus. The Sermon on the Mount, too, aims at a just society in which each individual has what she or he needs, but above all, a society in which all are righteous "before God" because they participate in *God's* saving righteousness. "Those who hunger and thirst for righteousness" are, first and above all, Jesus' disciples who allow themselves to be gathered to form the eschatological Israel.

The last, ninth beatitude shows how profoundly the whole text of the Beatitudes speaks of Jesus' disciples, those who follow him:

Blessed are you when people revile you and persecute you and utter all kinds of evil against you falsely on my account. Rejoice and be glad, for your reward is great in heaven. (Matt 5:11-12)

So in Matthew's version of the Beatitudes Jesus does not speak in generalities, not about all the people on earth; first of all, he speaks of the tiny group of disciples he has gathered around him. They have given up everything for the sake of serving the people of God, and to that extent they can indeed be called "poor" (Matt 5:3). They renounce all use of force (Matt 5:5). They try, among themselves, to live Israel's social order. They seek to deal with one another kindly and forgive each other seventy-seven times a day (Matt 5:7; 18:21-22). They strive to have a "pure heart," that is, they want to live the "righteousness" of the Sermon on the Mount undividedly, with their whole existence (Matt 5:8). For that they are reviled and persecuted like Jesus, because such a way of life calls into question the old society and its principles. So the Beatitudes are for Jesus' disciples. Matthew even says so explicitly in his introduction to the Sermon on the Mount:

When Jesus saw the crowds, he went up the mountain; and after he sat down, his disciples came to him. Then he began to speak, and taught them . . . (Matt 5:1-2)

So in Matthew the disciples are those who hear the Sermon on the Mount directly. This great discourse is primarily for them. It is they who may rejoice and be glad (Matt 5:12) because they are already living under the promise and have a share in the reign of God (Matt 5:3, 10). For them, the fulfillment of the Beatitudes has already begun.

Jesus' Realistic Way

Then what about the poor of this world, those who throughout every country are abandoned, despised, deprived of all rights, trodden into the dirt? They are by no means left out of the Beatitudes in the Sermon on the Mount, but here, too, the Sermon chooses the realistic path—the way God began by calling Abraham and telling him he would become a "great nation" (Gen 12:2) so that one day all the peoples of the earth would receive blessing (Gen 12:3).

The community of disciples to whom the Beatitudes are addressed does not in any way exist simply for itself. The disciples are servants to the whole people of God, and the people of God is in service to all peoples. The Beatitudes expand their space to the degree that belief in God's promises spreads through the world by means of the witness of the disciples and the living example of the people of God. In that way the poor and the victims of violence can be aided everywhere. Alms are not enough; they are nothing but a drop on the hot stone. In the long run nothing can help but the new community life that Jesus inaugurated with the Sermon on the Mount.

That, at any rate, is how Matthew sees it. For him, certainly, the disciples are the immediate audience of the Sermon on the Mount. But representatives of all Israel are already gathered around the disciples (Matt 4:23-25; 7:28-29). The disciples are sent to them (Matt 10:5-6). The church, the eschatological Israel, is already revealing itself in the listener scenery of the Sermon on the Mount.

After Easter the view will expand again. Then the Risen One will send his disciples into the whole world (Matt 28:16-20). They are to "make disciples of all nations," that is, found communities everywhere and teach them everything Jesus has taught his disciples. In Matthew's thinking such "teaching" refers, above all, to the Sermon on the Mount and also, of course, to the Beatitudes with which the Sermon begins. The Beatitudes change the world as soon as they find hearers who receive them in faith and anchor their lives to them.

Naomi and Ruth

The little book of Ruth shines like an especially precious gem among the many-hued stories in the Old Testament. It is a masterwork of ancient Hebrew narrative art.

Here we have the story of a family; we could also call it a story about refugees. The book's action takes place in the time of the "judges" (1200–1020 BCE). The story begins with a famine in Israel. Driven by deprivation and hopelessness, a Jewish family leaves its home town of Bethlehem and emigrates into pagan territory—namely, the land of Moab, east of the Jordan. The family consists of a man named Elimelech, his wife, Naomi, and two sons named Mahlon and Chilion. After they have settled in Moab, the father dies. The two sons then marry Moabite women, and after about ten years the sons, too, die. Naomi remains alone with her two pagan daughters-in-law, Orpah and Ruth.

But that is only the introduction to the real story, which is about the struggle of two single women for survival: the mother, Naomi, and her daughter-in-law, Ruth. After so many years Naomi wants to leave that foreign land and return to Israel, where the famine has now ceased. She advises her two Moabite daughters-in-law to remain in the security of their homeland and return to their parents' house. Orpah, after polite hesitancy, follows her advice, but Ruth insists on remaining with Naomi and going with her to Israel: to poverty and an uncertain future. Ruth's words to her Jewish mother-in-law are unforgettable:

> *"Where you go, I will go; where you lodge, I will lodge; your people shall be my people, and your God my God. Where you die, I will die—there will I be buried. May the* Lord *do thus and so to me, and more as well, if even death parts me from you!"* (Ruth 1:16-17)

Thereupon Ruth, together with Naomi, sets out on the road to Bethlehem, and we have arrived at the heart of the book. Exciting episodes then tell how the need of the two women is met in Bethlehem. Both have lost their husbands, and they have no sons. What that meant in those times was that they were without protection or anyone to defend their rights. But their situation is resolved through the cleverness of Naomi, Ruth's trust in her mother-in-law, and the circumspect concern of an Israelite man.

The narrative reaches its climax in an event that takes place around midnight, on the edge of the threshing-floor at Bethlehem (Ruth 3:1-15). Naomi has advised that Ruth dare something highly extraordinary and Ruth has trustingly agreed. But it turns out well because God is an invisible actor in the scene.

What we are told here is an almost modern woman's story with the patriarchal structures of the ancient Near East as background, structures she coolly breaks through: two women dare to believe in the God of Israel—and they are given a new future. The Moabite, Ruth, in particular gains our affection right away. Just like Abraham of old, she leaves father and mother, land and relations, and takes shelter with Naomi's God (Ruth 2:11-12).

In the marvelous figure of Ruth the narrative also reveals its secret meaning: Ruth shows us how people from the pagan world can receive a portion among the people of God and find a home with the true God—and not only a home: the pagan Ruth joins the company of the "great mothers" in Israel. She will become the great-grandmother of King David (Ruth 4:13-22).

The Treasure of "Now"

This took place not long ago, shortly before Christmas, in a family I know (the mother told me the story): She had fetched her little Micah from the kindergarten and the two were back at home. She noticed that he was much quieter than usual. He had something on his mind. Being a wise mother, she did not press him, knowing that it would soon come out. It did, in the evening, before the good-night kiss.

"There are children who are starving because they don't have anything to eat," said Micah suddenly. "Petra told us about them." (Petra is the head of the kindergarten.) He added: "Somebody should do something about it." "Certainly we must do something," said his mother. "What?" asked Micah. "For example, we could do without any Christmas presents and give the money we save to feed a child in Africa so that it won't starve." Micah's forehead suddenly wrinkled a little. "I need to think about it," said he. "I was hoping for an Erector set."

Next morning the mother looked questioningly at her Micah. "Have you thought about it?" "Yes," said Micah. "What you said yesterday is a good idea. We will do that for the African child next Christmas. This year, though, the Erector set!"

That was the story. Is it just a tale about a five-year-old? No, it is a story about all of us. We all do the same. Doesn't it happen that we suddenly think that something has to be done, that we have to help? No, we think: *I* have to help. *I* need to give something, perhaps some of my time.

And then we do what little Micah thought of: we delay the thing that had suddenly dawned on us until next week or next year or sometime or other.

And because we have delayed, God cannot do what God wanted to do in the world through us. It simply doesn't happen. A little bit of the world that could have been different remains as it was. No, wrong! The little bit of the world that could have been different does not remain as it was: it is poorer. For the world is designed, is crying out, to hold more hope, more mutual aid, more peace within itself. But we put everything off until later . . .

How was it with Mary? Did she tell the angel "I'll have to think about it"? If she had even thought that, there would be no Christmas.

Or the shepherds: did they say "Well, that is very interesting about the child that is supposed to be the Messiah. But at the moment we have a lot of work to do with our sheep. We will look for that Messiah-kid next week." If they had said that, there would be no Christmas, for the shepherds are essential to what happened in Bethlehem. In Luke's story they represent the people of God.

Or take the example of Stephen: If he had said to himself: "There are people in the synagogues who are offended when I speak of Jesus as the Messiah. They could be dangerous to me. I had better be quiet for a while. Next year I can make a new attempt after the situation has quieted." If Stephen had thought and acted that way, Jesus' cause would not have been carried forward.

"Later" is a bad thing. It is an obstacle to an infinite number of things in this world. We need to see through the devilish game that "later" plays with us; we have to recognize the evil trick and stand up against it. How?—by simply asking ourselves: "What is really most important in my life?" And the most important thing in our lives is always God and God's cause. Jesus dared to say:

> *"Seek first the kingdom of God, and everything else will be given to you."*
> (cf. Luke 12:31).

Do I have to say how Micah's story played out? He really wanted both things: to help the child in Africa and to have his Erector set. So his mother suggested: "You can have the Erector set four weeks from now, when it is your birthday. For Christmas we will go to the attic and bring down the toyshop your papa played with when he was your age, and we will set it up again. And this year Papa and Mama will not give each other presents at Christmas. We will use the money we save to help in Africa."

Little Micah not only agreed; he was happy. He would help another child, and what was still more important, he had learned not to say "Later!" but instead "Yes, today!"

Can Memory Save?

"Remembrance is the secret to redemption," reads a prominent inscription in Yad Vashem, the Jerusalem memorial to the victims of the *Shoah*. The much-quoted statement is supposed to come from Israel ben Eliezer (the famed Baal Shem Tov). The full quotation reads:

> *Forgetfulness leads to exile, while remembrance is the secret to redemption.*

Israel ben Eliezer, the founding figure of Eastern European Hasidism (ca. 1698–1760), can only have been referring to the return to Israel of Jews scattered throughout the world. According to this maxim Jews must never forget their true home or they will never return to it. Still, the short form of the sentence that is so often quoted also makes sense, and even says something essential about the historical awareness of the people of God.

How can Israel be redeemed through memory? The answer is not difficult. If God's promises to the patriarchs, the exodus from Egypt, the covenant, the exile, the persecutions were all forgotten—in short, if Israel were to forget its history with God—it would soon no longer be a people but would dissolve among the nations, and then the possibility for true liberation and the distinction between good and evil would no longer exist in the world.

The same is true for the church, which stands entirely on the ground of Israel: obviously, for it, too, the mystery of redemption means remembering. If the church were to forget the history of its origins, from Abraham to John the Baptizer; if it were to forget Jesus, his Sermon on the Mount, his death, and his resurrection, the time of the apostles, the way of the early communities—then there would soon be no church in the world any longer and no good news of our redemption.

Forgetting as Healing

"Remembrance is the secret to redemption." But doesn't that saying also contain dangers and traps? Is it true that memory only and always heals? Can it not also be destructive? Can it not be a heavy burden that weighs a person down? Aren't there many people who really die because of their memories? And cannot the church itself suffocate from the pressures of habit and the weight of outworn tradition?

Modern medicine, especially psychiatry, has long since recognized the problem of destructive memory and seeks to remedy it. Brain researchers are analyzing, with ever greater precision, the ways in which memory and conscience work. They can now localize the processes that take place in particular parts of the brain. Knowledge of brain function is growing, and with it the possibilities for directing the brain's workings.

A recent article in the journal *Science* included a long account of how many laboratories are seeking a means to induce forgetting. Of course, the scientists have to be extremely careful: not all the contents of the brain should be erased. In that case the patient would become an empty shell. Only burdensome, destructive, traumatizing thoughts and images are to be eliminated—more precisely, they are to be curbed through the use of special medications ("memory-blockers") so that they are no longer present to the person in question.

How is that supposed to happen? The research study asserts that scientists are on the point of finding a way simply to make intensively present to the patient—visualize—the contents of memory and the images that the patient wants to get rid of and banish forever from her consciousness: then the chemical "erasers" are brought to bear simultaneously.

Wouldn't that be a great thing? Haven't we always wished for something like that? The depressing thought of the school year that had to be repeated because I didn't make the grade—away with it! The hideous experiences of a prisoner of war dragged off to Siberia that repeatedly torture him in his dreams—vanished once and for all! The dreadful image of how a schoolchild falls under a streetcar and is crushed—erased!

All the insults, humiliations, and sorrows, the bitternesses and griefs of life, the disgraces and embarrassments that rise in our mem-

ory again and again—we just take the proper pill and destroy them.
All that remain are the successful, happy hours. The laboratories in
Atlanta and Harvard, Lille and Tel Aviv are working at high speed
on behalf of our future. Our grandchildren will lead happier lives.

Really? Aren't the shadows part of our past? Surviving through
dark hours—hasn't that made us more human? Sorrow—do we not
need it if we are to experience the exaltation of happiness? And
doesn't the *Exsultet* in the Easter Vigil sing of the *felix culpa*, the
"happy fault" that is called happy because, while it was real fault,
it was transformed by repentance and forgiveness? Would not our
"I" fall apart if we took away part of its past? Wouldn't the human
being, in fact, be destroyed by that?

"That's all rhetoric," says the woman who has been raped in the
most brutal way possible. "If I could finally get rid of that trauma,
I could live again." "And that's really all we want," say the psychiatrists. "We just want to bring a partial amnesia to people with severe
post-traumatic disorders. Haven't you ever encountered deeply trau-
matized people?"

The physicians are right. Who wants to deny that chemistry can
help people as much as the scalpel? There are depressions that can
only be resolved by medicines. However: there is also suffering that
can only be relieved by consolation, and there is guilt that can only
be dealt with through forgiveness. And there are the ravaged parts
of the soul for which only a new, healing community in faith can offer
help.

Faith that faces its history can transform. In that transformation
even a forgetting that heals can come about—but only when at the
same time there is new and liberating experience. In this sense the
Bible also speaks of an all-transforming forgetfulness:

> Do not remember the former things,
>   or consider the things of old!
> I am about to do a new thing!
>   Now it springs forth, do you not perceive it? (Isa 43:18-19)

Memoria, remembering in the biblical sense, is nothing like merely
looking at the past—as one might page through an album in which
the pictures are already yellowed and their corners torn. That is not
what biblical memory is like. "Remembering" in the biblical sense

always opens a new future. It frees us from every form of self-torture. It allows us to encounter God's mercy. It bestows discernment and so makes us free of all the burdens that are superfluous and senseless.

Liberating Memory

"He makes his marvelous works to be remembered" (Ps 111:4).[1] The context shows that the "marvelous works" are God's actions in freeing Israel from slavery in Egypt, feeding them in the wilderness, and making an everlasting covenant with them at Sinai. The people of God are never to forget those saving deeds. Hence their great festivals, above all the Passover, where they do nothing but remember.

The church has entered into this great "remembering" of Israel. It prepares for its "paschal feast" over a period of forty days; on the evening of Holy Thursday it remembers the hour in which Jesus established the memorial of his death; in the Easter Vigil it celebrates Israel's rescue from the power of Pharaoh and, at the same time, the rescue of Jesus from the power of death; and then, for fifty days longer, it celebrates this mystery of death and resurrection out of which it lives.

If we look more closely we see that the church celebrates this foundational memory every Sunday in the Eucharist, which is likewise the saving "memorial" of Jesus' death and resurrection. The eucharistic celebration proper is preceded by a Liturgy of the Word that repeatedly recalls the foundational history of the church so that the assembled community may measure itself by that history.

Finally: Jesus himself promised his disciples that the Holy Spirit would "remind" them of everything he had said (John 14:26). The Holy Spirit, the Spirit of Jesus and the Father, will thus repeatedly recall to the church the power and discerning force of Jesus' words— and not only recall, but again and again interpret what the earthly Jesus said and did in its full scope and consequences. In just that way the church will remain a living place of discernment in the world.

---

[1] Quoted from the Psalter in the *Book of Common Prayer*. AV is similar. NRSV "He has gained renown by his wonderful deeds" eliminates the focus of remembering in Israel.—Tr.

"Remembrance is the secret to redemption." The statement is true, but it does not speak about oppressive, destructive memories such as—God knows—are everywhere in the world. Instead it speaks of the one great, liberating memory on the basis of which the world really lives.

The gospel and the liturgy are and always will be for Christians a "dangerous memory," because this memory demands of those who enter into it that they dedicate everything they have so that the world may be dragged out of its dumb forgetfulness and into the true freedom into which God wants to lead it.

Spiritual Communities in Light of the Bible

There are no "spiritual communities" in the Bible. There is Israel, there are Jewish synagogue communities, there is the church, and there are Christian communities—but no "spiritual communities." Nevertheless, the many and varied new forms of community that arose in the church in the twentieth century, and that are nowadays mostly spoken of under the rubric of "spiritual movements," have something very biblical about them. They have to do with the Bible to a great, indeed decisive, degree. In order to show that, I will have to go into more detail.

God Needs a People in the World

When the Old Testament tells about God's self-revelation it is always about God's creating a people in the world. The self-revelation of God in the Old Testament never has the sense of opening up "the depths of the godhead." The "depths of God" (1 Cor 2:10) are God's hidden plan of salvation. The purpose of revelation is that God may gain a people in the world that distinguishes itself from the other peoples and precisely in that way can become a blessing for them in order that by that means the nature of the true God may be revealed to them.

This is especially evident in the story of the burning bush in Exodus 3–4. There God reveals Godself to Moses. Moses asks God about the divine name in order to be able to legitimate himself before the Israelites. In doing so he is still thinking within the world of the ancient Near Eastern religions, for in them every god had a name and, with the name, his or her own "portfolio"—even when that portfolio is governance over all the other gods. But God does provide a name in answer to Moses' request. God's answer, "I will be who I will be" (Exod 3:14), is equivalently a refusal to give a name. The Israelites will only recognize *who God is* when God delivers them from the house of slavery in Egypt and, at Sinai, gives them an alternative social order.

All Israel then gathers at Sinai, women and men, to receive that alternative social order, that is, the Torah, which is part of the covenant. That covenant constitutes Israel as God's people. The book of Deuteronomy calls that day at Sinai the "day of assembly," *hēmera ekklēsias* (Deut 9:10 LXX).

Here we must insist that what is really decisive for Israel's being a people is not biological descent or territory or a central government, but the covenant offered to them, the covenant that Israel freely accepted on the "day of assembly" (Exod 24:7; cf. Deut 26:17-19).

According to Deuteronomy 31:10-13 this "day of assembly" is to be repeated every seventh year, each time at the Festival of Booths, with the reading of the whole Torah. In this way Israel will be returned every seventh year to its original condition and must learn anew what it is there for and what its way of life is to be. The regular "assembly" of the people of God that would later be so important to the church is established here. The theological origin of the concept of *ekklēsia* (= assembly) is Sinai.

Beyond the reading of Israel's social order every seventh year, the people of God gathers each year in Jerusalem for the three great feasts: Passover, the Feast of Weeks (Pentecost), and the Feast of Booths (Sukkoth). All are to gather: men, women, children, male and female slaves, and even foreigners (Deut 16:11, 14; cf. 29:9-10). Israel lives from feast to feast. The fact that all assemble in one place is a real symbol of the unity and the solid togetherness in the people of God.

But how does that togetherness hold together in daily life? In the ancient Near East the extended family played a crucial role. It protected individuals, guaranteeing them solidarity and support. In the Torah the ancient Near Eastern family structures remain in place at first. But the solidarity within the family is now extended to the whole of Israel. That is precisely what is meant by the command in Leviticus 19:18: "You shall love your neighbor as yourself."

After all, that "yourself" is not the individual, as countless modern sermons claim, not the "I" who is to be cultivated in order that one may love others; it is a collective. It is one's own family. And the "neighbors" are not just any fellow human beings; they are the members of the people of God. Thus the commandment of love of neighbor in Leviticus 19 means showing the same solidarity to all members of the people of God as one gives to the members of one's extended family. That solidarity is due even to the "aliens" among the people of God (Lev 19:33-34).

Jesus and the Eschatological Assembly of Israel

Jesus took the commandment to love of neighbor in Leviticus 19—that is, the extension of family solidarity to the whole people of God—quite as a matter of course and combined it with the principal commandment to love God from Deuteronomy 6:5 (Mark 12:29-31). What was new was the clarity and unambiguousness of that combination.

That Jesus spoke separately and explicitly of love of enemies was also something new. In principle, love of enemies was also prescribed in Leviticus 19:17-18 and quite certainly in Exodus 23:4-5, which says one must help an enemy whose donkey has collapsed under its load. That is nothing other than love of enemies, because in the Bible "love" does not refer to emotions but to practical action.

Likewise a matter of course for Jesus was the institution of the regular assembly of the people of God. He routinely journeyed to Jerusalem for Israel's feasts. However, he radically eschatologized that gathering of Israel: now, as the reign of God is breaking in, God is definitively "gathering" God's people. Jesus says: "Whoever [now, in this eschatological hour] does not gather with me scatters" (Matt 12:30). And in the Our Father he has his disciples pray in the very first petition for the "gathering" of Israel, in accordance with Exodus 36:22-28. "Hallowed be thy name" means first and above all: "Gather, unite, and sanctify your people Israel so that your name may be hallowed."

Jesus introduces a strategy for this end-time gathering of Israel that he learned from the prophets: he gathers people who follow him, so that a circle of disciples is created around him. The model is primarily Elijah's calling of Elisha as related in 1 Kings 19:19-21.

From within that circle of disciples Jesus chose twelve men (Matt 3:14). They were sent forth in pairs (Mark 6:7) as official witnesses to proclaim the inbreaking reign of God in Israel and, as a sign of it, to drive out demons and heal the sick (Luke 9:2).

However—and this is important in our context—the assignment of the Twelve was not exhausted by that mission. Mark 3:14 says explicitly that they are to be "with Jesus." Apart from their apostolic "journey" (they return very quickly) they are thus to be constantly around Jesus—naturally not as a kind of "court," but as the realization of the new togetherness in the reign of God.

Beyond the Twelve there must have been a larger circle of disciples (Luke 6:17) who accompanied Jesus, at least sometimes (Luke 8:1-3). Together with Jesus and the Twelve they made up the growth center of the eschatological Israel-to-be-gathered. According to the gospels—this is evident especially in Mark—there was thus not only a *missio apostolica* (an "apostolic mission") but also a *vita apostolica* (an "apostolic life"). Both are necessary, and the two must augment each other. The longing for the New Testament *vita apostolica* will play an important role in the church's history. Especially in the Middle Ages, that concept would become a programmatic call of many movements of church renewal.

Apostolic Life

The gospels, especially Mark's, even give more space to the *vita apostolica* than to the *missio apostolica*. Concretely, the conflicts within the group of disciples and the corresponding instruction given them by Jesus play an unusually large role in Mark's gospel (but not only there). Moreover, many sayings of Jesus that the gospels now direct to the crowds were originally addressed to the disciples.

One theme of this instruction for disciples (and thus of the orientation to apostolic life) is the demand to leave everything, even one's own family, in order to live totally and undividedly in service to the gospel. That theme appears repeatedly, in many variations (see especially Matt 19:29). The historical context is the calling of disciples to follow Jesus and their unsettled wandering through Galilee with him.

In connection with the readiness to leave everything we also find the theme of "renunciation of possessions" (see especially Mark 10:17-31). It does not mean that having possessions is something evil in itself, but rather that they can get in the way of the "totality" of surrender to the reign of God, and often do.

Another theme of the orientation to the apostolic life is Jesus' demand that the disciples resist the elementary impulse to lust after power, to seek recognition, reputation, and influence. The disciples are not to build themselves up but to serve one another (see especially Mark 10:35-45).

The degree to which all these themes concern problems among the disciples is indicated also by the demand that they continually forgive (Luke 11:4). Jesus radicalizes the subject of reconciliation by using the example of someone who interrupts his sacrifice in the temple in order first to be reconciled with his sister or brother in faith. The example even leaves open the question of which is the guilty party. Reconciliation with one's sister or brother in the people of God is the precondition for all liturgy, and it must take place without delay (Matt 5:23-24).

The continuing formation of the group of disciples also includes the theology of the cross. Jesus probably did not develop it only as he was on his way to his Passover death in Jerusalem (Mark 8:31-38). As shown by the parables of the sower and the endangered seed (Mark 4:1-9), it was part of the preaching of the reign of God from the outset.

Finally, a crucial element in orientation to the *vita apostolica* is the theme of unconditional trust in the care ensured by the Father in heaven (Matt 6:25-34). That theme also shapes the Our Father, which is a prayer for disciples. It appears not only in the address, *Abba*, but especially in the fourth petition (Matt 6:11; Luke 11:3). The prayer for tomorrow's bread belongs to the disciples who are on the road in Israel and do not know in the morning whether anyone will receive them at sundown and give them lodging and food to eat.

The Self-Gathering Community

The community of disciples that gathered in Jerusalem after Good Friday evidently lived according to the instructions for disciples Jesus had given them and the pre-Easter experiences of the group he had gathered. Those who had followed Jesus fled at first but later reassembled in Jerusalem. They joined their lives together, not only because of the appearances of the Risen One but also under pressure from their Jewish society. Hence it is inappropriate to read the summaries in Acts (especially 2:43-47 and 4:32-37) simply as utopian or as whitewashing.

The charge of utopianism is also inappropriate because Luke does indeed tell about problems and conflicts in the Jerusalem community. We can think, for example, of the betrayal by Ananias and Sapphira (Acts 5:1-11), the neglect of the widows among the Greek-speaking part of the community (Acts 6:1), and the quarrel about circumcision of Gentile Christian men (Acts 15:1-7).

In the context of these conflicts Luke shows how solutions could be arrived at, using the example of the so-called apostolic council: the whole community gathers around the apostles and elders (Acts 15:6, 22); God's actions in the most recent past are narrated and interpreted (Acts 15:7-12); the current event is measured against what Scripture says (Acts 15:13-21).

Moreover, Luke presents the Christians of his time (and thus, of course, ourselves as well) with what had proved within a few decades to be the enduring structure of the church as the eschatologically assembled (and to be reassembled) Israel—especially in the conflict with Gnostic false teachers (see Acts 20:20, 29-30). Luke wants to show what church is, and he does so especially by telling repeatedly about assemblies of the Jerusalem community.

The community of the first chapters of Acts—at the same time the "primal image" of Christian existence—gathers regularly, not only for prayer but also to consult together about their problems. It strives for unanimity (Acts 1:14; 4:24; 15:25) but knows that such unanimity is the work of the Holy Spirit. It gathers around the table of the Eucharist "in gladness and singleness of heart" (cf. Acts 2:46) because it knows that the Risen One is in its midst. But it shares more than the eucharistic bread; it lives a shared life. It seeks, for example, as Torah prescribes, to achieve an enduring equalization between rich and poor (Acts 4:32-37).

This community is a visible assembly around the twelve apostles, as the number 120 in Acts 1:15 shows. It is a visible gathering in which each is aware of the bad and good fortunes, the cares and joys of the others. How would it be possible to sustain responsibility for the faith of others in a mega-community?!

The basic realization of this primal image of the church, however, is not simply the assembly, although *ekklēsia* means nothing else. There are countless assemblies in this world. The carrying-out of the church's existence happens only in the kind of assembly that is fully and completely a listening plea and that begs for the coming of the

Spirit (Acts 1:14) because it knows that by itself it is completely help-less and unable on its own to establish anything even resembling community. That could only end in irresolvable rivalries.

Paul and Community

Naturally, the image Luke draws for us leaves quite a few things open. New problems arose in the communities around the Mediter-ranean with their port cities reveling in freedom and harboring many private cults. For these we must turn to Paul. A great deal could be said about the "encouragement" of the communities (*paraklēsis*) that takes up so much space in Paul's letters. I can only mention a few things. It will appear that the concept of "community" for Paul, just as for Luke, is the unavoidable and fundamental basis for Christian life. For example, Paul speaks of the "*ekklēsia* of God that is in Corinth" (1 Cor 1:2; 2 Cor 1:1). He means to say that the eschatological com-munity of salvation created by God, beginning in Jerusalem and al-ready spreading to many other places, is also present in Corinth (and equally in all other Christian communities). The "collapse of com-munity theology" recently proclaimed by some theologians in an almost triumphal tone is far removed from the New Testament, in-deed from the whole Bible.

For Paul, just as for Luke, the joining together of Christians' real lives plays a decisive role. It appears in his writing in the frequency of the reciprocal pronoun "one another" (*allēlous*). We meet it again and again in the genuine Pauline letters. To give only a few examples: "love one another with mutual affection" (Rom 12:10); "live in har-mony with one another" (Rom 12:16); "welcome one another" (Rom 15:7); "instruct one another" (Rom 15:14); "wait for one another" at the eucharistic meal (1 Cor 11:33); "have the same care for one an-other" (1 Cor 12:25); "through love become slaves to one another" (Gal 5:13); "bear one another's burdens" (Gal 6:2); "encourage one another" (1 Thess 5:11).

Striking among these examples is the admonition to mutual "in-struction" or "correction." Loving correction of one another and humble reception of the correction demand a high degree of Christian discipleship and a corresponding ethics of discipleship. The crisis in our contemporary parishes is evident, among other things, in the fact that there is scarcely any fraternal or sororal correction or instruction in the biblical sense, even though Paul speaks of it so often (Rom 15:14; Gal 6:1; 1 Thess 5:14).

A special characteristic of the Pauline mission was the multitude of household communities, about which we read both in Acts (18:7; 20:8, 20) and in Paul's letters (Rom 16:5; 1 Cor 16:19; Col 4:15; Phlm 2). The communities met in the houses of well-to-do members (see Acts 12:12), and the latter placed not only their houses but also their lives at the service of community building.

We can get a good insight into this place of Christian common life when we look at the household of the Jewish couple Prisca and Aquila, where not only a local community assembled—in Corinth, Ephesus, or Rome. Aquila and Prisca's house was also Paul's base for mission over a long period of time. It was precisely the household communities where Christians grew together to become "the body of Christ" as they celebrated the Lord's Supper.

Paul founded his idea of "mutuality" in the community in his calling it "the body of Christ" (1 Cor 12:27) or "one body in Christ" (Rom 12:5). Ultimately that ecclesiological metaphor is rooted in the tradition of the Lord's Supper (1 Cor 10:16-17). Christ's surrender of his life and the power of his resurrection bind Christians together in the Lord's Supper and make Christian sibling love, *agapē*, possible.

This *agapē* is first and above all the power, given by the Holy Spirit, that enables and characterizes mutuality in the community. In that sense it cannot be equated simply with universal human love, as unfortunately happens too often. For Paul the noun *agapē* (and the verb, *agapan*) always refers to community life, just as it does in the Johannine writings (see especially Rom 13:8; Gal 5:13; 1 Thess 4:9). Paul prefers to speak of relationships *to* non-Christians or the actions *of* non-Christians in terms of "doing good" (Rom 2:10; Gal 6:10; 1 Thess 5:15).

This high degree of awareness that, in light of Christ, the community is one body bound together in sibling love corresponds to the contrasting function of the Christian community in relation to pagan society (Rom 12:2; Phil 2:14-15). Paul and his followers developed that contrasting function in various ways, especially through the "once/now" paradigm (Rom 6:19; 2 Cor 5:17; Eph 5:8; Titus 3:3-7), and by contrasting pagan vices with the "fruits of the Spirit" (Gal 5:19-26) or use of the concept of "sanctification" (Rom 6:19; 1 Cor 6:11; 1 Thess 4:2-8). The features that recall this contrasting function of Christian communities are not popular today, at least in Germany. Instead of "contrast," people prefer to speak of necessary "compatibility" between church and society or to emphasize that the church's *ethos* needs to be "low-profile."

In Face of the Imperial Church

This last observation sounds an echo of the whole problematic of the next period, when the church of the martyrs and confessors was gradually transformed into an "imperial church." The little communities, which from their whole context and history were the opposite of pagan society, were transformed between the fourth and sixth centuries into administrative districts to which everyone in the empire had to belong. Being Christian was no longer a matter of free choice; it was a social requirement, and the *parochia*, that is, the "parish," far too often ceased to be the place for vital Christian experience.

It would be impossible for me even to sketch the process of that stepwise transformation of the earlier church of free choice into a blanket "empire-wide" organization. I can only point out what this development necessarily brought about within the church: a series of new fellowships that sought just what the early church had displayed in spite of all its failures, sins, and divisions: namely, that there was such a thing as free choice of a Christian existence, that there was discipleship, life on the basis of the gospel, mutual commitment of lives, *vita apostolica*.

From the fourth century onward (in rapidly Christianized Egypt even earlier), many Christians turned to a radically ascetic way of life and an internalization of Sacred Scripture. This was most manifest (especially in Egypt) in "withdrawal into the desert." Whole colonies of hermits or anchorites arose. There were, certainly, many reasons for this "exodus"—for example, the pressure of taxes or of military recruitment. More important was a motivation derived from ancient philosophy: that genuine insight and true wisdom could be obtained only through a strictly ascetic way of life. The crucial reason for the exodus of so many Christians, however, was something else: the longing, as already mentioned, for a realization of the whole gospel. It was, in fact, just at the time when the former charisma of the church communities was fading that the exodus of the anchorites and monastics began. That temporal correspondence cannot be mere coincidence.

In the beginning this exodus was truly flight from the world into individual solitude, but that changed rapidly. The withdrawal of the early Christian ascetics into the desert soon acquired its specifically "Christian" shape from the men and women who created a form of community from the ascetic movement. First and foremost among these was the Egyptian Pachomius, the father of "cenobitic" monasticism. In about 320–325 he founded the monastery of Tabennisi in Upper Egypt. By the end of his life Pachomius had founded nine monasteries of men and, with the help of his sister, two of women, totaling altogether more than ten thousand monks and nuns.

The isolated lives of many anchorites had now incorporated table fellowship, common prayer, organized common work, the companionship and assistance of a "new family" in the gospel sense (Mark 3:34-35). Thus something of what existed in Christian communities from the beginning was carried forward and given new forms within a society that was descending into a Christianity-of-habit.

Continual Development of New Forms of Church Community

This community movement that began in the fourth century has never ceased. Again and again new orders and institutions of common life, new spiritual communities and movements have emerged, sustained by the longing for a radical life according to the gospel and moved by the yearning for a more solid community in faith. The most influential texts were those of Jesus' instruction for his disciples (especially Matt 19:16-30), the summaries in Acts (especially Acts 2:43-47), and Paul's *paraklēsis* for his communities (especially Rom 13:1-13).

It is impossible to offer even an overview of the unbelievable multitude and variety of these church community efforts. Speaking from the point of view of Catholic Christians, let me first name various *forms* of such community structurings apart from the usual parishes: Monastic communities arose, following the rule of Saint Benedict; since the mid-eleventh century the so-called "canons regular" were created on the basis of the Rule of Augustine—for example, the Augustinian Canons and the Premonstratensians; beginning in the thirteenth century the preaching orders, Dominicans and Franciscans, with a structure completely different from that in the Rule of Benedict; in the sixteenth century came the Jesuits, again with a new and revolutionary form in which mission, disposability, and mobility play a central role; there are even so-called "Communities of Common Life"—the Oratorians, for example.

Parallel to nearly all these orders of men, orders of women were likewise founded not only for contemplation but later also for teaching in schools, care of the sick, and apostolic works. The nineteenth century saw a total number of women's congregations almost beyond counting: communities whose members took only "simple vows" and were active primarily in the social sphere. Also characteristic of the nineteenth century was the creation of many missionary societies such as the "White Fathers" or the "Spiritans."

In the year 1933 René Voillaume, inspired by the life of Charles de Foucauld, founded "The Little Brothers of Jesus," who were quickly followed by the "Little Sisters of Jesus," once again a new and quite inspiring form of order whose members simply seek to live among the poor and share their lives. Somewhat comparable is the multitude of "secular institutes" founded in the twentieth century. Finally, since the mid-twentieth century new spiritual movements have arisen: for example, *Comunione e liberazione* (Communion and Liberation), the Neocatechumenate, the Focolare movement, the Community of Sant' Egidio, the Immanuel Community or *Cursillo*—to name but a few.

Still, that by no means begins to exhaust the list of various types of common life, for within the history of the church there have been some quite different ways of life shaped by the gospel: in the first centuries, for example, the so-called family- or house-cloisters in which a family (usually well-to-do) gathered friends around them and tried to live with one another as followers of Jesus. In the Middle Ages and the Baroque period the so-called "brotherhoods" played a particular role. We should also mention the "third orders" (tertiaries): groups of Catholic laity, usually married couples, that formed around one or other of the classic Orders. We may also think of the Beguines and Begardes (since the twelfth century) and the "Brothers and Sisters of the Common Life" (since the fourteenth century)—or of the Christian villages in the Jesuit "reductions" in South America (seventeenth/eighteenth centuries)—or the Christian villages in East Africa founded in the nineteenth century by the Spiritans, communities made up of enslaved persons whose freedom had been purchased. All of them led, from morning to night, a life deliberately formed on Christian principles, a life similar to that of an Order, but often as married persons. A great many more could be named.

Above all, I ought to list corresponding spiritual communities and movements within the churches of the Reformation and characterize them according to type: from the Moravian Brethren to Dietrich Bonhoeffer's "Bruderhaus" to the "Bruderhof" to the "Brotherhood of Jesus" and many other more recent community foundations outside the official parish or congregation. But that would explode the limits of these reflections. It is more important to draw some conclusions from what has been said. I will begin with the early communities of monks and sisters.

The Institution of the "Monastery": Gains and Losses

The Rule of St. Augustine says at the very beginning: "First, the reason that you are gathered together in one is that you dwell with concord in the house: and that you possess but one soul and one heart in God." The reference to Acts 4:32 is clear. The monastic community is to be a "new family" in the sense of the Gospels and Acts. "This longing for the earliest church is the origin of all the great religious foundations."[1]

But if this is a *"new* family," it must necessarily be accompanied by some aspect of a new society, a new culture, and a transformed world. In fact, many monasteries that began as new foundations in waste places soon became successful economic centers. They shaped their environment not only by faith but also culturally and in the context of a civilization.

Thus here it is also clear that faith must incarnate itself. It cannot be otherworldly. In its innermost being it aims to penetrate all the believer's life-circumstances and give them a new, redeemed form. Faith, of itself, presses toward changing social relationships and shaping the material of the world. It is no longer at all clear to many Europeans how much the world in which they live has been civilized and humanized by Christian faith.

At any rate the monasteries of the West carried forward the exodus-character of the people of God. Above all, in times when scarcely anyone had the freedom *not to be a Christian*, they became signs of the freedom to follow Jesus. At the same time they retained an aspect of the early community-church with its unity of faith and life.

---

[1] Hans Urs von Balthasar, *Die Grossen Ordensregeln* (Zürich: Benziger, 1961), 55.

It is true that there were dangerous developments in Western monasticism as well. Regrettably, the freedom we are speaking about here was narrowed in the Middle Ages by the institution of *oblatio*, whereby children could be dedicated to a monastic life by their parents. Any later attempt to leave the monastery was followed by excommunication (Fourth Council of Toledo). Cluny made the first attempt to minimize the numbers of oblates in its own monasteries, and the Cistercians were the first to refuse in principle to receive any more oblates. However, the institution continued in many monasteries and did immense damage to the monastic communities.

Another abuse was the medieval "proprietary church system." This led to a situation in which many monasteries were the property of noble landowners who, while they protected their cloisters, likewise exploited them as family property.

Nevertheless, despite abuses the monasteries were a source of abundant blessing for the church. The same is true of the later communities in which faith in the gospel took on spirit and form.

Certainly the monasteries and their unusual role in Western history (and the same is true for the East) also involved losses: while they regarded themselves as monastic "families," they consisted only of men or women. For many centuries—with important exceptions—there was no opportunity within the Catholic Church for married persons to pursue discipleship in a biblically constituted way of life.

Certainly countless mothers and fathers lived exodus and discipleship, mostly in silence and hiddenness, through a love of neighbor that often meant sacrificing their lives, but they were often denied the support of a living Christian community. Certainly for a very long time they lacked the opportunity to participate in a mutual community of life through which they could offer service to the community and share in preaching the gospel.

It was different with the churches of the Reformation. Here I want to mention again, as a particularly prominent example, the church of the Moravian Brethren, which has spread throughout the world. There were many other examples, especially the communitarian structures in the so-called "free churches." In Germany in recent decades it is precisely in the evangelical part of the German Lutheran Church that an extraordinary number of house-churches have arisen; in them people read Scripture together, pray, and invite those who are strangers to the church to join in conversation.

Beginning in the twentieth century and especially since Vatican II there are increased numbers of ecclesiastical movements or "intentional communities"[2] in which not only the unmarried but families also join their lives together. In this regard we must speak of a new breakthrough both in the Roman Catholic church and in the churches of the Reformation. The reason for this is, among other things, a renewed view of the Bible that now has a scholarly foundation. It was not accidental that at the beginning of these reflections I spoke of God's will to have a *people* in the world—a people that continually carries out the exodus anew and becomes a unity in faith and life.

One other reason for the growth of new ecclesiastical movements, however, is that the society in which we live is more and more segmented and that many seek a way of life as individuals, with freely chosen relationships that, however, in most cases remain nonobligatory. Obviously this unwillingness to commit has a huge effect on parish life. More and more Christians sense, however, that Christian "communities" are in their innermost nature more than attendance at Sunday worship and religious community life.

Certainly it is true that a communitary binding of Christian families brings problems with it unlike those that existed in the classic Orders and were probably one reason why for such a long time the Roman Catholic Church suppressed communities of life involving families, or else regarded them with great skepticism: I am thinking here primarily of child-rearing and with it the protection of the necessary intimacy of the family. Children need a natural family, and young adults need the freedom to make their own decisions about their lives (in accord with their age level, of course). Certainly adults must also make a fully free decision for a community life, but in doing so they enter into obligations that younger people cannot yet adopt in the same form and should not be required to do so.

Jesus' Strategy

It makes sense, then, at this point to take another look at Jesus' strategies in his eschatological gathering of Israel. Here he is exceptionally and astonishingly straightforward. He has with him the

---

[2] In the Roman Catholic Church "ecclesiastical movements" is the preferred term; other churches and groups speak more of "intentional communities."

group of the Twelve and the larger circle of disciples with their correspondingly radical ethos of discipleship. And as we saw, the circle of disciples was the center of Jesus' initiative toward incarnation of the reign of God.

Still, there were also local adherents of Jesus who did not travel with him throughout Israel; their most important task was to receive the disciples into their homes in the evening, give them something to eat, and support them. Beyond those, there were friends, sympathizers, and helpers attached to the Jesus movement, people Jesus did not take into the circle of disciples but sent home to tell about his work (see, for example, Mark 5:18-20).

Still more distantly, there were occasional helpers who were promised a higher reward for handing a cup of water to the passing disciples (Mark 9:41), and on the very edges of the movement there were those who made use of Jesus' cause, not joining with him but profiting from the Jesus movement: people such as the man who drove out demons in the name of Jesus (Mark 9:38-39). Jesus' humorous and pragmatic judgment on him was: "at least he won't be able to speak ill of me."

This unbelievable openness of Jesus and the strategy of concentric circles should also be important for all new church communities. There has to be discipleship in them, but there must also be many others surrounding that center who, sustained and inspired by it, lead their Christian lives in freedom and personal responsibility based on their baptismal promises. Also, it is precisely in terms of this Jesus strategy that we can look for what is right about the slippery and often-condemned idea of the "national church."[3]

The Goal: Communities in the New Testament's Sense

I began by speaking at some length about the nature of the people of God and of community on the basis of the biblical record. That was necessary. The "community" as Luke and Paul envisioned it is the real internal structure of the people of God as Israel had received it, and in every community—depending on the concrete callings of individuals—there should be discipleship, an ever-renewed exodus

---

[3] Volkskirche.

from society, and people who devote their whole lives to building up the community.

Because, since the fourth century, there have often been no such communities and Christianity repeatedly lost its "salt," the multitude of monasteries and later the spiritual societies and movements became "surrogates" for the exodus and for the communities as understood by the New Testament. This elementary link to the church made up of communities is also visible in the fact that at the beginnings of monasticism no special vows were pronounced. The monks and sisters regarded baptism as their vow. Later, when profession of vows was introduced into the Orders, it was regarded as a realization and actualization of baptism.

For this very reason monasteries and ecclesiastical movements have something preliminary about them. The goal must be the biblically-constituted community, but for that very reason they have the character of a sign. Ecclesiastical movements are not islands, nor are they reservations where a fulfilled Christian life can be lived. They are here for the church—and thus for God's plan with the world.

Perhaps we could also, with Norbert Lohfink, call the Orders "God's therapy for the church."[4] They are prophetic reminders that the church may not accommodate itself to the spirit of the times. They are prophetic signs that there really must be Jesus-discipleship in the church, always and everywhere—and that means in every parish. There must be discipleship, exodus, sending forth, radical living according to the gospel, joining of life, mutual help in spiritual and secular matters, new community, brotherly and sisterly companionship, places for silence and meditation, adoration, and not least the biblical freedom from worry that Jesus taught us.

I have said that monasteries and ecclesiastical movements have something preliminary about them because they are to be "signs" for the parishes. One might dare the hypothetical proposition: if we had biblically-shaped communities, the monasteries and all other Christian-communitarian projects would be superfluous. But that "if we had" is unrealistic and unbiblical. Israel already knew that

---

[4] Norbert Lohfink, "Die Orden als Gottes Kirchentherapie: Biblische Überlegungen zur Not der Kirche und zur Not vieler Orden," paper read before the Wanderakademie für Ordensleuten [Itinerant Academy for Religious Orders] in the Archdiocese of Cologne, 7–10 October 1985.

there would always only be a "remnant" of the people who repented (Isa 10:22), and Jesus speaks of the "little flock" (Luke 12:32). So orders and ecclesiastical movements remain always as God's necessary help for the church.

But are monasteries and ecclesiastical movements only there to save and help? Aren't they more than that? Aren't they also anticipations of the ultimate and eternal community—a little bit of heaven, a first glimpse of the new Jerusalem—and, despite all their troubles and imperfections, still the beginning of the heavenly wedding banquet that knows no nightfall? Yes, they are—and yet they are what the "normal" Christian community should be, the community that gathers around the table of the Eucharist and shares not only bread and wine but life as well.

It is probably no accident that it is precisely in the countries where the church is hated from without, forced underground, persecuted and silenced, that Christian communities are often finding their way back to their ancient biblical form: joining their lives together through mutual solidarity in Christ.

Part II

Festivals and Feasts

Advent Eschatology

Advent means "arrival." That does not refer only to the birth of Jesus; it is also about the coming of the reign of God as well as the coming of Jesus Christ on the Last Day, when our time flows into its eternal fulfillment. So the weeks before Christmas not only look forward with joyful expectation to the birth of the Messiah in Bethlehem; they look far beyond. That is why, for example, we hear in the Gospel for the First Sunday of Advent how Jesus Christ appears on the clouds of heaven—with great power and glory (Matt 24:30; Mark 13:26; Luke 21:27).

Imminent Expectation

"He will return in glory." That statement in the Nicene Creed summarizes the fundamental hope of the very earliest Christian communities, and it was combined with a burning expectation. We encounter this expectation of the imminent return of Christ and with it, naturally, the end of the world, at many points in the New Testament: in the Gospels of Matthew and Mark, in the authentic Pauline letters, in the book of Revelation. The question for us, of course, is: What shall we do with this excited anticipation that marked the first decades of the church's existence? But first we should ask: how did Christians deal with it in the further course of church history?

A number of sects, from the Montanists to the Adventists, have pursued a completely delusive resolution by repeatedly stoking that early Christian expectation in new ways. They have proclaimed the "thousand-year reign" or the end of the world with Christ's reappearing as imminent—despite the biblical "about that day and hour no one knows" (Matt 24:36), often giving a precise date. Then, when at last the promised day arrived and the clock struck the longed-for hour, they all stood waiting—but in vain. Still, that momentary disappointment was never the end for those sects because their leading prophets were always able to give reasons for the delay of Christ's appearance: specific obstacles that supposedly prevented the return from happening as they had calculated.

The larger church took another direction from a fairly early date: as more and more generations of Christians were born and the return of Christ had still not come about, the phenomenon of "imminent expectation" dimmed, and with it the power of the corresponding New Testament texts faded from the forefront of believers' minds. At some point apocalyptic expectation ceased to be discussed, and the texts referring to it were suppressed—at least, that was the case for the mass of churchgoers.

The Revival of Imminent Expectation

It was only in the nineteenth century that biblical scholars discovered how deeply Jesus' preaching of the reign of God was *eschatologically* shaped and filled with urgent expectation—and so also the expectation of the early communities. Since that time theologians have been trying to deal with eschatological expectation, and some quickly found an elegant solution: they reduced the expectation of the imminent coming of the reign of God in Jesus' preaching to a timeless *ethos*.

One example we might mention is the German Lutheran New Testament scholar Herbert Braun. In his book on Jesus he wrote: "The essential intention of Jesus' preaching about the end is not entertaining advice about events in the near future but an unprecedented sharpening of accountability."[1] The assertion here, then, is that when Jesus said "the reign of God is at hand" his aim was ultimately to establish a new ethical position: the reference to the reign of God is not *temporal*. What was meant, instead, was a very particular quality of our ethical behavior. A Christian's whole thinking and doing should be directed by the sense of an ultimate responsibility for the world.

---

[1] Herbert Braun, *Jesus of Nazareth: The Man and His Time*, trans. Everett R. Kalin (Philadelphia: Fortress Press, 1979), 41.

What should we say about that? Obviously, Christians are responsible for the world, but Herbert Braun's position simply ditches a crucial element of Jesus' proclamation of the reign of God. It makes Jesus' preaching and that of the early church *a-historical*. Living hope is turned into sharpened "accountability." There is no salvation that comes to us from the future, the promised future already in the process of fulfillment. We could also say: there is no more Advent.

However: besides theologians who reduce Jesus' expectation to mere ethics there are others who interpret it *existentially*—in terms of human existence. A particularly impressive example is that of the New Testament scholar Hans Conzelmann. In his *Interpreting the New Testament* he wrote:

> *Jesus is not interested in the question of the interval of time in itself. If the expectation of the kingdom is understood radically, then "enggiken" [the kingdom "has come near"] does not represent a primarily neutral statement about the length or brevity of an interval of time, but a fact that determines human existence: man has no more time left for himself. He must respond to the kingdom in the present moment. It is still not there; otherwise the opportunity for this response, for repentance, would be past. The kingdom would no longer be preached. But it is so near that a man can no longer ask: "For how long can I postpone repentance?" There is no more time. Now is the last moment for those who are addressed.*[2]

That is exceptionally well stated. An existential theology of this kind does, in fact, reveal important elements in Jesus' preaching and practice. Above all, it makes it plausible that the delay of the imminent end did not represent too much of a problem for the early church: in its repentance, in its ever-renewed expectation of the Holy Spirit, and above all, in its sacramental life it experienced that "last moment" again and again.

On the other hand, though, the existential view has a deficiency: it considers imminent expectation from the point of view of the individual, and therefore history falls out of the picture. We need a better explanation for Jesus' imminent expectation and that of the early communities.

---

[2] Hans Conzelmann, *An Outline of the Theology of the New Testament*, trans. John Bowden (New York: Harper & Row, 1969), 111.

The God Who Is Continually Coming

Since the creation of the world—to speak for the moment in the categories of time, although God is beyond all time—there has been no "moment" in which God does not contain and sustain the world with anticipatory action, with providence, with love, with constant coming. God is always coming. But in Jesus of Nazareth that grace and care that are and always have been coming to the world attained their goal.

Prepared by Israel's history since Abraham, God found in Jesus the "place" to which God could ultimately and finally come. With that, the end-time has come. With that, the reign of God breaks in. Even if, all the same, it is not yet whole and without diminutions, often scarcely visible at all, that is not because God is still withholding it but because we have not yet grasped it. Blindness and unbelief predominate everywhere in the people of God and in the world. The reign of God cannot yet be full reality. What in principle is already present in Christ since his coming has not yet made its home everywhere; indeed, it often meets bitter resistance. But that is not God's fault. It is ours, because of our lack of repentance. From God's side everything is already present, everything is offered.

At this point, then, the existential interpretation given by Hans Conzelmann also makes sense. Its only deficiency is that it does not take into account the *historical* dimension of this salvation that is already available to us. After all, the world is not made up of individuals who repent or do not. Rather, the decisions of each individual are sustained and limited by the choices of many others to whom the individual is tied or in whose steps she or he follows—and the decisions of every individual likewise create a history, opening or closing doors to others. To put it another way: we are located within a history of salvation and anti-salvation, and it is essentially determined by whether we, as church, live as a believing community or not. In the church, in its liturgy and life, the end-time salvation of God is constantly coming to us, desiring to transform the world. Here, then, we live in eschatological expectation—in a space where God's promises are, or can be, unceasingly fulfilled. But if we do not believe God's promises they are not fulfilled and the ultimate arrival of the reign of God is delayed.

It Happens Every Moment

We must locate the New Testament texts of imminent expectation within this field of tension: of salvation already being fulfilled and also repeatedly delayed. Imminent expectation must then mean reckoning, in every hour, that God wants to show us new ways; expecting in every hour that God will open new doors for us; believing in every hour that God is transforming evil into good, damnation into salvation; awaiting in every hour that the impossible will be made possible. Imminent expectation means that we never say: "Later!" but always "Now!" We always have only this hour, and this hour is already the hour of Christ's coming.

One day, then, the time will come when the many hours in which Christ has already come will be gathered together into the single moment in which all the hours of our life will be collected and brought together. Then Jesus will finally come for us. That is the hour of our death. It is close to all of us. When, in death, we leave earthly time behind us, all earthly time and history will also have reached their end. Then our own hours and those of the whole sweep of world history will be gathered before Christ, the judge of the world. All that is very close to us—much closer than we think.

Thus the texts of imminent eschatological expectation in the New Testament are not something embarrassing that we should be ashamed of, nor are they something time-conditioned that we can leave behind us. No, these texts are at the center of what is Christian, and that is why they are placed at the very beginning of the new church year. They show the kind of time in which we live: the end-time that has dawned with Jesus Christ, the time when we can no longer ask: "how long can I delay my repentance?" Not a minute longer! The last hour is always here. It is especially Advent, the beginning of the church year, that aims to open our eyes to it.

How the Son of Man[1] Comes

The Advent liturgy makes no pretenses. It is hard and clear. It does not try to enchant us with soft, sweet "pre-Christmas" images. The gospels with which Advent begins in the several cycles speak of a catastrophe—*the* catastrophe. They talk of the darkening of the sun, the fading of the moon, the tossing of the sea. They say that the stars will fall from heaven and all the powers that hold the universe together will fail. They speak of the end of the world (Matt 24:3-31; Mark 13:3-27; Luke 21:7-28).

End of the World?

There are various ways of dealing with such texts. Some see in the images real disasters that are approaching humanity: climate catastrophes, environmental catastrophes, nuclear catastrophes, pandemics. Others say that these biblical horror scenes of the end of the world, these threatening scenarios, are part of apocalyptic, which arises out of a worldview that nearly always emerges in times of crisis. But we are not tied to a concept of the world born altogether from the experience of disaster. Still others limit the catastrophic images in these texts to internal events in the human soul.

All those positions fall short. We may not locate the Bible's images of horror simply in the fear-induced disaster scenarios of our contemporaries, nor may we make light of them. All these images are

---

[1] The Aramaic words traditionally translated "Son of Man" simply mean "a human being"; see NRSV at Daniel 7:13, "one like a human being." In the time of Second Temple Judaism it could be used in ordinary speech to mean "a person" or even "I," but the gospel writers often understood Jesus to be referencing Daniel 7:13 when he called himself "the Son of Man" and thus to be claiming the status there described.—Tr.

very old, originating long before so-called "apocalypticism." We must consider what they really mean to tell us.

The Fundamental World Catastrophe

These images are not about *some* disaster or other; they concern the fundamental catastrophe of the world: unbelief. From its first page to its last, the Bible tells us that unbelief is never something that happens only in the interior of the human being. It arises, certainly, in heads and hearts, but it does not stay there. It pushes outward. It makes itself at home in the world, replacing a part of it. The mistrust that is unbelief destroys the world that could be Paradise.

The immense pride of which human beings are capable, the pride and avarice that blind them and cause them to forget all fear of God: these create world catastrophes. We can almost count on it that these catastrophes will grow increasingly intense as more and more technical and digital possibilities are made available to people in the future.

That, then, is the first thing the horrific apocalyptic images in the Bible want to tell us: unbelief is the fundamental world catastrophe. It does not stay in hearts; it causes evil on earth, and when it is the unbelief of many it will become a comprehensive, global context of blindness.

The Coming of the Son of Man

All that is, of course, more the presumption than the proper statement of the gospels for the first Sunday of Advent, for their center is the coming of the Son of Man in power and glory. It then appears that the world is being shattered not only by unbelief but ultimately by the coming of the Human One, the "Son of Man" himself. What really causes the world to totter is the confrontation between unbelief and the returning Christ.

Jesus Christ, indeed, is the absolute reality, God's own reality. When he appears, the true condition of society is uncovered. The old world, with its pride and arrogance, falls to pieces before him. It cannot stand before the truth that appears in him. It collapses, and a new world is in the making. But when will all that happen?

We may and must say: since the appearance of Jesus this new world of God has been on the way. It can already be seen with the eyes of faith, even in the midst of our old situations. Again and again the truth of the gospel shows itself, the miracle of faith happens, people allow themselves to be called into discipleship, following Jesus, and the church takes the path of repentance. And again and again the miracle of reconciliation happens.

Of course, this inbreaking of God's new world into the old one is not without peril. The coming of the reign of God has consequences. Therefore the gospel is right when it describes that coming as a shattering of the world, a cosmic drama. Letting Jesus into our world threatens uproar—not only in our insides but far beyond. After all, we don't want the upheaval by which Jesus becomes master of our lives—and the society around us most certainly does not desire such a thing. Society's models and its self-made gods are so powerful that their overthrow is like a complete collapse. Then "stars" indeed fall from heaven, and people experience profound fear.

Thus Jesus is already coming, today, in this life. Like a thief in the night, he is suddenly there. We do not know in advance when that will be. It can happen in very many ways, differently for each individual. It can be an event that shakes us, an accident, an illness, a fatality—but for the most part God speaks to us through human messengers. The "end of the world" begins for us—to speak in theological terms—at the moment when we suddenly know: I can no longer escape. Now, for me, it is no longer about this or that; it is about God's very own cause, God's reign, God's rule.

Such a moment can take one's breath away. We are profoundly shocked—which is why angels in the Bible always say "Fear not!" In precisely such a moment, when in the midst of our life we grasp that it is now about a change of ruler, we are confronted with the end of the world: namely, the *end of our old world* and the beginning of the new world that lies before us.

Fundamentally, this is good news: we can put the old, used-up thing aside and enter into God's new world, the world Jesus Christ spreads before us. That is the merciful kindness of our God: that year after year, in Advent, the door to repentance, to new beginning, to the coming of Jesus is opened anew. We only have to enter it. Those who dare to do so will realize that the church's penitential time before Christmas bestows a blessed stillness on us, something altogether different from the supposed blessings of the Christmas frenzy that is building up around us.

Threefold Advent

Advent celebrates the "coming" of Jesus. After everything I have said, we have to understand that coming in a threefold sense. Advent reaches out to the coming of the Son of Man as judge of the world at the end of time. The gospels for the first Sunday of Advent speak about that.

But Advent also means the coming of the reign of God that has already arrived in Jesus. Jesus has already broken into our world like a thief in the night. He has broken into our society, which tries to close itself to him and yet cannot. He comes toward us, unceasingly: in the Gospel we hear, in the sacraments we receive, in the great saints given to the church again and again, and in the upheavals through which God renews the church that is God's.

Also, the days of Advent want to prepare us for the child lying in the manger. That was the beginning of all the advents of the Son of Man, the Human One. We want to kneel before this child, forget ourselves, and give him our hearts. Maranatha! Come, Lord Jesus!

Christmas without a
Manger or Shepherds

The Gospel of Luke shapes the picture most Christians have of Christmas. For them, Luke 2:1-20 is *the* Christmas gospel. Its inventory includes the emperor Augustus, his imperial command to register the population, the journey of Joseph and Mary from Nazareth to Bethlehem, the birth of Jesus, the manger, the swaddling clothes, the announcement to the shepherds, and the heavenly host proclaiming peace on earth. Luke 2:1-20 has had an unbelievable impact. We cannot imagine a Christian Christmas without that text.

However, the church's liturgy is much richer and more nuanced than it often seems. At Christmas it offers us not only the images in Luke's Christmas story. The Mass for Christmas Day is shaped by the Prologue of the Gospel of John (John 1:1-18), which sets different theological accents than does the text of Luke. And the Mass "on Christmas Eve" (not to be confused with the Mass "at Midnight") presents us with Matthew's Christmas story. It, too, is different from Luke 2:1-20. For that very reason it is worthwhile to take a look at Matthew's text for a change. Although Luke's Christmas story is by no means sweet and charming, there can be no question of such a false interpretation in regard to Matthew.

Here the birth of the child is only told in two subordinate clauses (Matt 1:25; 2:1). There is no emperor Augustus and no imperial census, no journey to Bethlehem, no manger, no swaddling clothes; there are no shepherds and no heavenly hosts. But above all: the heavenly messenger does not appear to Mary but to Joseph—and in a dream (Matt 1:20-21). For Matthew, then, it is not Mary but Joseph who is the principal figure. The basic question in Matthew's story is: How does the "savior" (Matt 1:21) come? How does the "Messiah" (Matt 1:16, 17; 2:4) enter the world? The question is likewise: how

does a messianic people come to be in the world? The two are inseparable. Matthew gives a threefold answer to the two questions. First
of all, he shows that

The Messiah Does Not Fall from Heaven

Of course Matthew does not say it that way but instead uses a long
genealogy of no fewer than forty-seven names (Matt 1:1-17). Thus
Jesus is shown to have a long prehistory: that of the people of God
since Abraham. Really we should not call it a "prehistory" because
it is about much more: the basis on which Jesus stands, the root of
his existence. Without the long history of Israel extending over centuries there could have been no Jesus. Without the fidelity in faith of
many individuals in Israel, without the long and complicated history
of the Old Testament people of God, which included Gentile women
such as Ruth (Matt 1:5) and other women such as Tamar and Bath-
sheba (Matt 1:3, 6), there would have been no Messiah.

Correspondingly, it is a fact that without the history of Israel there
would not have been a history of the church as a "messianic people,"
as Vatican Council II rightly called it (LG 9). Matthew speaks not only
of the Messiah but always of the Messiah's people as well. That is
true even in the Old Testament. Adam always represents not only an
individual but humanity as a whole. Abraham always represents his
descendants, too. In just the same way, the Messiah always represents
the messianic people, a people for God.

Not Just the Product of Israel

Thus the Messiah and the Messiah's people come from a long history, that of Israel. The history by no means ends with Jesus and those
who follow him. While it has found its fulfillment in Jesus, it must
continue in order to reach the whole world. Still, even though that is
all true, the Messiah and his people are not simply a product of
human history; the Messiah is not just the product of Israel.

That is the second answer Matthew gives to the question: how
does the Savior, the Messiah, come into the world? Jesus is not just
the sum and consequence of everything that had happened in Israel
since Abraham, for with him the Matthean genealogy places the long

list of "witnesses" on a completely different level. When it comes to Jesus, it no longer says "Jacob was the father of Joseph, and Joseph was the father of Jesus," but "Jacob was the father of Joseph the husband of Mary, of whom Jesus was born, who is called the Messiah" (Matt 1:16) and a little later: "the child conceived in her [Mary] is from the Holy Spirit" (Matt 1:20).

By suddenly interrupting the long, stereotypical sequence of begettings at this point, Matthew intends to say that as unthinkable as Jesus would be without Israel's history, as that people's best and most precious heir, in him Israel itself is confronted with a miracle. The coming of one like him was pure grace, pure gift, something that could not be planned or made. No human being, no people could produce him of itself.

In the same way we must also say, in Matthew's sense, that as much as the church comes from Israel—is, indeed, nothing other than the eschatological Israel—it is not simply the sum of Israel's history but something new, rising from the cross and resurrection of Jesus Messiah.

The Reception of the Child

Matthew goes still one step further. He gives yet a third answer to the question: "How does the Savior, the Messiah, come into the world?" He says: not only could the people of God not simply produce its Messiah; it had also to *receive* and *accept* this Messiah, for without that the Messiah could not have come.

"It had to receive and accept him, or he could not have come." That seems like a paradox, and yet it is true. We only have to think of a gift that someone wants to give to someone else. If the other does not want the gift, rejects it, and withdraws her hands, it will not be given. In many African tribes it is a fact that one must always receive a gift in both hands. To extend only *one* hand counts as terribly rude. It says, "I really don't want this gift." Then it can happen that it will not be given at all. It is no accident that the "acceptance" of the Messiah plays such a major part in the narratives of both Matthew and Luke.

For Luke that "acceptance" is depicted in the person of Jesus' mother. Mary makes the all-decisive statement: "let it be with me according to your word" (Luke 1:38). Matthew tells of the same thing, but entirely from Joseph's point of view. That particular part of Matthew's "Infancy Narrative" deserves closer examination, because here Matthew reflects in the subtlest possible way not only the "acceptance" of the Messiah but the conditions for the possibility of a messianic community.

In Israel girls were ordinarily betrothed as early as twelve or thirteen. Legally, a betrothal was as valid as a marriage. A year or so later the girl was then "taken home," that is, ceremonially led to the husband's family and received into it. Sexual union began with this "bringing home."

Joseph, according to Matthew, was suddenly confronted with the fact that Mary, before being "brought home," had become pregnant (Matt 1:18). According to the provisions of Torah, Joseph had two choices in such a situation: he could accuse his betrothed before the court and prove by the testimony of two witnesses that she had willingly had intercourse with another man. If there were such witnesses—at least according to Deuteronomy 22:23-24—she was subject to stoning, but in any case to public humiliation. Otherwise he could release her by giving her a writ of divorce as prescribed in Deuteronomy 24:1. That would allow her to marry another man (Deut 24:2). Matthew speaks of the two possibilities:

> *Her husband Joseph, being a righteous man and unwilling to expose her to public disgrace, planned to dismiss her quietly.* (Matt 1:19)

So Joseph means to give Mary a writ of divorce, which would allow him to separate from his betrothed without too much publicity and without exposing her. (The writ of divorce had to be signed by two witnesses, however.) The phrase "being a righteous man" refers simply to Joseph's devotion to Torah. The story means us to understand that Joseph is a Jew who holds to the law from Sinai. He lives according to the provisions of Torah. In his everyday life he tries to live the written will of God—not, of course, in the sense of a stupid legalism, because that is not what fidelity to the law meant in the Old Testament. One need only read Psalm 119 to know that.

And at precisely this point, in Matthew 1:20-25, another significant piece of theology enters our story: to live carefully according to Torah, Matthew says, is good, but it is not enough. When the miracle of the Messiah happens in Israel, more is demanded. Then God is acting anew in God's people and everything depends on whether this people will receive the new thing and allow itself to be led by God.

The narrative expresses this in highly visible terms: Joseph is not only to be just, to listen to Torah, but also to hear the living voice of the angel who will now lead him. He is to bring Mary home to his parents' house (Matt 1:20). Being just is a good thing, but something essential must be added: faithful listening to today, to the angelic voice, entering into the living guidance of God.

Joseph obeys. "He did as the angel of the Lord commanded him; he took her as his wife" (Matt 1:24). Therefore the Messiah can come into the world—but not only the Messiah: his people as well, for the messianic people of God lives by the same inner law. The messianic, eschatological Israel rests entirely on the Torah, the direction of the commandments; that is true. And yet there is more.

The church shows itself to be a messianic people—and we all call ourselves "Christians," that is, the Messiah's people—only when we act out of the living will of God, trust to God's guidance, and live in such a way that we daily, in fact hourly, rely on God's acting and respond to it. Only then is the church—only then are we—a truly Christmas people of whom it can be said: "As the bridegroom rejoices over the bride, so shall your God rejoice over you" (Isa 62:5).

A Longed-for Child

Many years ago, on the morning before Christmas Eve, I had a brief conversation with a neighbor from across the street that, oddly enough, I have not forgotten to this day. Calling it a "conversation" is really an exaggeration: it was only a brief exchange of words. At that time I was living on the outskirts of a city in the south of Germany, in a part where people still knew their neighbors. The house across from me was the home of a doctor and her husband. They had a five-month-old son of whom they were very proud, as they often showed.

So as I was standing in front of our house the door on the other side of the street opened and our neighbor came out with the child in his arms. He called to me across the street: "Have you already put up your Christmas crèche?" Without waiting for me to answer, he bubbled: "*We* don't need a crèche! This is our Christ child." He hugged the child as if it were a marvelous toy. I laugh, he laughs, and we wish each other happy holidays.

But seeing the neighbor's baby "as the Christ child"—that preoccupied me. How would things go for the neighbor's child? How will it be when the baby is six years old, twelve, fourteen, eighteen?

I don't know what happened to the neighbor's child; I only learned that his parents got a divorce. Three years after that December 24 there were loud arguments, and they sold their house. That I know for certain; I know nothing about the child.

The Promise Finally Fulfilled

I do know what has happened with other children. Every child is really an infinite promise. Certainly, babies are a lot of work. They cry; they keep their parents constantly on the move; they know how to assert themselves. But they manage to melt your heart the first time they smile at you. Even later, when they grow to be adolescents, the flame of promise is still alive in them. They are not satisfied with the way the world is—just as children are not satisfied when the situation surrounding them is not right.

Still, the promise that shines from the eyes of so many children and still twinkles in adolescence is not always fulfilled. All too often the child's longing is dulled; trust turns into mistrust, ability to let oneself be touched becomes hardness, even cynicism. The shining eyes lose their luster. As adults they have learned to get along—to accommodate to themselves and the state of the world. The promise that lies in every child: what will become of it in the slaughterhouse of life?

Truly there is an infinite amount of attention, dedication, care, and devoted commitment to children. For the most part it happens quietly, and society gives too little thanks to the mothers and fathers who sacrifice part of their lives for their children. But despite all the care and devotion, we are all aware of what falls short of fulfillment in our growing adolescents, every month and every year, and we certainly know all that has not been fulfilled in us.

I think it is for that very reason that we love to look at the child in the manger, and that is why Christmas is such an ineradicable feast. For one of the mysteries of Christmas is that something succeeded here that had never succeeded *in this way* before: in this child all the promises were fulfilled. In the child of Bethlehem nothing was buried and nothing was stunted. What could be sensed already in the child in the manger was realized, in full purity and without distortion, in the adult Jesus. And more than that: in him was realized everything that a human is meant to be. This child was what the human being should be, according to God's plan: the true human person.

But can we say that? Wasn't everything different for Jesus from how it is for us? After all, he came from God; he is God's son. Wasn't he an exception?—not really a human being like all of us but something unique, an extraordinary appearance, a singularity, a privileged individual, a higher being? Those who ask such questions are pointing to something correct, but with dangerously false words.

Jesus indeed comes entirely from God. He is really the "Son of God." But our faith also confesses that he is truly human. The fact that he is a true human person is as much part of him as the mystery that he is truly God. So we also have to see Jesus as one person within the long history of humanity, one who is the result of an unimaginably long biological evolution. But the long historical development of humanity was always driven by the hidden goal that someone like him would come, that somehow, somewhere, the miracle would occur: a child who would not be damaged by its prehistory, its parents, or its environment—and that child would also not damage its own life.

Jesus' Prehistory

Certainly it is not enough, when we speak of Jesus, to talk vaguely about his "prehistory," because his prehistory is Israel. It includes Abraham, who left his land, his people, and his father's house because he listened to God's call (Gen 12:1-4). His prehistory includes Moses, who applied all his strength and craft to avoid having to approach Pharaoh on behalf of his oppressed people, and then did go after all (Exod 3:7–4:18). Jesus' prehistory includes Israel's prophets, who put their lives on the line for the message they had received. His prehistory includes the poor and silent in Israel who relied on their God with their whole existence. Finally, his prehistory includes his mother, who softly and trustingly said to the angel "let it be with me according to your word."

That is why it was possible, one day, for a person to come into the world who was only truth, who was absolutely open, and who was pure trust in God. In Jesus what the human being is meant to be was finally realized, and in its realization it was pure grace. In Jesus, contrary to all human experience, the miracle happened: a human being grew up without wanting anything for himself but solely and entirely what God wants. Therefore God could be fully expressed in him; therefore God could dwell in him; therefore the reading for Christmas Day says of him, "he is the reflection of God's glory and the exact imprint of God's very being" (Heb 1:3).

"In Christ"

Since humanity finally succeeded in him, it can also succeed in us—presupposing that we want to share in him; presupposing that we are "in Christ," as Paul says, and that means that we are baptized into him, that we are part of his "body," that we are his community.

So the New Testament dares to say that in Jesus Christ we can become daughters and sons of God, "children of God" in communion with him.

From that point of view my neighbor was theologically correct when he called his baby boy a "Christ-child." It is only that he had no idea what that can mean. The statement I somewhat casually wrote—that from the very beginning there is an endless promise in every child—can, to be precise, only be said in light of Jesus. Only since Jesus came do we really know it. Only since Jesus does every child have the real opportunity to be the kind of human being who pleases God, truly a child of God.

But that can only take place in faith, in the space of Christian community, in the realm of biblical confidence. Only there is it possible that our children's eyes never lose their shine, that children are never smothered, even before they leave the womb, with the cares, plans, wishes, ideas, and interests of their parents.

It is so easy nowadays to complain about Christmas in the society in which we live. It is so easy to make fun of the shopping frenzy, the Christmas fairs, the inflated plastic Santas, the orgies of holiday lights, the sybaritic holiday feasts, and the annually repeated advice of concerned veterinarians about how one should treat one's dog, cat, and guinea pig at Christmas and New Year's. It is so easy to feel superior to all that, but I find it harder and harder because I see the people's longing for the real Child who fulfills the promises.

Certainly that longing is kneaded, exploited, trivialized, and perverted by a vast and efficient Christmas industry. But it is there. If there were no such longing, Christmas would long since have faded out. Isn't it our task to see to it that this longing doesn't dissipate into nothing? But we can only do that if we are the Body of Christ and allow ourselves to be touched by the real joy of Christmas, to be moved by the words of the Christmas reading: "A child has been born for us, a son given to us" (Isa 9:6)—and if we believe that this is, at last, the child in whom all the longings of the world are fulfilled, not least the longing of our own heart.

Christmas Peace Is Different

It has been some years since the media reported an archaeological sensation: In Rome, deep in the Palatine Hill (the hill on which the Roman emperors' palaces stood), scientists, with the aid of sound equipment, had found a cave adorned with marble and shells.

Ancient literature had already informed us of the existence of such a cave. It was considered the most important cultic place in ancient Rome, for there—according to legend—a mother wolf had suckled the twins Romulus and Remus. Romulus then went on to found the city of Rome. It was possible that the ancient cultic cave had been rediscovered. Though some doubts were expressed, Italian antiquarians were ecstatic.

Two Caves

When I read about the sensational discovery I thought immediately of another cave: the one in which, according to tradition, Jesus was born. We usually imagine Jesus' birth as taking place in a stable. Often enough the "cribs" we create are real works of art and a delight not just for children. But the ancient church tradition (for example, the so-called *Protoevangelium of James*, 18), and especially the long tradition of the Orthodox Church, depict Jesus as entering the world not in a stable, but in a cave.

Historically speaking, there is much in favor of that: at that period in Israel the stables for domestic animals were often dug out of the soft rock of an overhang. Jesus may indeed have been born in a cave. At any rate, Luke writes that Mary laid the newborn baby in a manger (Luke 2:7). It could have been in a place that at other times sheltered goats and sheep.

I felt moved to compare the two: the cave of the Roman twins and that of Jesus. To put it more precisely: what interested me was not the caves as such but what happened there according to the two stories. I could also say I was drawn to a comparison of what came out of the caves.

Two Brothers Contend

The abandoned twins, Romulus and Remus, were suckled by a wolf: so the story goes. Evidently that was good fortune for them. They grew tall and strong. The wolf in them only appeared later when each of them wanted to found a city: Romulus on the Palatine Hill and Remus on the Aventine—one for each of them. That already meant division. But then it got worse. Romulus had two white oxen yoked to a plow and drew the "sacred furrow" around the Palatine, the outline of the city he planned to build. He called the furrow the "moat" of his future city and the earth that was thrown up he dubbed its "wall." But Remus jumped over that tiny wall and laughed at his brother. Romulus flew into a rage and slew his brother, saying: "Thus shall it be with anyone who jumps over my wall."

That is Rome's foundational statement and, like any saying, it contains some truth. The little city of Rome became a world empire, one that, like every human empire, was built on violence. According to Virgil (*Aeneid* VI, 853) Rome's eternal duty was

> *parcere subjectis et debellare superbos* (to spare the vanquished and sub-due the proud).

That is: the peoples who freely submit to Rome will be spared (they only have to pay a heavy annual tribute), but those who resist Rome will be cut down. In any case the Western Roman Empire endured for more than a thousand years.

And the Roman world power that, in line with its basic principle, was built on violence is only *one* in a long series of great empires. All states are built on violence, whether it is that of wolves dressed as statesmen or measured violence that attempts to create law and order so as to secure social peace. Without this state monopoly on violence, chaos would immediately erupt even in the most admirable of states under the rule of law.

So even a contemporary democratic constitutional nation is built on violence: it needs police, prosecutors, and prisons because other-wise order could not be kept. It even needs armies because, if necessary, it must protect itself against enemies. There is thus a *legitimate* state violence—and yet it is sadly the case that even truly democratic states often become oppressors. The bias toward violence and the urge to steadily increase power are deep-seated forces within human beings.

An Anti-History

The story associated with the other cave of origins, that of Luke (Luke 2:1-20), knows all about that. Luke is aware of what Rome and the Roman world power mean. He sees the law, and with it the order, that this world empire has brought with it, but he also sees its demonic side. Thus it is no accident that he begins his story with the emperor Augustus, who was regarded in the Western empire as the great bringer of peace and was celebrated, at least in the East, as the "savior" (*sōtēr*) of the human race." Augustus's official, legal name was

IMPERATOR • CAESAR • DIVI FILIUS • AUGUSTUS
(RULER • CAESAR • SON OF THE DIVINIZED ONE • THE SUBLIME)

Augustus had taken the name of his adoptive father, Caesar; he now has himself officially called Caesar as well. In addition, his name "Divi Filius" indicates that his adoptive father had been officially divinized. After his death in 14 CE, Augustus himself was declared by the Senate to be *Divus*, that is, "the Divinized One," a state god. All that must have been echoing in Luke's ears when he began his narrative with the words:

> In those days a decree went out from Caesar Augustus that all the world should be registered. (Luke 2:1)

Such a "census," that is, a tax list, was an important instrument for exploiting the conquered provinces. We need to listen to the background noises in our Christmas gospel: a ruler who has himself celebrated as "Emperor" and "Savior" and will be declared a god by the Senate after his death; a state power that pictures itself as the continuation of the Roman republic but is really a sophisticated monarchy; an imperial tax system that exploits other peoples and degrades them into poverty.

Against that background Luke tells a counter-story, one about the real bringer of salvation. The "angel of the Lord" proclaims him to the shepherds as the true "savior" (*sōtēr*), and that high and lofty concept known throughout the ancient world is then coupled with the biblical concepts of "messiah" (*christos*) and "lord" (*kyrios*) (Luke 2:10-11). He alone is the savior, and he will bring the peace the world longs for—not the phony peace brought by heavy boots and blood-spattered military uniforms (cf. Isa 9:4). It is an altogether different kind of peace, one that comes not from human beings and not through violence. The signal of this different peace is the helplessness of the child in the manger, together with the proclamation of the angelic host:

> *Glory to God in the highest heaven, and on earth peace among those whom [God] favors!* (Luke 2:14)

That is: this true peace, the peace all nations so long for, comes only from God—and the helpless child in the manger is the true bringer of peace. With this it is clear: he only comes through absolute nonviolence. Thirty years later Jesus prefers to let himself be executed for his message rather than use violence. This same genuine peace then comes through people who follow Jesus and begin by being peaceful among themselves. The shepherds who run peacefully to the manger are the first of Jesus' many disciples.

Christmas and Ourselves

The story of the child in the manger, of the shepherds with their flocks and the angels above the fields of Bethlehem is thus not a pleasant idyll. It is a story about all or nothing, namely, the question of how peace can come about in our world. The weapons of the Roman legionnaires were lances, swords, and catapults. Meanwhile the world has developed more effective weapons that could kill millions of people in a few minutes' time. The all-decisive question for us and our children is whether there will be peace in the world—against the lust of shameless dictators for power and the fanaticism of blind terrorists. Peace cannot be created simply by a humane attitude, no matter how much dialogue is conducted and how urgent the appeals to world-brotherhood and -sisterhood. Humanity is much too fascinated with power for that; we have too much wolf blood in our veins. Romulus slew his brother Remus. That is the norm. It lies in all of us, but normally we do it more subtly and behind the façade of hypocritical civility.

The Christmas story says: there is only *one* way to world peace, to peace in our families and in our hearts. It is the way of the child in the manger. We ourselves cannot create the peace we long for by our own initiative, but as disciples of Jesus, in the company of the shepherds who already foreshadow the future communities—there peace is possible.

Moreover, the peace the angels announce means more than just not-biting, not-scratching, not-killing, not-exploding. This peace means reconciliation, opening one's heart to the other, sensing where the other is hurting, binding up wounds, being sisters and brothers to one another.

Thus the two caves bear the thickest kind of symbolism. One is the symbol of obsession with power and the struggle between brothers, the other of the love between sisters and brothers and the renunciation of power. The latter does not happen because we can produce it of ourselves—by our own power we cannot even will it—but because God wants to give us that peace in his Son, the child of Bethlehem. That is the good news of Christmas.

It would be a good thing if each of us would go to the crib on Christmas and in the days after and pray: "My Lord and my God, give me and those who belong to me this Christmas peace. Make my heart open and quiet and believing. Make me an instrument of your peace. Teach me to see my sisters and brothers in faith anew and to follow your way with them: the way of the gospel, the way of discipleship."

Then it could be Christmas for us.

The Astrologers from the East

The story of the stargazers is found in Matthew's gospel (Matt 2:1-12). It is told quite simply, and yet it is theologically significant and broad in its implications. Over the centuries this story has moved many people. At a very early period the stargazers (we would say "astrologers" now) were interpreted, in light of Psalm 72:10-11, as *kings*, and in order better to imagine them, people took their gifts of "gold, frankincense, and myrrh" to indicate that there were *three* kings. In the sixth century names were invented for them: Caspar, Melchior, and Balthazar. In the Middle Ages the "three kings" were unimaginably popular. In Germany the names of taverns and hostelries recalled them—because, of course, they had traveled such a great distance. Still today many older inns are called "At the Sign of the Crown" or "At the Sign of the Star" or "At the Sign of the Moor."

Even today groups of children parade through the streets before the "Feast of the Lord's Appearing," dressed as the "three kings" and their entourage. They sing at the house-doors and collect money for children in need. A rich folklore has developed over the centuries around the story of the stargazers, and in art galleries countless paintings, many of them very famous, tell of the encounter of the "three kings" with the child-messiah.

Forms of Prayer

Let me select a single sentence from the powerful story of the stargazers from the East. In the middle of it Matthew writes:

> . . . *they knelt down [before the child] and paid him homage.* (Matt 2:11)

The word "homage" in itself leaves a lot open. In paying homage one knelt, bowed low, and kissed the earth—or perhaps the feet of the one being honored. One might pay homage to a king or a person of higher rank; in the ancient Near East there were many highly placed persons who received homage. Or one could also pay homage to a god through worship. In Matthew's text the corresponding Greek word *proskynein* has this deeper meaning (see Matt 4:9, 10; 28:9, 17). The wise men from the East pay adoring homage to the "Son of God" (see Matt 14:33).

Have we ever reflected on what "adoration" really means? Of course, it is not the only way one may pray to God. There are a great many varieties of prayer: not only adoration but lament, petition, and thanksgiving.

Yes, even lament before God is genuine prayer. We may complain to God about our suffering; we may even shout our need and our misery to God with loud cries. But we can also petition. We may ask God for everything we need—so long as we also say "not what I want, but what you want" (Mark 14:36). We may also thank God for everything good and beautiful that we encounter every day, even the tiniest things. During a single day there are a thousand reasons to lift our faces to God.

Lament, petition, thanksgiving—these are elementary forms of prayer. But on the "Feast of the Lord's Appearing" we look to the travelers from the East who have made the long journey to the royal child in order to *worship* it, to pay it homage. What they do is the most elementary thing a person can do: worship the great, holy, incomprehensible God.

Why is worship of God so elementary, so moving, and ultimately also so beneficial? In adoration we ask nothing more of God. When I lament to God I am only thinking of myself. My suffering is the starting point. Even when I ask God for something, the cause is my own. I need something from God. And even when I thank God, my own ego is the starting point: I have had good luck or I have experienced something beautiful: a little flower has enchanted me or a child has smiled at me. But when I adore: then I abandon my own ego and look only to God.

What I have just said is not altogether true. Even when I complain to God about my suffering I look to God and say: "Why are you doing this to me? Why are you treating me this way? *You* are the one who says you will help, will listen to every prayer! Why did you bring me this misery?" Or we complain: "Why do you allow Christians to be persecuted, ridiculed, dishonored, and killed throughout the world? Doesn't it matter to you?" Even lament ultimately turns our minds away from ourselves and seeks the face of God, however agitated and upset we are.

Likewise, petition and thanksgiving do the same. When I implore God from my heart, I tell God: "I need you. I cannot help myself, but you can." So I acknowledge who God is: the only all-powerful one, the only merciful one, the only one who can save. My prayer of thanksgiving also looks first to the gifts received but then immediately directs my eyes to the Giver of those gifts. After all, isn't the church's most important prayer the Eucharistic Prayer at Mass? In it the priest, in the name of the assembled community and the whole church, thanks God for the greatest of gifts, the gift God has given us and through which God saves us: Jesus.

The Most Important of All Prayer Forms

All that is true, and yet in adoration something happens that extends even deeper because it is completely unexpected, because it makes us forget ourselves, our needs, and our joys and—simply adore. In adoration we look wholly and only to God, leave everything else behind, and praise God in pure wonder that God alone is the Holy One, God alone is the Glorious One, God alone is the Almighty. Everything else falls away and it is only about God's glory. That we can even do such a thing, that we can forget ourselves and our great importance, is a miracle—a miracle that is only possible because God places the Holy Spirit in our hearts and invites us to praise.

The celebration of the Eucharist would not be the greatest feast and the highest solemnity of Christians if it did not also contain pure adoration. The Mass includes lament and petition, and its center is thanksgiving. But obviously it also contains adoration: at the center of the Eucharistic Prayer, in the "Holy, Holy, Holy." When the gathered community sings or says this "Sanctus" it is one with the eternal adoration of all the people who are already with God, and with the adoration of all the angels. When we speak the "Holy, Holy, Holy" we are already in heaven. Then we live in anticipation of what will one day be our never-ending, unspeakable happiness: the eternal adoration of God.

We cannot understand now that this adoration will be endless bliss. We always want to be doing something. We want to act, take hold, change things. We want to accomplish something, achieve something, shape something. And rightly so! That is our duty. But in death, when we arrive in God's presence, that all ceases. Then our existence will be pure amazement, pure seeing, pure praise, pure adoration of God—and precisely that will be an unspeakable and unimaginable happiness. Every time we praise and worship God we experience something of that in advance.

Beyond all that the church knows a form of adoration that uses no words at all. Lament, petition, thanksgiving, and the ringing "Holy, Holy, Holy" are all made up of words. But there is another form of adoration in which we are completely silent—with all our senses. We simply hold out our life to God, in silence. Then adoration is the presentation of one's whole life to God; it is simply surrender. The believer who prays this way holds his heart in God's light. She comes to complete rest. She wants to be silent before God because God is ungraspable and far beyond all our ideas and windy words.

Once More: The Stargazers

I think of all that when I read the gospel for the feast of the Epiphany and come across the sentence "they knelt down [before the child] and paid him homage." Then I think: the astrologers in this story are not naïve. Today we would say they are scientists, because they study and observe the heavenly bodies. Today we would also have to say they are theologians, because they are trying to learn the will of God. Besides, they are not poor people, because that kind of long journey was much more expensive then than it is now.

The fact that precisely *these* people fall down before the little child and place their hearts at his feet seems to me the most beautiful part of this marvelous story. Should we not ask God that our lives might manifest the same gesture, the same movement, the same silent surrender to God?

Why Did Jesus Let Himself Be Baptized?

From Nazareth, where Jesus grew up, to the river crossing where John baptized in the Jordan was a two- or three-day walk. The same was true for many others who were baptized by John in the Jordan (Mark 1:5).

How should we picture those baptisms? The usual preparation was hearing John's preaching of repentance. Then individuals probably confessed their sins, one by one (Mark 1:5), and allowed John and his helpers to immerse them in the river. That immersion in the Jordan was apparently seen by John's contemporaries as so striking and unusual that they called him "the one who immerses," which is the meaning of the Greek word *baptistēs*.

Why Wasn't the Baptizer an Itinerant Preacher?

But why did John have people come to him at the Jordan—and at a particular point opposite Jericho? He could also have moved from village to village as an itinerant preacher, but that is just what he did *not* do. People had to leave their cities and villages and come out to him in the Jordanian wilderness, in an uninhabited place, and then they had to get into the water. Why?

It has to do with the great, wrathful divine judgment the Baptizer was predicting (Matt 3:7). A tempest of fire would break over the people of God (Matt 3:11-12). Israel could only escape that impending fiery judgment if it publicly confessed its guilt and repented, letting the water protect and seal it against the fire. Only in that way can the people of God go on as before. It must make a new beginning.

Thus John's baptism means more than a non-binding statement of intent and more than a bag of good intentions. The Baptizer tells the people of God: if you do not radically change your lives—that is, from the root—you will not escape the catastrophe. "Even now the ax is lying at the root of the trees" (Matt 3:10). The one who will separate the chaff from the wheat is close at hand (Matt 3:12).

Therefore the people have to leave their homes and come to the Jordan, because a change of life that extends to the depths, to the root, is nearly impossible at home. There people are constantly surrounded by the same walls, the same objects, the same faces, the same habits. Life goes on in a fixed pattern. Only those who dare the Exodus, the departure from their old world, at least for a space of time, can begin anew. That is why the Baptizer has the people come to him in the Jordan desert. There they will find the strength to see and order their lives anew. It would have been much more difficult at home.

Something similar happens now when we engage in a retreat. We usually do not do that at home; we go away to a house where retreats are conducted. A retreat demands a new place, a different environment, an altered daily routine so that we can look at our lives from an unaccustomed direction and newness can enter into our old life. The Baptizer demands of Israel a radical repentance and renewal in the name of God, and repentance includes leaving the old behind and letting something new happen to us.

Why Did John Baptize in the Jordan and Nowhere Else?

John's baptism, then, included a complete immersion in the waters of the Jordan. But why the Jordan in particular? There would have been fresh, flowing water at other locations in Israel, and enough deep water in Lake Gennesareth. Why did the Baptizer baptize in the Jordan—and at a particular place? The answer is intriguing. John apparently baptized where, according to the book of Joshua, the Israelites had entered the Promised Land centuries earlier, crossing the Jordan (Joshua 3–4). Repentance and exodus are thus not all that John has in mind. They are the beginning of something much bigger.

The Baptizer is convinced that if the people of God abandons its false security, if it moves out of the past, if it repents and allows God to forgive its guilt, then now as once before under Joshua it can enter into the promised land. Then God will lead God's people anew, once and for all, into the Land of Promise.

Why Did Jesus Let Himself Be Baptized?

Many people in Israel listened to the Baptizer's call and went out to him in the Jordan desert. Jesus, too, heard about what was happening there. He left his parents' house in Nazareth and allowed himself to be immersed by John in the Jordan waters so that he, like the others, could reach the threshold of the Land of Promise—the point at which the new life of the people of God would begin.

We should consider the fact that Jesus does not begin with self-glorification. First he follows another. He surrenders to the Baptizer's preaching of repentance. In just that way he gives God, his Father, the opportunity to begin that overwhelming new thing in which even the "least" is greater than John the Baptizer (Matt 11:11). If Jesus had stayed in Nazareth, or if he had said "I will choose my own way," God's history would not have continued.

At the beginning of the twenty-first century the church is suffering from the fact that it has many individual activists but too few who join together on the way. It suffers still more from the fact that many people already know exactly how the church could be renewed, but there are too few who take the time to ask how *God* wants to renew this people of God's own possession.

The fact that Jesus went out to John in the wilderness and let himself be baptized like all the other people at the Jordan created extraordinary difficulties even for the early communities. How could Jesus, who was so much greater than John, go to the Baptizer and join his renewal movement? But above all: how could the Son of God join the crowd of those who publicly confessed themselves sinners? How could the Sinless One allow himself to be baptized with a "baptism of repentance for the forgiveness of sins" (Mark 1:4)? The dimensions of the difficulty are apparent in the little dialogue Matthew inserts into the baptism scene: John hesitates at first to admit Jesus to baptism (Matt 3:14-15). That dialogue is missing in the baptism stories in Mark and Luke.

How could the Son of God let himself be baptized? It used to be said that Jesus wanted to give the people a good example, but that kind of fussy explanation falls far short. Jesus left his parents and his home town and went to John because he sensed that God was acting through the Baptizer. Israel was entering the decisive phase of its history, the time when all righteousness would be fulfilled (Matt 3:15).

For him, then, that meant he had to be where the fate of the people of God was being decided. He had to be where God was now acting in Israel. He had to be where God was fulfilling the promises and where the people were standing on the threshold of the promised land. The moral question of whether he considered himself a sinner does not touch the real point. Jesus is about the will and plan of God. In his baptism he surrenders himself completely to that plan.

When Jesus came up from the Jordan, the heavens opened. That is: heaven and earth are now bound together because at last there is One on whom the Father's whole favor rests and who is obedient fully and in all things. That is why the threshold to the promised land is crossed. Those who let Jesus gather them and follow his lead can, since then, live under an open heaven.

Why Do We Use Holy Water?

In every catholic church there is a baptismal font near the entrance. Catholics[1] are accustomed to crossing themselves with holy water as they enter and leave the church. Are any of them aware that the water at the church entrance is supposed to remind them of the water of baptism?

It is a fascinating symbol: we are not to enter God's house unthinkingly. We are always to recall the day when, by the water of baptism, we were incorporated into the scope of salvation, into the church. In light of John's baptism and the baptism of Jesus, however, we can understand our baptism even more profoundly: baptism not only as a formal incorporation into the church but as leaving the old human behind and beginning to make our way to the place where God is acting, gathering the people of God so that the Land of Promise may be visible in the midst of the world.

If we consider all that, then crossing ourselves with holy water at the entrance to the church is no longer as innocent as it seems at first glance. It draws into our presence, our current time, what was demanded when Israel went to the Jordan: namely, an exodus from the old world, a commitment to serious repentance, a fixed intention to

---

[1] In this context "catholic" includes not only churches in union with Rome but other churches in the Catholic tradition as well: Anglicans, Orthodox, Old Catholics, and so forth.—Tr.

be where God is renewing God's people and leading them into the Land of Promise.

What Were Jesus' Temptations?

The narrative of Jesus' temptations in Matthew 4:1-11 follows a strict outline: the tempter approaches Jesus three times; each time he uses every ounce of his cunning to divert Jesus from his mission. Three times Jesus rejects him with a quotation from Torah and thus remains true to that mission.

Still, the narrative is not only skillfully designed. It also uses images; it compresses; it even introduces fictive elements. For that very reason, though, it is also able to bring together in a single text Jesus' profound convictions about his mission. The story is packed with reality.

The Reality of Evil

Let us consider the figure of the devil, surely what creates the most difficulties for us in this text and may even prevent us from taking the full scope of the narrative seriously. "The devil" has so often been caricatured in words and pictures that it is easy to dismiss it as a figure of fun, but it represents a terrible truth: the reality of evil. Which of us can deny that there is evil in the world—with all the destructive energy it contains?

Evil possesses an immense power. It can be described as a potential that can increase in strength. There are potentials and fields of force not only in physics but also in individual psyches, in the spiritual depths of every nation, in the "tectonic" underground places of world society. The history of evil in the world has created powers and forces made up of the sum of countless individual decisions. How else can we explain that the seductive and poisonous power of Nazism is still with us and going about its death-dealing business?

The potential for evil, these powers and authorities, appears in our stories as a person—thus not *evil*, but *the Evil One*. Such personalization is quite proper; indeed, it is positively inescapable, for evil feeds on the decisions of many who have rejected God. Those rejections stem from personal freedom, and therefore evil can only be comprehended as a person, *the* Evil One.

If we think of it this way, however, we are only taking a distant view of the reality that is at stake in our text. The narrative says more: that this Evil One, of its very nature, is resistance to God's saving act. The Evil One takes action here at the very moment when God's plan with the world is about to succeed. Here, at last, is one who lives in ultimate obedience to and full unity with the will of God. Jesus has just left his family, gone to the Jordan, and has let himself be baptized by John (Matt 3:13-17). At that very moment the Evil One appears, armed with a terrible power of seduction.

Our text is not about the temptation to which we are all exposed, such as greed, falsehood, or the lust for power. It is, instead, about the fundamental sin of the people of God, the specific temptation that confronts believers in particular. The temptation story signals at the very beginning that Jesus has been led by the Spirit of God not just anywhere, but into the wilderness, and that he stays there for forty days—just as Israel was in the wilderness for forty years. Thus Jesus has to make his way through the history of the people of God as if in a time-warp. He is tested by God in person by being handed over to the powers of the world, just as Israel was tested by God during its years in the wilderness.

From that point of view it is no accident that Jesus answers the devil three times with a statement from the book of Deuteronomy: namely, Deuteronomy 8:3; 6:16; 5:9 + 6:13. The very first quotation, from Deuteronomy 8:3, is found in a context that interprets Israel's time in the wilderness as a testing by God. During its forty years in the wilderness Israel had to decide whether to trust itself to its God or not:

> *Remember the long way that the Lord your God has led you these forty years in the wilderness, in order to humble you, testing you to know what was in your heart, whether or not you would keep his commandments. He humbled you by letting you hunger, then by feeding you with manna, with which neither you nor your ancestors were acquainted, in order to make you understand that one does not live by bread alone, but by every word that comes from the mouth of the Lord. The clothes on your back did not wear out and your feet did not swell these forty years. Know then in your heart that as a parent disciplines a child so the Lord your God disciplines you.* (Deut 8:2-5)

Thus the one who just before this, at his baptism, was addressed as "the beloved son" (Matt 3:17) had to go through Israel's history of testing in the wilderness again. In doing so he was led and strengthened by the way of those before him in Israel who had believed. But on his shoulders lay also Israel's resistance to God, the people's murmuring, its ever-renewed rebellion, its self-glorification and its mistrust of its God.

Thus we see that the one who dares exodus and sets out on the way of faith will be no less tempted than others, but rather more. It can be no accident that Jesus had his disciples—those who had left their families and followed him—pray in the Our Father: "lead us not into temptation!" (cf. Matt 6:13; Luke 11:4). That is: do not lead us into testing situations that are too difficult for us.

The temptation into which the people of God are again and again led is something deeper than the ordinary immorality of society. The temptation of the people of God, and thus also of Jesus, begins *in the call itself*—in the midst of that for which Israel was sent. Israel was sent to live in the world as a people who honor God alone, take God as their only master, so that in this people others may see and read what it means to live rightly and in harmony with creation.

Self-Staging

But if God's people do not live for God but always and only for themselves—if they do not seek to glorify God but only themselves, and if God is simply used throughout as an instrument for the accomplishment of their own goals—then their calling and sending are perverted at their inmost center; then proclamation is replaced by self-presentation and service to others by service to oneself.

The story of Jesus' temptation reveals in drastic form the sin of the people who are called. First scene: People use the new opportunities presented by the sending of the people of God for their own needs and interests (getting bread for themselves). Second scene: People do not serve God but themselves instead by debasing faith to a mere *show*, thus also misusing Sacred Scripture (flight through the air). Third scene: Here, at last, we see what is happening at a deeper level in all this: Those who do not serve God but make use of God's call and mission in order to create their own mastery of others ("all the kingdoms of the world and their splendor") serve the devil.

Only when we have understood how narrow and dangerous is the way in which God is glorified and how quickly one's very faith and the calling to serve the people of God collapse into self-help and a using-of-God-for-oneself do we understand the salient point of the temptation story.

Jesus' Unambiguous Attitude

Here is what is so shocking (and reassuring): Jesus, too, was tempted to the very depths of his existence by all that. If we read Matthew's temptation story as if Jesus had cast the devil to the ground three times in succession, masterfully and without effort, we have misunderstood the whole thing. The scene on the Mount of Olives in Matthew 26:36-46 reveals it very clearly. There Jesus is tempted to the depth of his being to flee from a clear confession of his true self and thus from death. But he resists. In the desert also he withstands the tempter, but not by his own strength. He does so only because he holds fast to the word of God. That is why he quotes Sacred Scripture, the whole sum of Israel's knowledge about how to make decisions, and does so three times. That is why he quotes the book of Deuteronomy in particular, for, more than any other writing in the Old Testament, it again and again places the reader before the fundamental decision: *for or against God.*

In his temptations Jesus makes clear decisions, and he places himself with absolute clarity on God's side. In Genesis 3:1-6, one of the great Old Testament temptation stories, which in turn distills Israel's long experiences, the human beings lack that clarity, and the serpent from the beginning uses double meaning and suggestion as its tools: "Did God really say . . . ?" (Gen 3:1). Slyly, the serpent thus seizes a position that makes it seem to be judge over God: it interprets God's desire for salvation as resentment and envy.

The woman and man allow themselves to be seduced and ultimately fall in with the tempter's line: they, too, want "to be like God"—that is, to be masters themselves. Jesus did *not* want to be the master. He wanted God alone to be Lord.

The Problem with Resolving to Fast

"Good intentions!" Who doesn't have them? They are born on the eve of round-number birthdays (when, for example, one approaches forty, fifty, or sixty), or on the last day of the old year, or on Ash Wednesday, when Lent begins. Who isn't familiar with them—all the grand and now really unbreakable and "definitive" intentions that are made then? "Starting tomorrow I will quit smoking!" "From tomorrow on I will drink alcohol only under control and in moderation!" "Starting tomorrow I'm going to watch less television!" "Tomorrow and thereafter I am going to bed early every night!" Or: "From now on I am going to be more loving toward my wife/husband!" Or really radically: "Starting tomorrow, everything will be different!"

Why "tomorrow"? Why not "now"? The very use of "starting tomorrow" shows that there is a virus at work in these intentions. In reality nothing changes at all. Intentions on this level, those one has made firmly and "definitively," are quickly revised, even after only a few hours. First I allow myself a single exception; then I delay the beginning of the new life until next week. Next week, however, the whole situation has blown away and things go on as they always have.

Why is this so? Why do good intentions such as I have described scarcely bring us any further? Why are they so dubious? And what does the Bible say about it?

To begin with: there is no such concept as a "good intention" in the Bible. The idea derives from ancient philosophy, which considered that one can do good only when one has chosen it through an inner decision (*propositum*) and set one's sights on it. Since the Middle Ages this correct insight has been made part of the theology of the sacrament of reconciliation: contrition may not stop there; it must be combined

133

with a firm resolve not to sin in the future.[1] Thus the firm will to change one's life is rooted in the seriousness and the joy of the sacrament of reconciliation.

Repentance! Not Repairs!

As I said, the concept of "good intentions" does not appear in the Bible. Certainly the prophets and teachers of the people of God spoke about the subject to which the phrase refers, and in very radical fashion, when they called for "repentance."

Repentance presumes that one is going in the wrong direction and getting farther and farther from the goal. In contrast, the usual principles suggest that on the whole everything is fine. They presuppose that there are some aspects of me that could be improved. A little sandpaper could be applied here and there. Some things need to be repaired or better adjusted, but all in all the direction is correct. The improvements thus remain on the level of mere repair work.

Here the Jewish-Christian tradition thinks much more radically. On Ash Wednesday, as ashes are imposed on us, it says: "Remember that you are dust and to dust you will return." That is the real human situation, and in line with it the liturgy for Ash Wednesday quotes the prophet Joel:

> *Rend your hearts, not your garments, and return to the* LORD, *your God.*
> (cf. Joel 2:13).

As long as we have not recognized our true situation and it has not torn our hearts we cannot repent and grasp the one principle that deserves to be understood more than any other: that we are to serve God with our whole existence and give honor to God alone. "Good intentions" in the current watered-down sense deceive us about our true situation. They seek external cosmetic treatment when what we really need is a new heart and a new spirit.

"Good intentions" of the usual sort are also questionable, however, because they presume that we can change ourselves if we only try hard enough. Thus they degrade the biblical faith to moral armament, indeed to self-redemption. The one who says: "Starting tomorrow I will change my life" knows little about human nature and nothing

---

[1] *Catechism of the Catholic Church* §1451.

at all about what faith is. I cannot change myself by my own efforts. If I repent, if something new enters my life, it is always a gift to me, always grace, even though the repentance is my own and truly depends on my action.

The "Lamentations" that are appended directly to the book of Jeremiah in the Greek and Latin Bibles conclude with the plea:

> *Restore us to yourself, O LORD,*
> *that we may be restored;*
> *renew our days as of old . . .* (Lam 5:21)

In the Hebrew text "repenting/turning back" and "going home" are based on the same word. Israel will never "return home" to Zion unless it first "turns back." But that turning back, that repentance, must be the gift of God. Therefore: "Restore us to yourself, O LORD!" Repentance by itself, on one's own initiative, is impossible. Moreover, it must be a repentance *toward God*.

In the Force-Field of God's History

When Lamentations shows human repentance as happening from divine initiative, that is not merely pious babble. These songs look back at the destruction of the Southern Kingdom and of the temple in the year 586 BCE. They call up one of the most shattering convulsions in Israel's history. The "we" of these texts is the "we" of the broken and scattered people of God.

Evidently Israel, as long as it tied its faith to a political form of existence as a state, could not really repent. Only the catastrophe of 586 gradually opened its eyes. Now it begs for repentance, restoration to a new form of life.

This defines the place of all repentance. God does not give it magically, but by opening our eyes to the history within which we stand: our own history, that of the people of God, and that of the nations. Only a profound shock in light of this history of self-created evil leads to true repentance. Human beings must view the misery they themselves have made as well as the new thing that God is creating out of the nations' catastrophe.

There is still another aspect to the biblical idea of repentance: when it is genuine it always occurs within the field of force that is church and community. Repentance presupposes an encounter with people who reliably show us the way in the name of Jesus. "[W]e are ambassadors for Christ, since God is making his appeal through us," Paul writes in the New Testament reading for Ash Wednesday. He continues: "we entreat you on behalf of Christ, be reconciled to God" (2 Cor 5:20). That, too, belongs to the foundation of all repentance: others who speak in Christ's place, who open our eyes to our real situation and promise us God's reconciliation.

Repentance, then, is more than a dresser drawer full of good intentions. It is a profoundly moving event that incorporates us into the history of God with God's people and that, ultimately, is only possible through encounter with that history. Repentance presumes that we have tasted something of the new thing God is doing in the world. How could anyone change the whole course of her or his life unless that person has seen and tasted, has entered into a joy one never knew before?

Repentance Out of Joy

Repentance very often happens as a reaction to elementary crisis. We see that not only in the Old Testament book of Lamentations. The lost son in Luke 15 first had to lose his wealth, become a swineherd, and experience gnawing hunger before he could repent. But even that repentance based on misery would not have been possible for him if he had not recalled the picture of his father's house. There everyone got up from the table satisfied. What makes the lost son take to the road is the catastrophe of his life, but what draws him back home is the love of his father and the joy he hopes to find there.

The older brother of the lost son, too, who had more urgent need of repentance than the younger, could only turn back if he was willing to join in the rejoicing. What does his father tell him? "We had to celebrate and rejoice!" (Luke 15:32).

Thus repentance is a radical event with many components. One of those is the "good intention." In the case of the lost son it was "I will get up and go to my father." The Greeks were right: one can do the good and right thing only if one has anticipated it with an inner choice. The lost son's choice, his "I will get up and go . . ." changes his whole life. Paul describes this new situation that God gives us and that is so filled with joy by writing:

See, now is the acceptable time; see, now is the day of salvation! (2 Cor 6:2)

When they are located within this history of God with the world, "good intentions" have their rightful place. Then they are no longer something we think of for ourselves; they come to us from without, from the encounter with those who show us the way in the name of Jesus. Then they serve no longer to build up one's own person but to cooperate in advancing the work of God in the world. They arise out of joy: joy in the reign of God. And that is why they lead us further: into the new creation that God is building out of the dust of our mortality and our self-created catastrophes.

Jesus' Fear of Death

The narrative of Jesus' fear in the Garden of Gethsemane, in the face of death, reveals the depth and seriousness with which Mark tells of the way of the Son of Man (Mark 14:32-42). This one who has announced his impending suffering three times to his disciples (Mark 8:31-33; 9:30-32; 10:32-34), who evidently knows to the last detail what lies before him, who has long since said that he will drink the cup (Mark 10:38)—still more, who has just gifted the saving power of his death to the twelve disciples in the cup of thanksgiving (Mark 14:23-24)—this one now shrinks from that very cup.

The Jesus in this text is afraid of death. What he is asking for is not at all that his fear should cease, that it should pass from him—no, he is praying that he not have to die, that the "hour" may pass him by (Mark 14:35), that the "cup" be taken away from him (Mark 14:36). That means nothing other than that he should be spared from death, because the "hour" is the hour of his passion and the "cup" is the cup of death. The Son of Man, truly human, prays to his heavenly Father, in his fear, that he may not have to die.

Notice also that God gives him no answer to his prayer—differently from Luke 22:43-44, where (at least in some of the textual witnesses) an angel appears from heaven and strengthens him as he prays. Here God is silent. Jesus finds a kind of answer, at least, in the deathlike sleep of his disciples. Three times he prays to God to rescue him—and three times he finds his disciples sleeping. Their sleep seems like an answer from God to his prayer: cryptically shrouded and yet obvious. The answer, then, is that God is leaving him alone in this hour, just as his disciples leave him alone. Their sleep becomes a sign that he is altogether abandoned and now really and finally must drink the cup of fear, loneliness, and death.

Certainly this interpretation does not put anything into Mark's text that is not there, as Jesus' cry on the cross will show: "My God, my God, why have you abandoned me?" (Mark 15:34). That is not a cry of despair, because Jesus is quite obviously praying the whole of Psalm 22 as his dying prayer. That psalm testifies to an ultimate trust in God and at the end even witnesses to an unfailing hope for rescue (Ps 22:23-32)—and yet it is a cry out of the most profound distress.

Perhaps we may ask still more about all this—beyond Mark's Gospel. If this evangelist supposes that Jesus suffered an ultimate fear of dying, even that Jesus tried for a moment to escape the cup of death, should we not ask what really caused Jesus' fear and distress?

Was this simply creaturely fear of suffering and death?—or was it, beyond that, the fear of the human being who, theologically speaking, is falling into darkness? Is it the fear of a person who wants to do the will of God but does not know what God really wants? Darkness, after all, means that one cannot see—cannot grasp, cannot understand. Jesus surrenders himself entirely to the will of the Father (Mark 14:36). That is his meaning and his goal. But beyond that, was it possible for him to clarify that will to such an extent that his future lay clearly before him like an open country full of light?

May one therefore exclude the idea that Jesus had to go, theologically as well, into the darkness of death and thus into the obscurity and silence of God? In this context I recall a text from the great theologian Hans Urs von Balthasar—a text about Jesus' eschatological expectation—that is equally valid for Jesus' journey to death:

> *Jesus is truly human, and the unalienable nobility of the human being consists in the fact that [one] can, and indeed must, freely project one's existence into an unknown future. For a believer this future into which one throws [wirft] and projects [entwirft] oneself is God, in God's freedom and incomprehensibility. To remove this opportunity from Jesus by leaving him to walk toward a goal that he already knows beforehand and merely has to work out in time means, quite simply, to rob him of his human dignity.*[1]

Must not the seriousness of our theology consist precisely in thinking of Jesus in such contexts and not confining him too swiftly within our often all-too-convenient interpretations?

---

[1] Hans Urs von Balthasar, "Faith and the Expectation of an Imminent End," *Communio International Catholic Review* 26 (1999): 687–97, at 687. Translation by Nicholas Healy, III, ed. LMM.

Still, that is by no means all. Must not the seriousness of our theology really, and first of all, consist in our daring to risk our own lives—as we are able—like Jesus, in the darkness and immensity of God?

The Laments of the Crucified

Together with the liturgy of the Easter Vigil, that of Good Friday is among the most profound and beautiful the praying church has produced. I will take just one example: in the Good Friday service the veneration of the cross follows the great petitions. This tradition goes back to the earliest centuries of the church. At a very early date this context also incorporated the singing of the so-called "Laments of the Savior" or *Improperia*.

These "laments" are a kind of dialogue between the crucified Christ and his people, a dialogue rooted in the Old Testament. In the sixth chapter of the book of the prophet Micah, God says:

> *O my people, what have I done to you?*
> > *In what have I wearied you? Answer me!*
> *For I brought you up from the land of Egypt,*
> > *and redeemed you from the house of slavery;*
> > *and I sent before you Moses,*
> > > *Aaron, and Miriam.* (Mic 6:3-4)

and in the famous "Song of the Vineyard" in Isaiah 5, the prophet, who first indicates he is about to sing a secular love song, asks the inhabitants of Jerusalem:

> *What more was there to do for my vineyard*
> > *that I have not done in it?*
> *When I expected it to yield grapes,*
> > *why did it yield wild grapes?* (Isa 5:4)

The Laments of the Savior on Good Friday include such formal elements from the Old Testament. At three points a "chorus" is inserted, consisting of the "Holy, Holy, Holy" from Isaiah 6:3 in Greek, expanded in the *Improperia* as follows:

Hagios ho Theos,
Hagios Ischyros,
Hagios Athanatos—
eleison hēmas!

Holy God,
Holy and mighty,
Holy Immortal One,
have mercy on us!

With these elements of Old Testament language the suffering Christ speaks from the cross on Good Friday. While in the Old Testament it is God who speaks, laments, and begs the people to understand, here it is Christ who speaks. He speaks as the historical Jesus always spoke: as the one who stands in the place of God. From the cross Jesus poses questions to his people such as a lover would utter—a lover speaking to the beloved in order to win her back—knowing the beloved is unfaithful and intends to abandon the lover.

O my people, what have I done to you?
How have I offended you?
Answer me! . . .

What more could I have done for you
that I have not done?

And Christ the lover details all the common history between him and his beloved:

I led you out of Egypt, from slavery to freedom . . .
For forty years I led you safely through the desert,
I fed you with manna from heaven,
and brought you to a land of plenty . . .

The rest of the ever-new deeds of God in history that are listed are followed by examples of the people's evil responses, the ways it has responded to the works of its God. I will quote just one example:

I gave you saving water from the rock,
*   but you gave me gall and vinegar to drink.*

Parts of the *Improperia* are attested as early as the seventh century, but their origins go back still farther. One indication of the antiquity of the litany is the presence of Greek elements.

To take seriously the fact that these Laments of the Savior are still an essential part of today's Good Friday liturgy is to be clear about the fact that the killing of Jesus is here not simply pushed off on historical Israel. The reason for Jesus' crucifixion is named: the attitude of his "people"—and that includes especially the church—or, more precisely, the community that gathers for worship on Good Friday.

The whole thing is fully reminiscent of the accusations brought before a court of law, but Christ does not lament the breaking of the covenant. No statement of guilt is presented, only a plea: "Answer me!" Jesus the lover is unrelenting. He pleads for the return of that first love and the continuation of the common history.

This highly theological and altogether contemporary hymn can give us access to the meaning of Good Friday. The point of the liturgy for the day is not primarily a self-immersion in the pains of the Crucified. Rather, it is suffering with him in the sense that we allow ourselves to be drawn in, that we become passionate for the cause Jesus died for: namely, that God needs a people in the world through which to act—a people that lets itself be led by God—a people that lives in the holy community Jesus founded in the Last Supper as his Body in the world. The Laments of the Savior on Good Friday are Jesus' struggle for the church—a struggle for us.

We can only respond to Jesus' death by desiring to be members of his Body, the body of the church. It is not compulsion, but freedom. It is love returned for love. Christ does not want sympathy (suffering-with), but living-with and loving-with, in the being-with of the Christian community to which we belong. We have the privilege of sharing in God's work in this world. Those who only live out their own plans let life run through their fingers, but for those who let their lives be built into the work of God the resurrection is already beginning now, and their lives are eternal.

The Easter Alleluia

The church year, with its feasts and its liturgy, is a collective work of art. It grew through history—and yet it is the work of God. It contains a regular sequence of ordinary days, and then comes the shining Sunday, the "Day of the Lord." Since the early days of the church it has been "the first day of the week" (Mark 16:2), the day on which the Easter experiences began, the day when the disciples saw the Risen One and knew that "the Lord has risen indeed" (Luke 24:34).

And as the series of normal weekdays is interrupted by the Day of the Lord because after six days it is high time to stop, to rest, and to celebrate so that we can be drawn out of the banality of our lives—so also the church year has its ordinary times, but between them there are days and weeks that disrupt everything and lift us up to the mind of God, and not only to God's thoughts but to God's saving deeds that have happened among us. The church year is crowned by the great feasts of Christmas, Easter, and Pentecost. Unlike the United Nations, which in 1978 defined Monday as the first day of the week and continually creates new memorial days (from the World Day of the Child to the World Day of Wetlands), so that gradually the whole year is fully plastered over with memorial days, we Christians understand our great festivals and days as things not simply made by human beings. It is God who has created them to celebrate the "renown [gained by] his wondrous deeds" (Ps 111:4).

The greatest of the feasts is Easter. It is the only one preceded by forty days of preparation and repentance and the only feast that begins a fifty-day period of celebration. It is the only feast whose vigil celebration has developed into a long liturgy recalling the whole of salvation history. Originally that vigil celebration lasted all night and only ended with the rising of the sun, and it is the sole feast that

144

echoes with repeated *alleluia*s, because for the forty days preceding it no *alleluia* could be uttered.

Overflowing Joy

But what is it about this *alleluia*? What is its origin? It comes from the Old Testament—more precisely, from Israel. It is a cry of jubilation in the Hebrew language, based on the verb *hālal* (praise, break forth in joy), and the name *Ya[hweh]*. Translated, *alleluia* means "Praise YHWH!" or "Praise the LORD!"

But does it make any sense to translate *alleluia*? At some time or other we have to be told what language the word comes from and how it should be translated—but then we can forget all that. We *have to* forget it, because even the Septuagint, the pre-Christian translation of the Old Testament into Greek, did not translate *alleluia*, and neither did the church. It was retained in its original language. The church wanted to have it in its liturgy as an untranslated word: a word that is inexhaustible, a word that says more than all our concepts, statements, and definitions.

Because the *alleluia* sounds forth untranslated, it is akin to inarticulate speech and even to ecstasy. In ecstasy it can happen that one no longer speaks in ordinary words but stammers with joy. From that point of view the words spoken in God-given ecstasy are nothing like animal sounds; they are words beyond all conceiving. The sounds of such ecstasy express something beyond all understanding. So in the history of the people of God the *alleluia* has become the expression of overflowing joy. After all, the greatest joys contain something that, while it does not extinguish reason, leads it to unimaginable heights. The Easter Alleluia expresses a joy that only God and God's Holy Spirit can give.

We live now in a world where everything is for sale, from takeout food to adventure vacations—all of it well packed and loudly praised by a gigantic advertising industry. It is a good thing that Easter joy cannot be bought. It cannot be made; it has to be given to us. It is given when we have traveled the road to Jerusalem with Jesus during Lent, watched with him on the Mount of Olives, and wept and sorrowed beneath his cross. The Easter joy has its reasons and yet surpasses all explanations.

God's Saving Deeds

I spoke about the ecstatic aspect of the *alleluia*. Certainly there are many kinds of ecstasy in the world, both good and bad. There is the ecstasy one feels on hearing captivating music, the ecstasies of dancing and of love. But there is also the ecstasy of drunkenness, of unbridled fury, of fighting and of murder. One of the most profound desires of the human being is to grow beyond oneself, to melt and merge with another or with the crowd, and thus to let oneself be incorporated into something that is greater than oneself.

These examples are meant to show that ecstasy can do us good but can also be dangerous, corrupted, and inhuman. The church has never surrendered itself to excessive ecstasy in its liturgy such as one finds in many religions and quasi-religions. Paul calls for a "reasonable worship" appropriate to the *logos* (*tēn logikēn latreian*) in Romans 12:1.[1] The Easter Alleluia is surpassing joy that is yet bound up with reason. That connection becomes clear when we ask ourselves where in Israel it originated.

The place where the *alleluia* originates is in the Psalms. There are groups of psalms in which "alleluia" plays a special role: for example, Psalms 113–118. In Judaism that group of psalms is called the "Pesach Hallel" or simply "*the* Hallel." These psalms are sung especially on the evening of the Seder, after the Pesach meal. Jesus, too, sang them with his disciples after his last meal, which indeed was a Pesach meal (Mark 14:12, 26).

If we look more closely at this group of psalms we see right away that thought of God's saving deeds, especially Israel's rescue from slavery in Egypt, is central to them. Here we are, of course, at the very center of the Christian feast of Easter, because in the Easter night Christians celebrate both the Exodus from Egypt and their own exodus from the power of sin and death. Then, on Easter Day, the whole church sings Psalm 118, which is the climax of the Jewish Pesach Hallel. The Easter liturgy abbreviates it, containing only the verses:

> *This is the day the* Lord *has made;*
> *let us rejoice and be glad.*

---

[1] *Not* "spiritual worship," *pace* RSV, NRSV, NABRE. The Authorized [King James] Version is correct in writing "reasonable service."—Tr.

Give thanks to the L*ORD*, *for he is good,*
for his mercy endures forever.
Let the house of Israel say,
"His mercy endures forever."

"The right hand of the L*ORD* *has struck with power;*
the right hand of the L*ORD* *is exalted.*

I shall not die, but live,
and declare the works of the L*ORD*."

The stone which the builders rejected
has become the cornerstone.
By the L*ORD* *has this been done;*
it is wonderful in our eyes.

This is the day the L*ORD* *has made;*
let us rejoice and be glad. (Ps 118:24, 1-2, 16-17, 22-23)[2]

The book of Psalms also contains the so-called "Final Hallel," which is included in the Jewish liturgy. It consists of Psalms 145–150, that is, those that conclude the Psalter. It is a thrilling conclusion, like the finale of a great symphony. The whole world is summoned to praise God: angels and hosts, sun and stars, fire and hail, snow and mist, all wild animals and domestic ones as well, young men and young women, the whole people of Israel, the rulers of the earth and all nations—the whole cosmos. The universe dances in a ring before God. The accompanying instruments for this finale are harp and zither, cymbals and flutes, horns and tambourines.

Still, the Final Hallel of the Psalter not only embraces all creation: it is an *eschatological* Hallel. That is, it is an *alleluia* that has no end and flows into eternity. In that sense it truly belongs to Easter. And this whole song of praise is because of God's saving deeds, for it is God who has

. . . *made heaven and earth,*
the sea, and all that is in them;
who keeps faith forever;

---

[2] Translation from the *Roman Catholic Lectionary for Mass for Use in the Dioceses of the United States of America, second typical edition* (Washington, DC: Confraternity of Christian Doctrine, 2001).

who executes justice for the oppressed;
who gives food to the hungry . . .
The LORD *will reign forever,*
your God, O Zion, for all generations.
Alleluia! (Ps 146:6-7, 10)

Thus it is God's deeds, and above all, the raising of Jesus of Nazareth, that evoke the Easter Alleluia, the all-encompassing *alleluia* of the people of God and of all creation—and so the ecstasy of the *alleluia*, despite all its overflowing jubilation, is succinct, human, and rational.

Learning from the Disciples at Emmaus

The gospel story of the two disciples who encounter the Risen One on the road to Emmaus is one of the longest of the Easter stories (Luke 24:13-35) and also one of the loveliest. It is a profoundly theological and also a formally perfect narrative. In this story Luke shows us—among many other things—how one comes to believe.

After all, the starting point of the story is that the two disciples no longer believe. How do we know that? Just look at their feet: they are walking away from Jerusalem, away from the place where Jesus had called his people Israel to choose, and away from the place where Jesus' disciples, who at first had fled, are already reassembling. These two disciples are about to give up. They are very close to making an end with Jesus—and yet they come to believe again.

How does such a thing happen? Don't let anyone say: That doesn't affect me; I have believed for a long time. No one should rush to say that. There is such a thing as burnout, even in faith. Externally one goes on, still goes to church—at Christmas, anyway. Maybe one even prays, especially in a crisis. But faith is slowly and silently dying. It becomes a heap of ashes—perhaps without our noticing it. When something like that happens, everything depends on our coming to faith anew and learning again to be in God's company. But how does that happen? How do the two Emmaus disciples find the way back to believing in Jesus?

Talking Together

At the beginning of the story we read that the disciples were "talking with each other about all these things that had happened" (Luke 24:14). So they are not going their separate ways, and they are not feeding and coddling their profound disappointment; they are looking back with new eyes and speaking together about everything that happened with Jesus.

149

That is the first thing we must do in such a situation: talk together about our faith. We have to talk about what is happening in us and around us. Don't let anybody tell you that is easy. It is very difficult. We are blocked by a natural shame. We would prefer to be alone with our faith (or lack thereof). After all, faith touches the inmost part of us, and we do not want to open that part to anyone else.

So we must speak together about our faith—but we must do so as sensitively and carefully as the Emmaus disciples. Pay attention to how they speak! While the next speech is directed to the strange traveler who walks part of the way with them, they reflect what they had already been saying to one another:

> "[He] *was a prophet mighty in deed and word before God and all the people, and . . . our chief priests and leaders handed him over to be condemned to death and crucified him. But we had hoped that he was the one to redeem Israel. Yes, and besides all this, it is now the third day since these things took place.*" (Luke 24:19-21)

What precision we find in those statements! They are a cautious probe into something these disciples cannot understand. They both believe that Jesus was a prophet—which is to say that they had not really understood the mystery of him. But they tried. And they want to understand what happened to Jesus.

That, then, would be the first thing that leads to faith: talking about what is happening in us and around us—and speaking about it precisely and deliberately, with care and tact.

But with whom should we talk about our faith? The sentence I have quoted ("[He] was a prophet mighty in deed and word before God and all the people . . .") is addressed to Jesus. May we not conclude that in trying to deepen our faith or win it anew we should speak especially to Jesus? Is it not possible to pray to Jesus, to tell him "I want to believe, but I find it hard. There are so many things I can't deal with, a lot I just can't understand. Can you help me? . . ."

Not Extinguishing the Flame

But the story continues. After it has reached its climax, the disciples say to one another: "Were not our hearts burning within us while he was talking to us on the road, while he was opening the scriptures to us?" (Luke 24:32). That, evidently, is also part of what happens when one returns to faith: it starts to burn within us.

Suddenly there is a longing, a desire, a still or even painful unrest, a sense of being drawn toward God and God's cause. A silent fire starts to burn within our heart. Then everything depends on our not smothering it with our fears, our concerns, and the daily routine but allowing it to burn, and even feeding the flame.

How that fire begins to burn—concretely, how one encounters God in Jesus—can happen in very different ways. It could be a text from Sacred Scripture that seizes us. It could be a dangerous illness that forces us to reconsider our life. It could be the sudden loss of someone very dear. It can be a profound complaint to God that instead becomes understanding and praise. It could be the encounter with other believers.

God can ambush us and shake us back and forth, or God can speak to us very softly, depending on our situation. If we are completely frozen, God sometimes needs violence to pierce the armor of our indifference. But usually the Holy Spirit speaks within us, with the utmost tenderness, almost inaudibly. God does not want to infringe on our freedom. God has infinitely many ways in which to light that divine fire in us.

The hearts of the Emmaus disciples burned when they encountered Jesus, but it was an encounter in silent clarity. Jesus opened the Scriptures to them, and the Scriptures opened themselves to them. That, then, is the second thing that leads to faith: that we do not extinguish the fire that at some moment begins to burn within us.

Going Where Others Are Gathered

Even all that, of course, would not suffice. Equally important for our faith is what the two disciples do at the end of our story: they turn back and go to where the others are:

> *That same hour they got up and returned to Jerusalem; and they found the eleven and their companions gathered together.* (Luke 24:33)

They gather together with all the other disciples in Jerusalem, the place where Jesus had had to die—and in future they remain together.

The greatest illusion of our times is that each of us thinks it possible to deal with the question of faith on one's own terms. But in fact it is impossible, because faith in Jesus Christ exists only where the Twelve are—that is, where the apostolic tradition and the church are.

Those who think they can believe on their own are making a dangerous mistake. We can only believe together, when we tell each other what God has done in our midst. We can only believe where many little fires have combined into a great fire that warms and illuminates. We can only believe when Jesus is in our midst and breaks bread with us.

The Miracle of Faith

The story of the two Emmaus disciples teaches us how to come to faith. In the end, however, I have to admit that all of it can still not explain faith. When anyone comes to real faith, a faith that changes one's life, that is a miracle—an Easter miracle from God.

We can pray for that faith, hear stories about it, experience how others believe, talk with them—but no one can "create" faith. It must be God's gift to us. The Risen One gave back their faith to the two disciples on their way to Emmaus.

The Emmaus narrative is focused reality. What it tells is something that happened not only then but has been repeated thousands of times over. Again and again the fire of faith has flamed up in countless human beings. What a miracle is this faith—and how lovely it is when a person finds the way to the joy of believing!

The Longest Easter Story

At the end of the Fourth Gospel—in John 21:1-23—we find one of the most important Easter narratives in the four gospels. It begins with an appearance of the Risen One to seven of his disciples at Lake Gennesareth. They have been fishing all night and caught nothing. Jesus helps them gather a superabundant catch, gives them fish and bread to eat, and then installs Peter as shepherd of the church.

The whole is a coherent and artistically composed story. Certainly a number of pieces of tradition have flowed together in this composition, but all of them now make up a tightly woven unit that is nourished not only by the events immediately after Easter but by the experiences of the early church long after them. At a very early period John 21:1-25 was added to the Fourth Gospel as a redactional expansion that became part of the unchangeable corpus of the New Testament.

Flight and Regathering

It is striking that John 21:1-23 does not take place in or near Jerusalem, but in Galilee, on Lake Gennesareth. This reflects historical knowledge on the part of the first communities: after Jesus' arrest, most of his disciples evidently fled north to their Galilean homeland. There the Crucified appeared to them as the Risen One and gathered them anew. This flight of the disciples to Galilee is still discernible in Jesus' words in Mark 14:27-28:

> "You will all become deserters; for it is written,
>   'I will strike the shepherd,
>   and the sheep will be scattered.'
> But after I am raised up, I will go before you to Galilee."

The disciples' flight to Galilee is also evident in Mark's story of the tomb when the angel tells the women:

> ". . . go, tell his disciples and Peter that he is going ahead of you to Galilee; there you will see him, just as he told you." (Mark 16:7)

If, according to John 21, Simon Peter, the sons of Zebedee, and other disciples have returned to their trade as fishers on Lake Gennesareth, it is also evident that they knew that Good Friday, from a purely human point of view, had been a catastrophe. The most important disciples had given up and returned home. Jesus' cause was apparently ended.

An Image of What Church Is

But that is more the presupposition of our text. Its purpose is to show how something new comes out of this catastrophe. John 21:1-23 offers a summary of what constitutes the essence of the church—in terms of its very origins, for the church as reflected in John 21 is still close to its beginnings. It still has the unexpected thing, the incomprehensible fact of its existence before its very eyes.

What, then, is its essence? First of all: there is failure in it, including and especially among the professionals. The fishermen with Peter have sailed out and then caught nothing all night. Why, then, do we live with the idea that we must always be successful in our work of fishing for people? Then, in John 21, success does happen, even to an unbelievable degree. No fewer than 153 big fish are in the net. But that superfluity presupposes the disciples' experience that they have come to the end of their own capacities and have achieved nothing by them. The superfluity of the fish that have been caught also presupposes that they have not clung to their own experiences and favorite ways of doing things (if you don't catch anything at night, you certainly won't by day!). Instead, they have unhesitatingly trusted in Jesus' word.

But how does one experience his word? How can one see that it is he who is saying: "Cast the net to the right side of the boat, and you will find some"? How could anyone recognize someone standing on the bank, scarcely visible in the morning mist?

"The disciples did not know that it was Jesus," the text says. Not even Peter recognizes him, but only "the disciple whom Jesus loved." *He* says: "It is the Lord!" So there are people in the church whose eyes are first opened, who first understand. They live entirely in the company of Jesus. They have a special calling to which they respond with love, and therefore they are the first to see. The others can follow them—then they also see.

Peter follows the insight of the Beloved Disciple unquestioningly and does something that, again, the others do not do: he leaps into the water in order to get to Jesus more quickly. Odd paradox: the one is loved, loves, and recognizes. The other does not recognize, but he believes what he hears, and he acts. That is just how knowledge of faith comes about in the church: in the community of faithful seeing that comes from love, and out of daring and courageous action that jumps into the water.

Evidently the church needs both if it is to exist: people like the Beloved Disciple and people like Simon Peter. The two of them sit together in harmony, together with the other disciples, at the meal Jesus has prepared for them. All that does not mean, of course, that not everyone in the church must live in *agapē*, in love for Christ.

This is shown in our text by the subsequent conversation between Simon Peter and the Risen One. Peter had denied Jesus three times. Therefore he is asked three times about his repentance and his love. The catastrophe that had befallen his faith had made him incapable of carrying out his office. Here is affirmed again that only when we have reached the end of our own possibilities can we experience that it is not we ourselves who fill the net and sustain the church, but the Lord alone.

Gathered Around Peter

In this conversation something fully unexpected happens: it is not the Beloved Disciple who is entrusted with the office of shepherd for the church, but Peter. The Beloved Disciple is indispensable for the church and its right perception of the will of God, and yet the Risen One does not tell him: "Feed my sheep!" It would be too little to explain this turn in the narrative only as a matter of historical fact, namely, from the role that Peter played in the early church. The Fourth Gospel means to say that in the church there is a fruitful tension between the charism of office and other charisms. That tension must be maintained. There has to be the Beloved Disciple, who first understands, but there also has to be Peter, who leads the church humbly, admitting his own faults.

The Beloved Disciple was already ahead of Peter at the empty tomb (John 20:3-8). It is a mistake to think that a highly symbolic text like John 21 is only about the status of the historical Peter and not about the Petrine service as a whole (thus even after the death of Peter). Certainly it is about the church's origin, but that origin is a concentration of what the church is to be in all times.

Our text is one of the longest Easter narratives in the gospels—and it is only right that from it comes the longest of all the Easter stories: the history of the church.

The Voice of the True Shepherd

The Sundays between Easter and Pentecost reveal the fruits of Jesus' resurrection: the disciples, too, have arisen. The readings from the Acts of the Apostles place the fact before our eyes: the disciples' fear has become courage, their disunity is now unanimity, their divisions have surrendered to their dedication to the task before them.

In the city where Jesus was done away with they appear before the people, speak publicly about Jesus, and testify to him as the Messiah. That could cost them their heads, but they are no longer afraid. Those who believe in Jesus as the Lord of their lives need fear nothing.

What Should We Do?

Jesus' disciples find people in Jerusalem who are cut to the heart by their words. Luke speaks of a great number of Jews who are greatly disturbed and ask the apostles: "What should we do?" (Acts 2:37). The apostles' words have struck them deeply. They have no wish to enter into discussion, and they do not say, "Those are really good ideas you are presenting. We will think about them." That is just what they do *not* say. After all, the apostles had not offered ideas; they had reported an event, a fact, a new reality: namely, God's action in the Messiah, an action mightier than death. Because the people in Jerusalem hear about a fact, they want to respond with facts. Therefore they ask: "What should we do?"

They turn to those who have already experienced the new thing and ask to be shown the next step they should take. Faith is not a lovely thought-construction or even a new awareness; first and above all it is simply an action—one step at a time.

Still, there is something else that is remarkable about the question "What should we do?" It does not ask "What should *I* do?" but "What should *we* do?" The *we* is conclusive. Faith is not something for individuals. Individuals cannot achieve it by themselves. Social pressure and the oppressive guidelines of society are much stronger than any individual. It is only when people believe together that they can resist being led astray by the unbelief of those around them. Only when Christians believe together do they experience the whole joy of faith.

Recognizing Jesus' Voice

This is also the place for the image of the flock of sheep that the church's liturgy sets before us in the time between Easter and Pentecost (John 10:1-21). I know: at first glance it is a foreign image, one that is more repellent than fascinating. We don't want to be herd animals. We don't want to nod along, bleating behind the other sheep. But that is not what it means. Rather, it means that those who believe in Jesus must remain together. They are called to community.

Indeed, it means a great deal more. If we interpret the image of the good shepherd and his flock in John 10 rightly, it tells us that there is a community drawn from faith that society does not know. There is a mutuality in which no individual is alone any longer, and yet each is called by her or his own name—in which each individual's calling and path are taken seriously, so that individuals can be altogether themselves and yet be participants in the same cause, the great history in which the people of God are led and guided by God.

Jesus Christ, the "true shepherd," goes before those who believe in him. "They know his voice" (John 10:4) and "they hear his voice" (John 10:3). People today are surrounded by an infinite number of voices, above all by those that shout over one another and by the voices of the media that lecture them—voices that announce themselves as wise and moral, serious and progressive, and yet are often nothing but voices of utter emptiness. There are also the voices of self-dramatization, hatred, and aggression.

Such voices come not only from without; we do not simply hear them while channel-surfing or grab them from the Internet with the click of a mouse. They come from within ourselves as well, and often the greatest variety of different voices revolves within us. Sometimes we try to trust the voice of Jesus, believe it, follow the Good Shepherd—and then the voices of mistrust, resistance, confusion, and greed rise up again inside us. There are so many voices in the world and in ourselves . . .

Nevertheless, we have all heard the one voice that calls us by name and of which we can say: "Yes, that is The voice." It does not come down vertically from heaven. There is nothing magical about it. It comes from history. It is altogether human. That is just how God speaks to us. This voice is gentle; it wants us to be free. We receive it when we let ourselves be still and open our hearts in prayer. We embrace it when we hear the Gospel. We hear it especially when we are gathered together in faith. It is the voice of truth and life, and it is different from all other voices in the world. It is the voice of the one who said: "The thief comes only to steal and kill and destroy. I came that they may have life, and have it abundantly" (John 10:10).

A Caricature of Christ's Ascension

In 1943 Pope Pius XII, in his pathbreaking encyclical *Divino afflante spiritu,*[1] spoke of the necessity of paying attention to literary forms and narrative genres when interpreting the Bible. How necessary that was is evident in a best-selling book that appeared ten years earlier in Germany, the widely read *Das Leben Jesu im Lande und Volke Israel* by Franz Michel Willam.[2] That book, 551 pages long, was on my parents' bookshelves. I read it as a fourteen-year-old, and it is still in my workroom. The book was published by Herder in 1933 and continued through many editions until 1960; it was translated into eleven languages. (By 1937 the seventh German edition had sold 44,000 copies.)

The great thing about the book was that Willam took Jesus' existence as a Jew seriously. The Jewish way of life, rituals, customs, and lifestyles were presented to readers at length—and that was anything but a matter of course in those days.

A Painful Conclusion

Still, the book had its weaknesses. Willam made the gospel stories into a history of Jesus, and in doing so he violated precisely the principle that Pius XII advocated ten years later—namely, to keep the biblical form of presentation in mind. It is true that the narratives in the gospels retain an extraordinary number of *historical* facts, but they

---

[1] See *Divino afflante spiritu* §§27–30, at any of several websites, including https://www.vatican.va/content/pius-xii/en/encyclicals/documents/hf_p-xii_enc_30091943_divino-afflante-spiritu.html and https://www.papalencyclicals.net/pius12/p12divin.htm.

[2] English: Franz Michel William [sic], *The Life of Jesus Christ in the Land of Israel and among Its People*, ed. Rev. Newton Thompson (St. Louis and London: B. Herder, 1936). Translation here by LMM.

are also a *theological* interpretation of the figure and history of Jesus. That kind of interpretation is indispensable. Every historical presentation *interprets*; it cannot avoid doing so. The same is true of secular historical writing, but all the more so when the history of God with the world is the subject. Then we cannot avoid textual forms that work with images, symbols, and especially with metaphorical language. Obviously texts of that kind have to be heard or read in the appropriate way. They cannot be used to create a kind of documentary film of the life of Jesus.

Let me give one example of what I mean. At the end of his depiction of Jesus' life Willam uses the two Lukan narratives of the ascension (Luke 24:44-53; Acts 1:4-11) to give his book an impressive finale, yet he misses the mark very awkwardly, for (apart from a short sentence at the beginning of the passage) he does not tell of Jesus' ascension as Luke does, from the perspective of the disciples, but from that of Jesus. Readers begin to feel almost dizzy as they sweep higher and higher into the air along with Jesus, and as more and more of the Holy Land becomes visible below them. Willam's text reads:

> *Jesus blessed the faithful flock one last time. Then they saw how he rose from the earth; by his own power he lifted himself before their eyes.*
>
> *From [above] the Mount of Olives Jesus saw, below and around him, the places his earthly presence had hallowed from his birth to his death. On the heights to the east stretched the Judean desert with its pale brown hues; beyond it he saw the Jordan valley; to the west he saw the hill of Calvary outside the city walls; to the south were the pastures near Bethlehem.*
>
> *His view grew broader and broader as he rose ever higher. He saw the countless ridges of Judea beneath him like a frozen sea; cities and villages glinted on their slopes and in the hollows between them; then the Sea of Gennesareth appeared, with the wreath of settlements around its blue expanse; he saw Nazareth high above the plain of Jezreel. The higher he climbed, the more the places of his life converged and melded into one: the land of Israel, the land of the Redeemer.*

As well-meant as this text is, it unintentionally approaches satire, because one only needs to expand a little on the scenario Willam chose in order to make clear how nonsensical such a presentation is:

> *In the end Jesus saw the land beneath him only as a blue-green veil. Faster and faster he rose, and the higher he went the more inhospitable it became.*

Far above, out of an ever-darkening heaven, shone the sun, increasingly bright and dangerous, and at the same time the atmosphere grew colder and colder.

What is wrong here? It is that Willam ignored the literary genre of the Lukan ascension stories. Luke tells of Jesus' departure from his disciples and his elevation to God's right hand, something we cannot imagine, and he does so, from start to finish, from the perspective of the disciples who remain behind. But above all: he depicts Jesus' ascension in biblical imagery that needs to be understood *theologically*. Luke makes no attempt to give an account of Jesus' heavenly journey. Willam, by contrast, depicts Jesus' trip in a balloon and thus inadvertently gives his book a comic ending. The papal encyclical came too late for him.

The Cloud as a Theological Image

If we take the literary genre of the Lukan ascension stories seriously we must read from the perspective of the disciples: through their eyes, not those of Jesus. That certainly has consequences for a right interpretation of the narrative.

Take, for example, the cloud that conceals the departing Jesus from the eyes of the disciples (Acts 1:9). Its message for us is: there is a boundary beyond which all our ideas about Christ's elevation must fail. We cannot imagine it, and we have just as little idea about his glory at the Father's right hand. We should indeed live altogether in light of the Exalted One, but we need not paint a picture of his elevation to God's right hand.

The cloud conceals him from our eyes. If we have understood that, it will be clear that the cloud is neither a rain cloud nor a fine-weather one; that it is not a fog bank or some kind of meteorological elevator. The cloud is part of a biblical symbolic language that everyone understood at that time: the Old Testament, for example, tells how a cloud accompanied the people of God on their wilderness journey to protect and lead them (Exod 14:19-20; 40:34-38), and there is also reference to that illuminating cloud in the story of Jesus' transfiguration (Mark 9:7). This "biblical" cloud is an image for God's presence. God is close to God's people, is in their midst, goes with them, and yet is the Hidden One whom no one can control.

When it is said of the departing Jesus that a cloud took him, the image intends to say that Jesus now enters forever into God's glory. From now on he will be hidden, and yet he is near to his communities. He is in their midst. He is with them all days. He goes before them and leads them—as God led the people of God in the wilderness of old.

Two Men in White Garments

The cloud, however, is only one of the images that are part of the riches of the feast of Christ's ascension. Another is that of the two men in shining garments who suddenly appear and ask the upward-gazing disciples: "why do you stand looking up toward heaven?" (Acts 1:10-11).

In this way the disciples' gaze is brought back from heaven to earth. God's realm is not above the clouds; it is supposed to break into life on earth. The disciples are to act as witnesses to Christ, gathering people from the ends of the earth so that the reign of God may acquire a visible form. The reign of God is of the stuff of this earth. It is a transformed world. That transformation will begin on Pentecost and spread continually outward. We, too, as those who are baptized and confirmed, may join in the work. "Why do you stand looking up to heaven?"

Those are two examples of how we should read the ascension story. It does not describe a space journey by Jesus, but with the aid of the genre "rapture narrative" it speaks from the perspective of the disciples—and in doing so it turns its eyes to *us*, those who remain behind, we who look to the departing Jesus full of longing and whose eyes are diverted by the angels to the here and now.

In Expectation of the Holy Spirit

But also part of this here and now—and this is crucial—is the expectation of the Holy Spirit, to whom Luke's ascension narrative points clearly and unmistakably, for immediately before Jesus separates from his disciples he speaks his last words to them:

> . . . *you will receive power when the Holy Spirit has come upon you; and you will be my witnesses in Jerusalem, in all Judea and Samaria, and to the ends of the earth.* (Acts 1:8)

With these words of Jesus, immediately before his departure to the Father, Luke has practically given us an outline of the Acts of the Apostles; we might call it a table of contents for his second volume. The new community of disciples of Jesus will first witness to Jesus as Messiah and Lord in *Jerusalem* and nearby (Acts 2–7). Then, being persecuted in Jerusalem, they will go to *Samaria* and *Syria* and preach the gospel there (Acts 8–12). Then there will be more and more Christian communities until, symbolized by the figure of Paul, they will reach the capital of the empire in Rome (Acts 28). With its arrival in Rome the message will have attained the *ends of the earth.*

We can only celebrate the feast of the Ascension of Christ in its whole fullness when we pray and live in such a way that Jesus, exalted to the Father, will send the Spirit to us as well: the most precious gift he has left us, the loveliest there can be. For in this Holy Spirit Jesus will be very close to us, and in this Holy Spirit we will be enabled to become witnesses for Christ, here and everywhere, to the ends of the earth.

A Saga of Resistance

If we consider the history of religions we come upon a strange phenomenon: the ancient peoples loved to serve their gods. The Assyrians and Babylonians, the Canaanites and Egyptians, the Greeks and Romans—they were all happy to pray, enthusiastically brought their gods the traditional sacrifices, and lustily celebrated their religious festivals. They lived in harmony with their gods. (The critique of religion that occurred in the course of history at some times, especially in Greece—namely, a critique of prayer, worship, and especially of the portrayals of the gods—took place on a different level and has nothing to do with what follows. Our context is the broad current of "popular religion.")

The Grumbling of the People of God

The Old Testament does not reflect anything like this "natural harmony" in matters of religion. What it tells is often, in fact, a story of Israel's resistance to its God. Again and again the people grumble against Moses and want to return to Egypt. The resistance begins, in fact, immediately after their liberation from the power of Pharaoh (Exod 16:2-8).

In the same way the people murmur against the prophets who try to prevent them from turning away from God. Images of other gods are constantly being set up within the land. Israel wants to worship its God the way other peoples honor their own gods (Ezek 20:32). The people of God want to be like other peoples (1 Sam 8:5, 20). It is an unending story of stiff-necked behavior and rebellion against God. Consider only the great review of history in Ezekiel 20, where God recapitulates the way traveled with Israel. Over and over again God has to say: "But they rebelled against me" (Ezek 20:8, 13, 21).

How can we explain this phenomenon? Was Israel worse than the other nations? Was it less devout? Was it, in fact, depraved? No, this is about something different. The essence of most religions is that human beings make the numinous powers of the world their gods: the forces of Nature, fertility, Eros, power, money, the homeland, even war: people deify all those things, make them absolute, and submit to them. And it is not hard to serve the gods of power or the goddesses of love; people enjoy it. It suits them. It is even desirable: who doesn't want Eros? Who doesn't want to make the rules? Who doesn't want to dominate?

Israel, on the other hand, had come across the true God in the course of its history, and it realized very quickly that the will of this God did not always coincide with what we ourselves prefer. God's will is different. It often goes contrary to our plans, our ideas, our will, our deep-seated egoism. So Israel struggles throughout its history with the will of God.

On the one hand, it constantly resists this God. It would rather be like the other nations: hence the incessant grumbling. On the other hand, Israel certainly had sensed that the will of its God was more beneficent and reasonable than its own. It was better to follow the Lord than to serve the gods of this world. So it undertook the enormous effort to record the will of its God in writing, to be forever before its eyes. The Old Testament teaching, the Torah, on which Israel's theologians labored for centuries, is the mighty attempt to wed the people of God forever to the true will of God.

It did not help. Israel itself expressed the truth in a shattering image: the commandments were scarcely carved into the stone tablets when the people began to dance around the golden calf and shout: "These are your gods, O Israel!" (Exod 32:4-6). That is: the people wanted to worship their God the way gods were worshiped in the other religions, and that in turn means that they did not want to do the will of God, but their own. Ultimately, as Israel increasingly turned to its own will, followed its own plans, and practiced power politics like the other nations, it fell between the millstones of the powerful nations and was ground to pieces. It had to go into exile.

We Christians should not imagine that we are better than Israel. We are not. The same resistance to God is embedded in us. We do not want God to be our ruler. We grumble as Israel did. We sin like the people of God in the wilderness. We, too, worship our golden calves. Above all we want the church to accommodate itself to society, to adopt its befuddlement and its sicknesses in order to become "compatible" with it. It was not without reason that Paul warned his communities about it, writing to the Corinthians that they were in danger of succumbing to the same spirit of grumbling that overcame Israel in the wilderness (1 Cor 10:1-10).

Ezekiel's Vision

The prophet Ezekiel was one of the many people from Israel who were exiled to Babylon. There he reflected on the true nature of the will of God—and there he had a truly thrilling vision: couldn't it be possible that people could serve God with the same passion that drives their pursuit of their *own* interests? Couldn't it be possible that people could advance the plan of God with the same joy that drives them to conceive their *own* plans?

But how could it really be possible? Ezekiel is convinced that the will of God cannot be imposed on people from without; it must reside within, in the human heart. People have to bring the will of God into their innermost being. They must, so to speak, make the will of God their own will, so that God's will becomes their greatest joy and passion.

But is that realistic? Ezekiel knows that people are not built that way. They are incapable of doing it. They always want only to realize themselves and pursue their own dreams. When it comes to God's cause they are afraid of losing their freedom.

Then the prophet is consumed by a thrilling image: God is greater than everything we can imagine. What seems impossible to us is possible for God. What if God were to place God's Spirit within human beings and transform their stony hearts into hearts of flesh, so that people will only want, passionately desire, to do what God wants?

The idea becomes a gigantic vision for the prophet: Yes, that is how it will be! Someday it will really happen. Someday it will be fulfilled. Then the Spirit of God will re-create the human being and give it a new heart. The vision is narrated in the thirty-sixth chapter of the book of Ezekiel:

> *A new heart I will give you, and a new spirit I will put within you; and I will remove from your body the heart of stone and give you a heart of flesh. I will put my spirit within you, and make you follow my statutes and be careful to*

observe my ordinances. Then you shall live in the land that I gave to your ancestors; and you shall be my people, and I will be your God. (Ezek 36:26-28)

The Desire for God and for God's Will .

With Jesus, the vision of Ezekiel came to fulfillment. The gospels describe him as the first human being who lived completely by the Spirit of God and whose food it was to do God's will (John 4:34). The Acts of the Apostles portrays the origin of the church as the eschatological coming of the Spirit of whom the prophets had spoken (Acts 2:17-21). The Spirit of God who re-creates all hearts descends on all. The young community are no longer merely "followers of the law"— they are driven by desire for the great plan God has for humanity.

That is the true mystery of Pentecost. After a long history of struggle over the will of God, now Sacred Scripture can finally tell us about a whole community that does God's will together and in unanimity, with passion and joy. That way of acting in the Holy Spirit through that helping, vivifying Spirit of God that creates all things anew: that is offered to us as well.

Who Is the Holy Spirit?

Probably every one of us has at some point flown in a fully occupied airplane and suffered from the crowding. To begin with, standing packed into the plane's aisle is not particularly pleasant. You have to wait until at last you reach your seat, and before sitting down you have to stow your carry-ons. At last you sit, belted in, nearly cheek by jowl with your neighbor. There you are, wedged in. You can't even really read the newspaper because there isn't room to turn the pages, and you can't talk to the person next to you because she or he doesn't want to be bothered. So we sit as close as possible to other people—and yet in utter distance from them.

But that is how things are. The same is true of the checkout line in the supermarket, the packed movie house, the subway. Physical proximity does not eliminate internal distancing. It is possible to be physically very close to someone and still be worlds apart. There is no connection.

But the reverse can also be true: think of two people who love each other but at the moment are separated—maybe by thousands of miles! They don't even have contact by cell phone because some part of the technology is not working. But in spite of the distance they are close to each other. They think of each other. Each wonders what the other is doing just now. They picture each other. They share feelings. They carry on a conversation with the other in spirit.

This example shows that people can be spatially very distant and yet close to each other. In spite of all the distance one is *entirely* with the beloved person *in spirit*. We all know similar examples. The greatest possible crowding together—and yet unbridgeable distance! Or: spatial distance and yet inner closeness! What creates that closeness? What establishes this tie that is not physically measurable, that does not consist of any kinds of waves or vibrations and yet is so real that each can feel it?

The Holy Spirit Bridges Every Distance

We need to draw on such experiences to get an idea of how it is with the Holy Spirit. The Spirit is the "in-between" that links believers together, bridging every distance. The Spirit makes us belong together—Christians somewhere in East Asia and Christians in Europe, in America. The Spirit brings us near to one another.

The Spirit makes the church an international people of God, forms the communities into the Body of Christ because this is the Spirit of Jesus Christ. We who are so unbelievably different from one another and, by nature, have very little in common are brought together by the Spirit in unity and unanimity.

The Spirit continues the work of Christ because it is through the Spirit that Christ speaks to us even today. The Spirit renews the face of the earth, being also the creative Spirit of God who brings the world to its fulfillment.

The Spirit is invisible but is discernible in the works Paul calls "the fruits of the Spirit." He lists "love, joy, peace, patience, kindness, generosity, faithfulness, gentleness, and self-control" (Gal 5:22-23).

Kindness as Fruit of the Spirit

Let me take just one word from that long list: "kindness" (or "friendliness"). Does that have anything to do with the Holy Spirit? Of course! It certainly does not refer to some kind of superficial friendly attitude that is only a façade put on to achieve social status, one that only turns on its smile as needed and then snaps it off again. This is a kindness, a friendliness that comes from the heart, that is gracious and full of affection because the other person is also God's creation.

This is a kindness that can forgive, console, help where help is needed, that makes time for others, rejoices that others exist. That kind of friendliness comes from the Holy Spirit. It is more than a vague humanism; it reflects "the goodness and loving kindness of our God" (Titus 3:4).

On the day of Pentecost the liturgy begins its "Introit" with "The Spirit of the Lord fills the whole earth." That sentence comes from the book of Wisdom (Wis 1:7) and immediately before it are the words "Wisdom is a kindly spirit." So that kindly spirit of the Lord fills the earth—and how could those who are far from God and the church experience it except through the kindness we show them: a kindness that comes from the Holy Spirit?

Whoever looks at another with kindness and friendliness and desires only good for that person demonstrates by that very action that the Holy Spirit exists, and that the Spirit of God transforms the world.

The Spirit Wants to Be Invited

If we seek for the Holy Spirit in the Bible we quickly discover something very important: Luke writes in the Acts of the Apostles not only about how the Holy Spirit came upon Jesus' disciples on the day of Pentecost. Before that he describes something different: namely, that before Pentecost the young community gathered repeatedly for common prayer (Acts 1:13-14). They implored God, they waited in prayer—they endured, waiting and praying, until at last the day of Pentecost came (Acts 2:1).

Why was that so important to Luke? Why is the day of Pentecost preceded by these nine days of prayer? Why did the Jerusalem community, and why must we all, pray for the Holy Spirit? Why does the Spirit wait to be invited?

It is very simply because the Spirit of God is supremely free and therefore can only come to those who freely long for the Spirit—and the freedom to truly desire the Spirit and be entirely open to it is achieved through prayer.

Dictators can impose their evil spirit on crowds. They work with disinformation, pressure, violence, terror—all the time talking of unity and unanimity. But that is a false, even perverse unanimity imposed by manipulation and oppression. The Holy Spirit, in contrast, is pure love, and real love always desires the freedom of the other. Therefore the Holy Spirit comes quietly, softly, often in utter silence, longing for our love—and only when believers pray for the Spirit's coming, since the Spirit is absolute freedom that knows no compulsion and no pressure.

Can Anyone Experience the
Spirit of God?

The gospel for the feast of Pentecost tells how the Risen One appears to the disciples in the evening (John 20:19-23). He greets them by saying, "Peace be with you." He shows them his hands and his side. The disciples know him by his wounds. Then comes the decisive moment in this wonderfully simple, positively reticent text: the Risen One again speaks peace to the disciples and then sends them forth: "As the Father has sent me, so I send you." Then he breathes on them and says:

> *"Receive the Holy Spirit!*
> *If you forgive the sins of any,*
> *they are forgiven them."* (John 20:22-23)

Like the Breath of God

The allusion here is to Genesis 2:7: "The LORD God formed the human being from the dust of the ground and breathed into its nostrils the breath of life, and the human became a living being." That was, of course, a metaphor in Genesis 2:7, but one pregnant with reality. The "earth creature" (*hā ādām*) is dust and returns to dust, but the Spirit of God makes it a human being, a creature full of hope and longing. It often behaves like an animal and it can fall back into its animal nature, and yet it is constantly in search of truth, of good, of infinity—of what the Spirit of God has breathed into it.

Against this background of the creation of human beings from earth and spirit, John 20:22 depicts the *new* creation by the Spirit given by the risen and exalted Christ. This new creation of the world begins in the church: more precisely, it begins with the sending of the disciples. In the power of the Spirit that Jesus bestows on them they can forgive sins—and out of that forgiveness of sins the church arises as creature of the Spirit and beginning of God's new world.

So Jesus breathes on his disciples. Breathing is scarcely audible, and yet breath is perceptible. When the Holy Spirit is called breath (as the Latin *spiritus* maintains, linguistically as well), that says a great deal: the tenderness and softness of breath and its lifegiving and warming power; the quiet, almost imperceptible nature of breathing that, even and precisely through its softness, can change everything.

As on Sinai

Nevertheless, the Lukan Pentecost in Acts 2:1-13 at first glance sets a very different image before us. There the Spirit comes like a stormy wind and the disciples see tongues as of fire. The background here is not Genesis 2:7 but Exodus 19:16-19, where the community of Israel is gathered around Mount Sinai and receives the Torah in thunder and lightning, fire and earthquake.

The Christian feast of Pentecost is based on the Jewish Feast of Weeks (*Shavuot*). In New Testament times it was no longer only a thanksgiving festival; it had already become a salvation-historical feast celebrating the gift of the Law at Sinai. The community of the disciples had regathered in Jerusalem for this Jewish pilgrim feast, based on the appearances of the Risen One. There they had a profoundly moving experience of the Spirit that expressed itself in ecstatic speech. Very soon they came to interpret that experience in terms of the Sinai narrative, thus: as once the Torah was given to the people of God at Sinai, so now the newly gathered people of God, reconciled and sanctified through the death of Jesus, is given the Spirit promised for the end-time.

There is another text in Acts in which the coming of the Holy Spirit grips the whole community. In chapter 4 Luke tells how Peter and John return to the gathered community. They have testified without fear, before the Council, to Jesus as the Risen One. Their return leads to a spontaneous prayer of thanksgiving on the part of the community. Then:

> . . . *the place in which they were gathered together was shaken; and they were all filled with the Holy Spirit and spoke the word of God with boldness.* (Acts 4:31)

Again, as in John's gospel and most emphatically in the Pentecost narrative in Acts 2, the Holy Spirit is a perceptible reality. The room in which the young community is gathered shakes as though there were an earthquake.

And What about Us?

The objection arises: why isn't all that true of us? Wouldn't it be helpful if fiery tongues would appear over our community when it gathers for worship, if wild winds blew and the ground shook beneath our feet? Why isn't the Holy Spirit visible, audible to us, part of our own experience?

At first glance this objection seems to rob the biblical texts of their substance and reveal them as pious fairy tales. But if we look more closely it is evident that the objection misses the point, because the Holy Spirit is *discernible* among us also. We, too, can see, hear, sense, taste the Spirit—and be shaken by it.

Everyone will admit that a person who lives in God and allows herself or himself to be led by the Holy Spirit comes, in time, to look different from someone whose whole life is a lie. And everyone will admit that a believing congregation filled with the joy of the Holy Spirit appears even at first glance to be different from a Christian gathering in which people are fearful and under pressure, silent or divided.

Christian Community: Image of the Holy Spirit

It is no accident that there are almost no convincing images of the Holy Spirit in Christian art. (The dove is something of a makeshift symbol.) By now the reason should be clear: the real image of the Holy Spirit is the church, the gathered community. An assembly seeking the will of God, attentive to every individual, believing, telling of God's works—that is the loveliest and most accurate image of the Holy Spirit. That is how the Pentecost event has been depicted since ancient times: the Twelve, gathered in unity, and in their midst Mary, the mother of Jesus (see Acts 1:12-14). That is the classic Pentecost image—and, notably, it is an image of the visibility of the Holy Spirit. More important than the fiery tongues are the humility, the faith, the unanimity of those gathered. Precisely in these the Holy Spirit is visible.

John and Luke are therefore correct when they present the Holy Spirit on the visible level. Paul does the same. In 1 Corinthians 12 he speaks of the charisms, the spiritual gifts in the community. He lists the gift of sharing wisdom; the gift of conveying insight; the gift of strong faith; the gift of healing. He also speaks of the ability to work miracles, to speak prophetically, to distinguish spirits, to speak in ecstasy, and finally, the gift of interpreting that ecstatic speaking "in tongues" (1 Cor 12:8-10). At the end of the list Paul says:

> *All these are activated by one and the same Spirit, who allots to each one individually just as the Spirit chooses.* (1 Cor 12:11)

Here, then, the same applies: the Holy Spirit is perceptible, can be experienced—in the multiple gifts of the Spirit that are found in the community.

Consider, for example, what Paul calls "faith by the Spirit." Such a charism of faith does not remain hidden in the heart; it glows outward. The church and the local community can orient themselves to holy people who believe with their whole existence and can follow them on the path of unbending faith.

But the text continues: after Paul has listed the gifts of the Spirit he writes:

> *For in the one Spirit we were all baptized into one body—Jews or Greeks, slaves or free—and we were all made to drink of one Spirit.* (1 Cor 12:13)

That is: beyond all individual charisms the community as a whole, the church itself, is a visible, palpable miracle of the Holy Spirit that all can experience.

Comforter in Distress

Thus all the texts for the Pentecost feast speak of how the Holy Spirit can be perceived and known: the reading from the Acts of the Apostles, the reading from the first letter to the community in Corinth, the Gospel of John. But also (immediately after the second reading) the Pentecost sequence, *Veni, Sancte Spiritus*, speaks of how the Holy Spirit can be known. It is one of the loveliest of medieval hymns, probably written by the English archbishop Stephen Langton (ca. 1150–1228), among the greatest theologians of the Middle Ages.

Here the Holy Spirit is said to be light in our hearts, consoler in distress, rest for the weary, warmth for the cold-hearted, softness to those who are hardened, life-bringer for all in us that is dried out. Healing and restoring, the Spirit flows through us, becoming a sweetness we can never forget when we have once tasted it.

The sequence does not speak of human struggle, heroic effort, deeds of spiritual valor, overcoming, asceticism, moral achievement, or moral armament. Only at the very end does it speak of trust—and the whole hymn sings of childlike prayer. The Holy Spirit is pure gift. We only need to reach out our hands.

The Self-Giving God

From the time of the Pre-Socratics, Greek philosophers thought unceasingly about God. The process of reflection attained a unique pinnacle with Aristotle. For him, God is infinitely perfect spirit and the highest Being, existing from eternity out of and within the divine self. And because God is perfect spirit, God is pure thought. But what does God actually think? Aristotle asks that in the twelfth book of his *Metaphysics* (1074b). He answers: It is clear that God can only think the most godly and worthy thing there is—namely, "Godself."

What else could God think, within Aristotle's framework? God is absolute Being-in-itself. Were God to think of anything other than Godself, such as the world or human beings, God would no longer be thinking the highest and best; God would therefore turn away from Godself and by that very action would sacrifice divine perfection.

There is something attractive about thinking of God in that way. Given certain presuppositions, the idea is even illuminating—but in such a way that Aristotle simply could not conceive of any such thing as a creation or management of the world by this supreme spirit. It is true that for him God is the "unmoved mover" of the world and the "final cause" (*causa finalis*) of all motion in the world, but the world that God moves by simply being God exists from eternity.

Moreover, the moving of the world in no way happens by God's action as "efficient cause" (*causa efficiens*); God moves the world, says Aristotle in a much-discussed expression, "as the object of love moves the lover" (1072b). This means that the beloved can move another without itself being moved.

Later philosophers in antiquity also regarded God as removed from all relation to the world. God, the highest and best of all that can be thought, rests in Godself and thinks only Godself. If God were to become an efficient cause for the world, God would undergo change and thus damage the divine perfection.

As enlightening as that all may be at first glance, it is equally terrifying. Does it not make God the most holy Egoist, the epitome of ceaseless circling around the self, the apotheosis of the one who is in love with the self and the archetype of absolute autistic self-absorption?

The Descent of "Divine Wisdom"

Israel speaks differently about its God. In ever-new images the Bible shows how God attends to the world in creative love. One of those images is the Old Testament figure of Wisdom. The form of Wisdom says something essential about God's relationship to the world.

That is because Wisdom is not something apart from God; she is divine Wisdom itself. She is altogether with God. She plays before God "as a beloved child" (Prov 8:30),[1] and yet she is entirely in the world. She "[delights] in the human race" (Prov 8:31), for she is at one and the same time God's creative wisdom, the measure, the order, and the meaning God has placed in creation. In the figure of Wisdom the Old Testament shows how thoroughly God thinks the world "at the beginning of his work," loves it, acts upon it, and seeks a dwelling within it (Prov 8:22-36; Sir 24:1-22; Wis 7:22–8:1).

The New Testament takes up this fundamental experience of Israel and shows how the Old Testament's wisdom theology has been fulfilled (John 1:1-18). In Jesus Christ the Logos, the eternal Word, the eternal Wisdom of God has come to dwell among human beings. This Logos, who was already and had always been the meaning and measure of all creation, became flesh (John 1:14) and brought the glory of God into the world. "From his fullness we have all received" (John 1:16).

These basic ideas in the Prologue to the Fourth Gospel link directly to the wisdom theology of the Old Testament, and the ideas in the Prologue are continued and expanded as the gospel unfolds: Jesus Christ is entirely "in the Father" and the Father is altogether "in him" (John 14:10). Everything has been given to him by his Father. Every-

---

[1] NRSV "like a master worker."

thing the Father has is his also (John 17:10). But Christ does not retain it for himself. He gives the fullness and glory of the Father to his own; that is, the Holy Spirit, the Comforter whom he will send, takes from what Christ is and hands it on to the disciples (John 16:4-15). Thus God is shown to be overflowing, self-giving love. "God's love has been poured into our hearts through the Holy Spirit that has been given to us," as Paul had already written (Rom 5:5).

Ever-Deeper Incarnation

A fundamental movement between Old and New Testaments is visible here. We could describe it this way: The ongoing revelation of the true God does *not* show us a God who is more and more distant from the world, more and more hidden; instead, it reveals an incarnation that becomes more and more palpable, an ever-deeper saturation of the world with the Spirit of God. Obviously God is not the world. For Israel, that is a fundamental distinction. But within Israel's process of learning, God turns more and more radically to the world.

How does such experience fit with Aristotle's insights? Was everything he said false? It is not so simple. Christian theology has been glad to make use of Greek philosophy and its conceptuality and has increasingly thought about God in Aristotle's categories, among others. With Aristotle it has said that God is self-sufficient, self-directed, that—understood correctly—God even thinks Godself.

Is that a contradiction to what we have just said about the Bible? It would only be so if Christian theology had simply submitted to Aristotle's concept of God. But from the beginning—led by Israel's experience and the disciples of Jesus—it has gone far beyond Aristotle. The church does not think about a "highest being" but stands adoring before the triune God. It has adopted the God-image of ancient philosophy but at the same time has blown it open and transformed it.

For the church, God is not one who is self-enclosed and reflects in lonely splendor on Godself, one who can think of nothing else but God's own "I." God is already a "we" within Godself; God is relationship, threefold life, community—that is, the community of the Father with the Son and the Holy Spirit. And in the Son and the Spirit, who in an *inner-trinitarian* sense are a "procession" from the "Father," God enters altogether into the world. Thus incarnation and the sending of the Spirit become the perfection of God's relationship to the world.

Hellenization of Christianity?

Above all since the Protestant theologian Adolf von Harnack (1851–1930), a ghost has been roaming through theology: the thesis of the "Hellenization of Christianity." That grandiose idea still impresses people today. It asserts that the development of Christian dogma in the first centuries increasingly confined the statements of the Bible about God and the Messiah Jesus Christ within Greek concepts, and with the aid of those concepts developed a highly complicated Christology and theology of the Trinity, thereby falling away from the pure Gospel and the simple faith of Jesus.

In reality, matters were precisely the reverse. A hellenized Christianity would have spoken of a "divine" that was withdrawn from the world and absolutely distant, something of which one can only say that it is "the One." The development of belief in the triune God was precisely the path that enabled the church to hold fast to the biblical picture against the trends of ancient intellectualism—to hold to the God who wills the world from eternity, who created it, who fills it with the divine Spirit in order to renew the face of the earth. To repeat: behind the Prologue of the Gospel of John lies not Greek philosophy but the wisdom theology of the Old Testament.

Thus also the feast of the Holy Trinity is not a liturgical outlier, unconnected to the ancient festival of the fifty days of Easter and reflecting Greek philosophy; it is an adoring summation of everything the church has celebrated from Easter to Pentecost: that God is not merely self-possession but is self-donation; that the self-donation of the Father to the Son continues in the self-donation of the Son and the self-outpouring of the Holy Spirit.

Thus God is self-possessed and self-conceiving precisely in that God gives Godself. Out of love, in self-surrender to the Son and the Spirit, God thinks the world and calls it into being so that it may have a share in God's unending life.

The Triune God in the
Eucharistic Prayer

The confession of the triune God is one of the treasures of Christian faith—and yet how difficult it is to speak about this mystery! One thing is certain: when we confess God as triune and speak of the Father, the Son, and the Holy Spirit, we are not uttering words produced by theological speculation. This confession springs from the history of Israel.

Historical Experience

It comes from the encounter with the one, unique God who rescued Israel from Egypt and became its liberator and its entire hope forever after. The whole Old Testament tells how this one God struggled for this people and became more and more fully known by Israel, despite all its failings.

The confession of the triune God then arises from the encounter between Jesus and his disciples. They had the profound experience that God spoke in Jesus and acted in Jesus, who is the definitive word and presence of God in the world.

Finally, the confession of the triune God comes from the experience of those same followers of Jesus with the Spirit. After Easter, and in the time that followed, they were repeatedly seized by the Spirit of Jesus. They could only interpret that experience of the Spirit to mean that the eschatological Spirit of God, of whom the prophets had spoken, was now also acting through them, and that Jesus would now be in their midst forever in this Spirit.

That is the basis of Christian faith in the triune God. This experience in faith took place in the midst of Israel, in Jewish women and men, in real history. Through baptism every Christian enters into that history. Therefore we may never speak of the mystery of the triune God apart from that history.

The Church's Great Thanksgiving

Still more: not only must we constantly speak of the mystery of the triune God *in historical context*, but every correct speaking about that mystery is based in *thanksgiving*. If we were to describe the historical origin of our faith in the triune God as historians or students of religions do, in terms of certain historical phenomena, that would not be false—but it would most certainly be too little.

Where, though, is the crucial place, the location where we can speak, both in historical context (recalling the history of our own faith) and at the same time in thanksgiving for the mystery of the triune God? It is *the* place where the whole church gathered together gratefully recalls the great deeds of God. It is the eucharistic celebration; more precisely, it is the Eucharistic Prayer at its center.

Even many Christians who are faithful in their belief are often uncertain about what that Eucharistic Prayer really is, what happens in it, to whom it is addressed, what kind of speech it is, who speaks it, and that it has a basic *trinitarian* structure.

The Eucharistic Prayer—here clearly separated from the "preparation of the gifts"—begins with the priest's invitation to the assembled community, and the invitation is answered in dialogue by the community. The dialogue shows that this is about a common self-preparation for a great, solemn act of thanksgiving:

> *The Lord be with you.*
> *And with your spirit.*
>
> *Lift up your hearts.*
> *We lift them up to the Lord.*
>
> *Let us give thanks to the Lord our God.*
> *It is right and just.*

We can see right away that something unusual is about to happen; we are beginning a solemn address to God. No one would speak that way in everyday dialogue. No one would say "lift up your hearts!" But here it is so, and this unusual language is fully justified. In such a situation one cannot speak as one would in the street or at a popular holiday celebration. We are to prepare ourselves to stand, surrounded by the angels, as representatives of all creation before God the Father and give thanks with our whole existence. And the Eucharistic Prayer ends as unusually as it began:

> *Through him [Christ], and with him, and in him,*
> *O God, almighty Father,*
> *in the unity of the Holy Spirit,*
> *all glory and honor is yours,*
> *for ever and ever.* Amen.

Thus the Eucharistic Prayer is addressed to God the Father. It takes seriously the instruction of the Council of Hippo (393): "Every prayer should always be addressed to the Father." The church's whole liturgy lives from that. There are exceptions in which prayer is also addressed to Christ or to the Holy Spirit, but those few exceptions prove the rule.

Thus the Eucharistic Prayer at Mass is addressed to God the Father. But it takes place "through [Christ] and with him and in him." That corresponds precisely to what I have said about the historical origins of faith in the triune God: In Jesus, God has become eternal presence in the world—and for this reason, from that point forward all prayer and, above all, every thanksgiving prayer takes place "through Christ" and "together with him."

The Eucharistic Prayer remembers a great deal of what God has done in Christ, but above all, Jesus' resurrection, his rescue from the power of death, and at the center of the Eucharistic Prayer is the grateful remembrance of the evening before Jesus' suffering, of the events at the Last Supper.

We must always be clear that the so-called "words of institution" are not a magical formula. They are grateful "remembering," fully embedded in the great thanksgiving. This thankful "remembering"—always so consequential—transforms bread and wine, and with them the hearts of those who share in the celebration. But it does not do so through some kind of magic trick; it gives a physical sharing in Jesus Christ and the surrender of his life.

Who does the transforming? Not a formula, but the Holy Spirit, who is invoked over the gifts of bread and wine and on the assembled community. This "summoning of the Holy Spirit" on the eucharistic gifts in the so-called "epiclesis" is an absolutely necessary and essential part of every Eucharistic Prayer. Eucharistic Prayer II, for example, says:

> *Make holy, therefore, these gifts, we pray,*
> *by sending down your Spirit upon them like the dewfall,*
> *so that they may become for us the Body and Blood of our Lord Jesus Christ.*

In Eucharistic Prayer III the summoning of the Holy Spirit on the *believers* reads:

> *. . . grant that we, who are nourished*
> *by the Body and Blood of your Son*
> *and filled with his Holy Spirit,*
> *may become one body, one spirit in Christ.*

The Holy Spirit, "who renews the face of the earth," is thus summoned not only upon the gifts of bread and wine but also on the assembled community. That community is to be transformed just as are the bread and wine. All this makes it clear that the Holy Spirit also has an indispensable place in this solemn prayer of thanksgiving, as the church acknowledges.

The Many Petitions

I have been deliberately speaking of "thanksgiving" and "prayer of thanksgiving." That had to be emphasized, because in fact there are a great number of petitions in the Eucharistic Prayer, above all in Prayer I, which for many centuries after the Council of Trent was the only one permitted. What is the explanation for that? Don't the many, many petitions disrupt the thanksgiving and thus the basic structure of this solemn prayer?

I see it this way: the proper place for petitions within the eucharistic celebration is in the Prayers of the People after the Confession of Faith (the Creed). The petitions within the Eucharistic Prayer have a different function. They link the praying community to the universal church: the bishop of Rome, the local bishop, all bishops, all those who hold offices of service in the church, the saints, and all believers living and dead. Thus the petitions within the Eucharistic Prayer are intended to create *communication* with the whole church throughout the world, and indeed both on earth and in heaven. That is their proper function here. We are not alone when we speak the Eucharistic Prayer in our local churches. Here, too, we are between heaven and earth.

Who Speaks the Eucharistic Prayer?

I have just written "when we speak the Eucharistic Prayer." But isn't it the priest who speaks? Isn't it reserved for the priest alone? Yes and no! It is reserved for the priest because the priest speaks officially in the name of Jesus Christ. But it is spoken also in the name of the assembled community. The community adds its voice at the Sanctus and after the words of institution: "We proclaim your Death, O Lord . . ." Both are parts of the Eucharistic Prayer itself. Finally, the whole assembly responds to the solemn conclusion of the Eucharistic Prayer with its "Amen." That is the most important and consequential "Amen" in all church liturgy, and we should speak it with full awareness—for this "Amen" means: What has just been spoken in this most important prayer of the church is the basis of our whole life and everything we do: namely, that we give honor to the triune God; more precisely that we are a community, that our common life magnifies the name of God. Still more precisely: that we lead our lives in such a way that even people who are far from God are again placed in a position to praise God.

"You Are God's Temple"

In Paul's first letter to the community in Corinth we find one of those seemingly out-of-the-blue statements that are typical of him: "Do you not know that you are God's temple and that God's Spirit dwells in you?" (1 Cor 3:16).

When we hear that statement we have to picture the tiny Christian community in the port city of Corinth—probably not more than one hundred to two hundred women and men, and not exactly a group of saints and heroic figures. Thanks to Paul's two letters to them, plus the Letter of Clement, we know quite a bit about their problems. They struggled with every possible kind of difficulty, and they were deeply divided. Paul did not have as much trouble with any of his other communities as he had with Corinth, and yet he writes to them: "you are God's temple"!

The Beauty of the Ancient Temples

We only realize how daring that statement is when we understand what a temple in Greek and Roman antiquity really was, and what people of that time pictured when they heard the word "temple." It is no exaggeration to say that temples were the most precious objects in the ancient world. They were constructed by the very best master-builders, using only the costliest building materials. The Acropolis in Athens gives us some hint of what a temple compound in antiquity looked like, and the temple in Jerusalem was no less impressive.

The Herodian temple (the result of Herod's major renovation in the year 21 BCE) was built of white marble, and many parts of its walls were covered with gold. At sunrise it shone with a blinding light. There was a reason for such beauty: this was considered to be God's dwelling. Therefore the heart of the temple, the Holy of Holies, could be entered by none but the High Priest, and even he could only set foot in that chamber once a year, on Yom Kippur, the Day of Atonement.

The Jerusalem temple was regarded as holy; that is, it belonged to God alone. It was God's special possession, God's presence in the world. The temple was regarded as so holy that the scribes said it made the city of Jerusalem holy, and the city of Jerusalem made the land of Israel holy, and the land of Israel sanctified the whole world.

Clearly, then, what was said in the book of Exodus of the tabernacle was now applied to the temple. In Exodus 35–40 the tabernacle is described as the fulfillment of creation. Accordingly, the stone temple with its beauty and costliness was meant to make clear how God had conceived the world even before it was created.

Still, there was more: the temple was regarded not only as the model of creation and the symbol of the whole universe; Israel's theologians were convinced that where the temple stood, there heaven and earth were united. In fact, the gigantic outer curtain before the Holy of Holies in the Jerusalem temple colorfully depicted the universe with all its elements. "This curtain had also embroidered upon it all that was mystical in the heavens, excepting . . . the [twelve] signs, representing living creatures" (Josephus, *Bell.* 5, 212-14).[1]

It is against this background that we have to hear Paul's question: "Do you not know that you are God's temple and that God's Spirit dwells in you?" Now we can understand all the echoes here, and we can sense the audacity—indeed, the enormity—of those words.

The Assembly of Believers

When we realize what Paul is saying here, it follows that the assembly of believers for worship is the most precious thing in the world. Then God and the Risen One dwell within our assemblies even though we are weak and sinful human beings. Then should be visible in us what God always intended creation to be. Then, in the place where the community gathers, heaven and earth are joined. Then the Easter perfection of God's creation begins already today in the midst of the Christian community.

---

[1] *The Works of Josephus*, trans. William Whiston (Peabody, MA: Hendrickson, 1987), 707.

Hence we can only shrink from the promise "you are God's temple," for our lives remain far behind what Paul is saying. Therefore it is necessary to reflect, again and again, on Paul's statement. It has to make us uneasy.

A Very Consequential Revolution

I would like to add a few historical notes to Paul's culminating statement. In late antiquity—that is, in the second, third, and fourth centuries CE—a highly consequential revolution took place in Europe. At that time, in the Roman imperial period, it happened that many intellectuals no longer regarded the temples as dwellings of the gods.

There were in those centuries more and more writers and philosophers who called the whole of the ancient temple cult into question. They made fun of the priests, who smeared themselves with blood like butchers as they prepared the sacrificial animals. They ridiculed people who went to the temple compounds to beg and cry to the local gods for help, filling the court before the temple with sacred shouts. Many regarded the expensive temples simply as masterpieces of architectural skill that were worth a visit but were no longer sacred, separate places.

More than that: in late antiquity many intellectuals no longer believed in multiple gods at all. They believed in the inseparable ONE, the absolute HOLY, the perfect SPIRIT, the UNNAMEABLE. They believed in *the* DIVINE. They said: all that matters is that this DIVINE be honored within oneself. Animal sacrifices are ridiculous, just as is a multiplicity of gods. They also said: everyone who lives a pure and holy life can be the dwelling of the divine spirit. Finally, they said: there is no further need of priests. Philosophers are the true priests. The true temple is the understanding of the wise and the wisdom of the great, enlightened thinkers.

The whole was an incendiary critique of religion without which Western culture would be unimaginable. This critique of the temple and its sacrificial cult was in full spate by about the second century CE, the work primarily of the philosophers of so-called "Neoplatonism." Following the great Greek philosopher Plato, who had lived many centuries earlier, these later Neoplatonists developed an enlightened critique of religion: all sacrificial worship is false and meaningless; we no longer need temples.

The Biblical Critique of Temple and Sacrifice

Obviously, this ancient critique of religion, which had many aspects and which I have described in very broad strokes, is well known to intellectuals in our own time and especially to specialists in the history of religions. They say that our enlightened awareness would be unthinkable without this ancient critique of religion. But what many do not know—including many among the so-called "intellectuals"—is the role Israel played in that whole development.

Israel's critique of religions and that of the early church is, after all, much older than the criticism developed by the Neoplatonists. The Old Testament already contains the idea that God dwells in the midst of God's people (Lev 26:11; Zech 2:14) and that a temple made of stones cannot contain God (1 Kgs 8:27). In the Old Testament the prophets tell the people again and again that for the true God social justice within the people of God is more important than all sacrifices (Hos 6:6; cp. Psalm 50; Prov 21:3). More significant than all animal sacrifices is the "sacrifice of praise," that is, prayer that comes from a surrender of one's whole existence (Ps 51:19; cf. Rom 12:1).

Long before Neoplatonism, in Israel the move from a temple of "dead stones" to the temple made of "living stones" had been accomplished. The Jewish community behind certain scrolls from Qumran rejected the Jerusalem temple and its cult and saw itself as the holy temple of the End Times. Note: here the community itself is the temple.

In fact, Jesus brought an end to the temple cult at the Last Supper by interpreting his coming death in such a way that his surrender of his life replaced the temple sacrifices. Jesus himself thus became the sacrifice, and the Letter to the Hebrews rightly interprets it: with this, all cultic sacrifices in the temple are perfected and at the same time are superseded. Thus every temple made of stones becomes superfluous (Hebrews 9).

The seer of Revelation then, consistently, depicts the new Jerusalem as the eschatological city in which there is no temple (Rev 21:22). God now dwells personally, immediately, in the midst of God's people, and now and forever there stands in place of the ancient statues of the gods and all temple sacrifices the sacrificed Lamb: Jesus Christ (Rev 5:6; 21:22).

Here above all, in this line of Old Testament–Christian theology, long before Neoplatonism, occurred the revolutionary enlightenment that put an end to the old sacrificial worship, with sweeping consequences: a more profound image of God, a clearer image of the human being, a more humane view of society. It is from this point that the ultimate question could be posed: Who, really, is God? One who requires sacrifices and demands of human beings nothing but sacrifices in order that God may be gracious to them? And who is the human being? Someone who must unceasingly placate God? And what is society? Does it continually demand human sacrifices that it first calls scapegoats and afterward destroys so that it can live in harmony, at least for a little while?

The only right answer to those three questions is found in the Jewish-Christian history of enlightenment. Athens and Rome assisted and helped to prepare the ground.

God in Our Midst

If what I have said is true—if God's dwelling is no longer to be sought in dead stones but in living communities, and if indeed a whole people is to become God's holy habitation—there must be consequences. Then God does not dwell only in our churches—more precisely in the Holy of Holies, housed in the tabernacle and deriving from the memorial celebration of the Last Supper. Then also God does not dwell only in our hearts through the Holy Spirit whom we received in baptism and confirmation. In that case God dwells, above all, in our midst when we gather to hear the word of God, to reflect together on what God desires of us now, in this hour, and how we can be reconciled with one another. Then God dwells in our assemblies through Jesus and his Holy Spirit. "For where two or three are gathered in my name, I am there among them" (Matt 18:20). Then every gathering is already an Easter assembly, with the Risen One among us.

In the Easter celebration, the most important of our assemblies, we celebrate the one sacrifice that has completed all sacrifices and links us to the true temple of God no longer made up of dead stones but visibly, tangibly, and really of the gathering together of living people.

There Have Never Been
So Many Martyrs!

Haven't we already worked our way through the whole church year with its great calendar of saints and their special days? Then why, shortly before the end of the church year, do we have another feast of *all* the saints? Isn't that really over the top? Those who think that way can be helped by a glance at history.

The Oldest Feast of All Saints

Originally, All Saints was not celebrated on November 1 but on the octave of Pentecost, which today is Trinity Sunday. The earliest witnesses to that come from the fourth century.

The sense of that oldest All Saints feast was as follows: The whole church, every congregation, is made up of saints (cf. Rom 1:7; 1 Cor 1:2; Eph 1:1; Phil 1:1, etc.), for all Christians have been made holy through baptism and bound together in Christ as a single "body." All Saints was thus originally the feast of the church sanctified by Jesus Christ. We could also say that the old All Saints feast on the Sunday after Pentecost revealed the fruit of Good Friday and the fifty-day feast of Easter: the holy church. The Orthodox churches and Catholics of the Byzantine rites still celebrate All Saints on that first Sunday after Pentecost. They have thus held to the original date and so to the inner tie between Easter and All Saints.

But that genuine feast of All Saints had another special accent: besides celebrating the church made holy by Christ it also celebrated the Christian martyrs of the first centuries. Why? It is true that many martyrs were known and commemorated by name, but there were also many others whose names had been forgotten. The church did not want to forget them.

These countless martyrs, known and unknown, had preferred to let themselves be slain rather than abandon their confession of Jesus Christ. Therefore they were unimaginably close to the crucified and risen Jesus. HE knew their names, and the church celebrated them, together with all other saints, on the one feast of All Saints.

Festival of the Dedication of the Roman Pantheon

In the East as in the West, the remembrance of all Christian martyrs is part of the feast of All Saints, and the Sunday after Pentecost was also the original date of the feast in Rome, but there, in the seventh century, the feast of All Saints migrated to a different day. The reason was that, as we know, Rome was the location of the impressive Pantheon, formerly a temple in which all the gods were worshiped. When the Roman state became Christian, the Pantheon was not torn down as were so many other pagan temples; instead it was turned into a Christian church. And who were those honored in that church? The Virgin Mary, who stood beneath the cross of her dying son, and all the martyrs, those known and those countless ones who are unknown. The many Roman gods were replaced by the many Christian martyrs, and so the day on which the church celebrated the consecration of the Pantheon (May 13) became the Roman church's feast of All Saints. However, May 13 was still very close to the Easter season. November 1, our present date, comes from Ireland and made its way into the Western church only later and very gradually.

That, then, is the original meaning of the feast of All Saints: on that day the church remembers that it is called to sanctity as a whole community, that it is a holy community before God, sanctified by the Easter mysteries. But then the genuine meaning of this feast is also the memorial of the countless martyrs who witnessed to their faith in Jesus Christ with the surrender of their lives. With their blood they remind us what church truly is: the community of people who are sanctified through Christ and for whom their confession of Christ is more important than their own lives.

The Liturgy

The liturgy for All Saints still clearly reflects this martyrdom aspect of the feast: at the gospel we read the Beatitudes from the Sermon on the Mount (Matt 5:1-12), ending with:

Blessed are those who are persecuted for righteousness' sake, for theirs is the kingdom of heaven. "Blessed are you when people revile you and persecute you and utter all kinds of evil against you falsely on my account. Rejoice and be glad, for your reward is great in heaven, for in the same way they persecuted the prophets who were before you. (Matt 5:10-12)

That is true for all who follow Jesus, even when they are ridiculed and excluded for it. And of course it is true also for all those who are persecuted to the point of martyrdom for Jesus' sake.

Christian Martyrs Today

The church today, when it celebrates All Saints, should recall this original meaning of the feast even more powerfully than in times past. It should especially remember the countless martyrs whose lives were destroyed in recent weeks, months, and years because they were Christians and confessed Jesus Christ, for there have never been so many Christian martyrs as there are today. It is utterly shocking how little aware many Christians are that the church of the twentieth and twenty-first centuries is living in a time when Christians are persecuted. The indifference of all too many Christians, corresponding precisely to the indifference of our society in this regard, is one of the deepest wounds of the church. The Christians of the early church did not treat their martyrs that way.

We should, for example, remember the Coptic Christians who are constantly threatened with death in Egypt, and the many who have already been killed there by Islamists—at the very time when they have gathered in their churches for worship.

We should also remember the Christians in North Korea who are relentlessly persecuted by the Communist regime. There are between 200,000 and 400,000 Christians there; they gather "underground" in some one thousand house communities. About 50,000 to 70,000 Christians in North Korea are imprisoned in work camps where their captors force them to perform inhuman workloads and subject them to torture in an attempt to move them to deny their faith.

Let us likewise remember the Christians in Afghanistan, all of them threatened with extinction at the hands of the radical Islamist Taliban now that they have regained power. In particular, Muslims who become Christians have to fear for their lives not only in Afghanistan but in other countries because Islamic religious law punishes apostasy from Islam with death.

But we should also remember the Christians in Pakistan who must live their faith entirely in secret because they dwell in the midst of an Islamic world that is easily roused to fanaticism. Christian girls there are regularly married to Muslim men so that they will convert to Islam. Others are raped by young men because of their Christian faith. They are fair game.

I could go on at length: consider, for example, the Christian martyrs in Nigeria. The Islamist group Boko Haram makes repeated attacks on Christian churches. Still worse: the Muslimist Fulani jihadists have managed to murder nearly twice as many Christians since 2015 as the "professional" terrorists of Boko Haram. The number of Christian martyrs in Nigeria alone has approached a figure in the thousands in recent years. Still the greater part of our mainstream media remains silent about this unceasing slaughter of Nigerian Christians. Is that accidental?

Thus blood-witnesses are not merely a phenomenon of the early church; they are our present reality. Seventy-five percent of all people throughout the world who are murdered for their religious faith today are Christians. We are experiencing a persecution of Christians at a level never before seen in the church's history.

On the feast of All Saints we should remember all these sisters and brothers in faith. They did not seek death. Innocent and nonviolent though they are, they are persecuted, despised, forced into hiding, mistreated, killed. Often merely possessing a Bible is enough to get them murdered. They are following Jesus. They are not nameless, even if we do not know their names. God knows those names and receives these martyrs with ineffable love into the "great multitude" we speak of in the liturgy of the feast.

All these martyrs, together with Jesus, are the loveliest and most precious part of the holy church. They want to tell us: You, too, should be living witnesses to the grace bestowed on you in baptism. You, too, are called to witness to Jesus Christ with your whole existence— as a holy community.

Our Service to the Dead

After the feast of "All Saints" the church celebrates that of "All Souls." The church year is approaching its end. The dark days of November in the Northern Hemisphere recall death and dying. Graves are decorated as people remember their dead. It is thus the right time to reflect on our relationship to the dead.

The Dangerous Dead

Among ancient peoples the dead played a role we can scarcely imagine. They had to be treated carefully: the burial ritual had to be followed exactly, the dirge had to be sung, memorial meals had to be celebrated, gifts had to be laid on the grave of the deceased, and people made an effort to say nothing but good about them.

Underlying all that were love and concern for the dead—and yet there was more. Deeper still there always lurked the fear that the dead could be dangerous if they were not approached in the correct manner and soothed in a variety of ways. Many cultures were convinced that "dead people can be dangerous." People were afraid that the deceased could return as ghosts and do harm to the living. That was also the real reason why one must only speak well of the dead: you had to be careful not to irritate them.

Many ancient tribal rituals show how dangerous the dead were thought to be. In West Africa, for example, among the Anyi people, the dead person was addressed with a dramatically enacted spell:

> *Why have you come back?*
> *Why do you not rest?*
> *After all, we are here.*
> *We are here for you.*

Leave us in peace!
You come to devour us.
Why? Why?

We are your children.
Leave us in peace!
We are here for you.
We did not banish you.
We did nothing bad to you.
Why do you come to devour us?
Why do you steal our flesh?
Leave us in peace!
We are here for you.

Then, in the dramaturgy of the spell for the dead, the whole sense of which is, of course, to soothe the deceased, the dead person gives a dreadful reply:

I had my house.
I had my farm.
Then I had to leave.
I had to go.
You lied.
You betrayed me.
I am alone.
I have no one.
I had to go forth all alone.
Now I am coming back.

"Now I am coming back." Fear of the dead rose in the ancient peoples, anxiety that they might come back as ghosts, spirits, and vampires and take vengeance on the living.

And let's not pretend that those are all "primitive" fantasies. Among us, too, the dead constantly return (in other ways, of course) and create havoc. The dead parents' lack of faith comes back on the children—the enmities the ancestors nurtured are pursued by the sons—the mother's lack of freedom continues in that of her daughters—the inheritance not clearly allotted by the parents leads to quarrels over the property and destroys whole families. Here, too, the dead come back. We have no cause to feel superior to the fears and rituals of the so-called "primitives."

Fascination with the Realm of the Dead

But ancient peoples not only *feared* the dead; they also experienced a *fascination* that emanated from the realm of the dead. The dead drew people into their spell; they lured people to magical participation in their world; they aroused unbridled curiosity about the Beyond. Thus the history of religions is full not only of fear directed toward the dead but also of spiritualism, invocations of the dead, and journeys to the underworld.

Biblical scholars have reflected at length on why the people of ancient Israel at first did not believe in an afterlife, the immortality of the soul, the resurrection of the dead. They believed that in *Sheol*, the underworld, people led only a shadowy existence. There is no real life after death. Hence people were convinced that everything depends on today, on the Now. We must praise God today, and it is in the present that life before God must develop its meaning.

This faith in the here and now was all the more amazing because all the nations around Israel, and especially the Egyptians, practiced a fascinating belief in the world beyond. How was it that only Israel, which lived surrounded by those peoples, did not originally believe in any world beyond this one?

The answer is: because belief in the Beyond among the peoples around Israel was imbued with an excessive cult of the dead and with practices aimed at securing for oneself a good place in that other world by acquiring a corresponding burial place in this one—something that, of course, only the wealthy could afford. The realm of the dead, with its dark secret and its fascinating aura, would have drawn God's people away from the *one* God whom one must serve on this earth and in this life. So ancient Israel refused any kind of belief in a Beyond, and Israel's prophets fought tenaciously against preoccupation with the world of the dead.

Only very slowly, when the dark and dangerous side of the cult of the dead appeared to have been banned from Israel, did belief in an eternal life find its place there also—but now nourished by faith in divine omnipotence, which desires life and had always rescued Israel from mortal dangers (Pss 16:9-11; 49:15).

Our Service to the Dead

On the whole we must say that fear of the dead and fascination with their world have one thing in common: we are never rid of the dead. Not being rid of them because of fear and not being rid of them out of fascination are two fundamental possibilities for our relating to the dead. Both are unbiblical; therefore neither corresponds to Jewish-Christian faith.

To begin with: those who believe in Christ are not afraid of the dead. After all, they have entered into the realm in which God's sovereign rule has already come to fruition—and, as Paul says, the rule and reign of God are "righteousness and peace and joy in the Holy Spirit" (Rom 14:17). Our dead are in the place where justice has been accomplished once and for all, where there is absolute peace and jubilant rejoicing. We need have no fear of these dead who are altogether with God. Quite the contrary: they are our helpers.

What we should fear is only the still-unresolved past that many of the dead left on earth before they arrived fully in the presence of God. As we have seen: when someone lives in chaos, strife, and unbelief, those are not removed from the world with the person's death. Their mass goes on growing in the world like a cancerous tumor that affects the children and grandchildren. The hard-heartedness of parents can continue in the hard-heartedness of children, the unbelief of ancestors in the unbelief of their descendants. Precisely because we love our dead we dare not cover up such connections. It may be that our dead have bequeathed much good to us, but it can also be that unbelief and things unredeemed have come down to us.

In that case there is only one solution: we must act differently. More precisely, we must repent and change our lives. In doing so we offer our dead the greatest and most beautiful service, because it is only through our repentance that our dead can be made altogether free of what still burdens them—everything they left in the world at their death that was still unresolved.

Those who believe in Christ are not afraid of the dead, or of ghosts, and want nothing to do with soothsayers who can supposedly contact the dead in order to reveal the future to us. We have long since been told what we need to know about our future, and we confess it every Sunday in the Creed: namely, that our God is a God who desires life, who raised Jesus from the dead, and who frees all those who believe in Jesus from death together with him.

Let me repeat: the best service we can offer our dead is to be steady in faith and to repent and turn to God ever anew.

I spoke about the disorders and darknesses that dead persons may leave to their descendants, but that is only one possibility. It can be altogether different. It may also be that they have left us faith, have shown us what constancy in faith is, that they have loved the church, that they were deeply concerned about whether their children would hold fast to Christian faith and not cast it aside. It can also be, and this is what I hope for us all, that our dead were pious in the best sense of the word: that they believed, hoped, and loved—perhaps much more than we do. We also serve such predecessors when we repent—in this case turning back to what they modeled for us and what they were.

So it can be said that whatever our dead have left to us—bad or good—we help and serve them best when we ourselves live in the faith of the church. That is more important than the flowers we plant on the graves of our dead. It is even more important than all our prayers for the souls of our dead, because the good of their souls includes our repentance.

Obviously what I have said is not a call to be indifferent to the external duties we owe our dead. That would be not only inhuman but un-Christian. Certainly we should also sorrow for our dead, decorate their graves, pray for them, and remain profoundly tied to them.

But still more important than all that is our constancy in faith and our ever-renewed turning toward God. That is how we can best help our dead and give them the most honor. It is precisely in that way that we are most deeply tied to them. Then they are with us; then they accompany us; then we will find them again, one day, with God.

Waiting for the Bridegroom

Somewhere along the way they are waiting for the bridegroom—the wise virgins and the foolish ones as well. They wait and wait. Finally they fall asleep. If we want to understand the parable of the Ten Virgins (Matt 25:1-13) rightly, we need to know why the bridegroom is so long delayed.

Marriage customs in Israel at that time required the bridegroom to go to the home of the bride's parents to fetch her and bring her to his own parental home, where the wedding would be celebrated. There is some indication that a particular ritual was performed as part of this conducting of the bride to her new home: the bridegroom's procession to the bride's parental house was halted repeatedly—by the bride's clan. This was not about negotiating the bridal gifts; those had long since been settled. Instead, the repeated delays were for haggling over additional gifts, according to the principle: the more beautiful and valuable the bride, the more numerous presents were due to the bride's family.

That is the only reason why the bridegroom is delayed. He is not one of those morons who forget their wedding date. It was in his own interest that the procession make repeated stops because that elevated the reputation of his bride. The delay had powerful symbolic value.

Without knowing that ethnic background we cannot understand the parable. Still, the young women with their torches who have traveled a distance to meet the bridegroom and are waiting for him at some crossroads knew the ritual. They had to have expected that it would be a long time before the bridegroom would arrive, and yet, even knowing that, only some of them prepared for the wait by bringing small jars of oil to moisten their torches. The others underestimated the quality of the bridegroom and bride. They expected an average wedding. So their torches are going out when, after the long wait, distant lights appear and they hear the cry: "The bridegroom is coming! Up! Go to meet him!" At that moment it is too late for the foolish maidens.

The Feast Has to Happen

Of course, nowadays our ingrained idealism asks: shouldn't the wise in that moment have shared their oil? Wasn't it time for solidarity, mutual aid, sisterly generosity?

But the wise maidens do not share, despite the urgent pleas of the other five: "Give us some of your oil. Our torches are going out!" They categorically refuse to share. According to the Greek text they say: "Never!" "Not on your life!" and add "Then the oil would not suffice for us and for you. Go to the sellers and buy for yourselves."

Suspicious Bible-readers find that the last statement in particular contradicts their social sensibilities; they read it as sarcasm, ridicule, and insulting of the poor young women who did not plan far enough ahead. After all, they say, it is the middle of the night! The shops are long since closed!

What these critics often fail to realize is that we are in the ancient Near East, where legal hours for doing business have not yet been introduced—oh, horror!—and the "sellers" are not supermarket owners but little shopkeepers who are happy to make a sale even in the middle of the night. No, when the wise maidens refer the others to the shops it is neither ridicule nor sarcasm. Moreover, the wise are completely correct as to the facts of the situation: if they were to share their oil with the others equally it would not suffice for the long trek to the bridegroom's village that lies before them. Then the bridegroom would arrive at his parents' house, where the real feast will begin, accompanied by a whole group of young women with dead, burned-out torches.

The wise maidens know what a feast is. It can only happen if the torches are burning. When the light goes out there is no more feast. If the festal procession were to arrive with burned-out torches it would be the talk of the village for years to come, and the honor of bride and bridegroom would be permanently damaged. So there is only one solution: those who are prepared and supplied receive the bridegroom and accompany him. The others go off to organize some oil, but they cannot catch up with the festal procession. For them it is too late.

The parable uses the metaphor of a marriage and images of a great feast: bridegroom, burning torches, festal procession, wedding hall. The images are easily translated: the feast of the reign of God is to be celebrated. God will hold a wedding with his bride: that is, with his people. God may hope that all those invited to the wedding are prepared and adorned so that the feast may sparkle, for only the fascination of the feast can rescue a darkened world, a world aimless and without hope. So God's feast must not be downgraded and deprived of its brilliance.

"I came to bring fire to the earth, and how I wish it were already kindled," Jesus said on another occasion (Luke 12:49). Our parable is about something similar. There must be people who burn with their whole lives for God's plan. Only then can the feast happen.

Jesus told the parable of the wise and foolish maidens when his situation was already perilous. The parable sheds light on the growing crisis. Israel knew that the inbreaking of the reign of God had been promised. It knew that the Messiah would come. It even prayed daily for that coming. But when suddenly it heard: "The bridegroom is here. Up! Go to meet him!" most people were not prepared for the day of the Messiah, the wedding of God and God's people. Other things were more important to them, or they had imagined the event altogether differently.

We are no better. We know the message. We have received the invitation. We pray, "Thy kingdom come!" We know how lost our society is without faith in Christ, and we sense what could happen if all the baptized were prepared with hearts and hands for the messianic renewal of the world to which the image of the wedding refers. That renewal is most powerfully endangered when we surrender what is our own: what our Christianity means. Our special duty, our Christian calling, is not up for negotiation. In this there can be no accommodation to society and no false sharing.

Are Our Lamps Burning?

It is worthwhile to locate the parable within the whole of Matthew's gospel. Its key concepts, namely, "wise" and "foolish," appear there earlier, at the very end of the Sermon on the Mount:

> *Everyone then who hears these words of mine and acts on them will be like a wise man who built his house on rock. . . . And everyone who hears these*

words of mine and does not act on them will be like a foolish man who built his house on sand. (cf. Matt 7:24, 26)

"My words" refers to the whole of the Sermon on the Mount. Having enough oil: that would be the believing acceptance of the Sermon's message and the readiness to live it—but not in the sense of an intensified moralism. Instead, it is to be lived against the horizon of the messianic feast God wants to prepare for the world through the Bride, the church.

Having no oil would then mean that we have not reckoned with the greatness of the feast, that we are not waiting and trembling in expectation of what is to happen in our midst, even today. There is great danger that, like the foolish maidens, we want to be present in some way—but only more or less and not with our whole existence.

But we dare not play games with God's invitation that is extended to us. Otherwise it could happen that one day it will be too late, and we in Europe or America or somewhere else suddenly find ourselves standing before closed doors. Those who accommodate themselves to everything and who minimize and waste the tradition entrusted to them will become "burned-out torches."

In that sense the parable of the ten bridesmaids, read almost at the end of the church year, is very serious. For Matthew it is a crisis parable—addressed not only to Israel but equally and even more urgently to Christians who have succumbed to weariness.

The "Now-ness" of the
Feast of Christ the King

Before a new church year begins on the first Sunday in Advent,
the Roman Catholic Church celebrates Christ the King Sunday.[1] This
feast is the conclusion, the crowning point, the sealing of the preceding year. "Christ the King" is one of the most recent church feasts,
introduced in 1925. Why? What was the occasion for adding a new
feast?

It may be that the minds of those who introduced it retained a bit
of nostalgia: beginning with the French Revolution, more and more
kings had vanished from European history. They were deposed,
forced to resign, or made purely representative figures. Democratic
governments took their place.

Many Christians in Europe were at first unable to deal with that
revolutionary change. They mourned the monarchy. In that situation
the church wanted to show that there is another, true, never-ending
kingship, that of the one who confesses before Pilate:

> *"You say that I am a king. For this I was born, and for this I came into the
> world, to testify to the truth. Everyone who belongs to the truth listens to my
> voice."* (John 18:37)

For us the reasons for the introduction of the feast belong to the
distant past. Has it then lost its significance? No, for as is so often the
case in the history of the church, what seems out of date and really
superfluous suddenly appears in a new light. Today there are very
few monarchs left who can show us what a king is, but there is a

---

[1] Some churches in the Anglican Communion that have revised their liturgical
books in the last several decades (e.g., those in Canada, Australia, and the United
States) also celebrate "The Reign of Christ" or "Christ the King" on the last Sunday
before Advent.—Tr.

growing crowd of rulers who have drawn a stage curtain of pseudo-democracy around themselves. It doesn't matter what these despots are called. What they all have in common is that they lie without restraint, tread human rights under foot, and rely on violence. Against that background the feast of Christ the King acquires a new force. It is the radical unveiling of all arrogated and unjust power.

Critique of Kings in the Old Testament

Many Christians are unaware that criticism of kingship already played a prominent part in the Old Testament. Israel did not have kings to begin with; it had no central government to lead it. It was not a "state" from the outset. Before Saul and David established something resembling a royal rule in Israel there were only allied tribes—a first, tentative attempt to live in freedom, equality, and brotherhood/sisterhood before the one God.

That loose confederation of tribes, described primarily in the book of Judges, was replaced by the kingship. Thus began an experimental phase in the history of the people of God, one that was fundamentally flawed. In retrospect—long after the beginning of the Exile—that kingship was criticized by Israel's prophets and theologians in the sharpest possible terms. For example, 1 Samuel 8:5, 20 says that Israel desired to be "like other nations." It no longer wanted God to be its ruler; it preferred an earthly king (1 Sam 8:7). But the Old Testament contains a great many other texts that criticized the royal period in retrospect (see, for example, 2 Chr 36:11-16). In the famous "Jotham's fable" in Judges 9:7-15 the kings are not only criticized but ridiculed.

The Torah, Israel's rule of life, which acquired its present literary form only after the exilic period, marginalizes the kingship. Israel's basic institution is not the king but the instruction from Sinai. In Israel power must be shared. Prophets, judges, and priests are mutually independent institutions. The king is to be a model Israelite: he must study the Torah daily (Deut 17:19). What is crucial for Israel is not the king but love and fidelity to God (Deut 6:4-5), social justice (Deuteronomy 15), and the ever-renewed gathering of the people of God for its great feasts (Deuteronomy 16).

However, the royal period, with its crises and catastrophes, accomplished one thing: it produced an increased longing for a future king who would finally bring law, justice, blessing, freedom, and peace. That was the longing for the Messiah. The word comes from Hebrew and means "Anointed One." As such the word could describe any king (or queen) or high official, but in its specific sense the concept of a "messiah" means the true, eschatological ruler installed by God in whom everything a monarch should be will be realized.

Jesus' Reversal of the Messianic Ideal

Jesus fulfilled Israel's longing for a real sovereign—but altogether differently from what was expected! In his public ministry he consistently avoided the concept of the Messiah and forbade his disciples to use it (Mark 8:27-30), because the idea had too much negative baggage. "Kingship" meant central rule, political state, government violence, wars with neighboring states, but the "dominion" Jesus proclaimed and lived was completely different: absolute nonviolence, living in service *to* others, free submission to the one God, and the assembling of the people of God *for* that God: in other words, the reign of God.

With all that, the radical demythologizing of human rule by force, already a central theme in the Old Testament, reached its climax. Jesus told his disciples, shortly before his death:

> *"The kings of the Gentiles lord it over them; and those in authority over them are called benefactors. But not so with you; rather the greatest among you must become like the youngest, and the leader like one who serves."* (Luke 22:25-26)

And the demythologizing of kingship went much further: the Messiah, the ruler of Israel, now dies on a cross, nonviolent and powerless and yet transforming his death into a radical "for"—that is, "for the many" (Mark 10:45; 14:24). He dies on a cross so that from his death might at last arise a people that lives without violence, that buries every form of sovereignty, and that is nothing other than service for others.

The People of God and the State

This people does not take the place of the state; it is not a theocracy. It acknowledges the legitimate government and recognizes the power of the state insofar as it is correctly exercised and respects human rights. It does not involve itself with the state because it is completely different. It is the continuation of what Jesus lived. It is a "messianic people"—thus Vatican Council II—and precisely in the sense that it follows the one who was the true Messiah: that is, the one who uncovers all false power and violence and shows what real "power" is.

States are necessary. Judges are necessary. Police are necessary. There is even need for something like a world police; otherwise the self-proclaimed authorities will destroy the world with their greed for power. But even constitutional democracies cannot create real peace. Jesus, the true sovereign, showed how it can be achieved: in his Sermon on the Mount and in his death. The church should follow him in that way, as a "messianic people."

That is the meaning of the feast of Christ the King for us today—and world history reveals more clearly every year how urgently we need it.

Part III

In the Joy of Faith

Zacchaeus's Joy

I still remember my first trip to Israel very well. At the time I was deeply impressed by all the places whose names were already known to me from the Old Testament or from the narratives in the gospels and Acts. But now I was *there*, and that was altogether different.

At some point our little tour group arrived in Jericho. Naturally, we all had the story of Zacchaeus in mind and were picturing the scene in which he climbs a sycamore tree in order better to see Jesus, because he is short and can't see over the crowd (Luke 19:1-4). So we asked our Israeli guide to show us some sycamore trees and peppered him with questions: "What does a sycamore look like?" "Do they still grow here?" "Is it possible to climb them?" It was not just a thirst for knowledge. If I am honest, I have to say that we also wanted to test the historical reliability of the Zacchaeus story a little.

When we then found ourselves standing beneath a mighty sycamore we had our answer: when these trees are old and well developed they are extraordinarily well suited for climbing. Even close to the ground they have thick branches that one can step up on without any difficulty. I felt a little ashamed. Once again the gospel text had proved to be very precise and accurate. (I am writing this in the hope that the sycamore trees in Jericho have not been trimmed up for the sake of Holy Land tourists.)

The Little Man on the Thick Branch

Obviously, then, sitting in the shade of a sycamore tree, we read the Zacchaeus story out loud. At first glance this narrative of the chief tax collector Zacchaeus offers no difficulties. It is smooth as a well-mixed cocktail. At last, a happy, satisfying story! The little man on the thick branch—Jesus down below in the passing crowd—the way Jesus invites himself to dinner and an overnight stay—the wealthy chief tax collector is all in with the idea—finally a religious happy ending: now, that is a *story* you could even tell in kindergarten.

Add to this that the story seems to be a superb match for the contemporary religious mind: a soft Christianity that does not like to give offense to anyone. We can describe this mentality, which massages the gospel to the point that it doesn't annoy anyone, in three principles: (1) Don't exclude anyone; everyone belongs! (2) I'm okay; you're okay; and God loves us just as we are! (3) If all of us treat one another with love and without fear, all the world's problems can be solved!

I don't want to say that those three statements are simply false. Christian truth is so strong that it shines through even such sayings. Obviously we must not exclude anyone, and it is also true that God loves us. And it is a fact that love—as the Bible describes it—is the only solution to the problems of our world. Only: how does that love come into the world, and which of us can say we have such love? And what happens to that love when it really enters the world?

We must not forget that in our story Jesus is already on his way to the capital city. From Jericho it is only *one* day's journey up to Jerusalem. And in Jerusalem Jesus, because of the way he lives the love of God, will be killed. So the story of Zacchaeus is not quite as harmless as it looks at first glance. What takes place between Jesus and the tax collector is not really a kindergarten story; it is an event played out against a dark background.

A Hated Man

After all, at that time toll collectors and tax-gatherers were instruments in the hand of the Roman occupying power and the lesser nobility dependent on Rome. At the beginning of every year they paid a considerable sum to the current governor; after that they were entitled to collect the money for themselves—under government protection, and with an added profit. They were exploiters. They shared in the guilt for the fact that many of the people suffered grinding poverty.

There is no excuse for such behavior. We can easily understand why the tax-gatherers lived in social isolation—that they were regarded as unclean because of their constant dealings with Gentiles—that nobody wanted to have anything to do with them—and that they were classed with criminals.

When Jesus speaks to such a man and says, "Zacchaeus, I must stay at your house today" (Luke 19:5), that was breaking all the rules. It was simply scandalous.

But this was not only about rules that get engrained in society. It was about God's social order, about the life of the people of God. Didn't Psalm 1 say that one should avoid the godless, not follow the path of sinners, and not sit in their company? With those warnings Psalm 1 gives the tone for the whole Psalter. It formulates a kind of motto for everything that is to follow: there are those among the people of God who hold fast to the Torah, the law of God, and base their whole lives on it. They keep clear of the godless. Those pious people will survive the judgment; their lives will be successful— unlike the lives of the godless, who are like straw that the wind blows away. They are like a trail that loses itself in the pathless waste. One must keep distant from them.

So how could Jesus invite himself to the home of a man like Zacchaeus, who did not live according to Torah, who trod the social justice of the people of God underfoot, who thus belonged among the sinners and the godless—how could Jesus possibly go to the home of such a man, sit at the same table with someone who behaved so indecently toward Israel?

The people of Jericho who were pressing around Jesus must have sensed the whole drama as a provocation. They could not allow it—for reasons of faith. Ultimately it was his association with sinners that cost Jesus his life. He was condemned to death by the highest court in Jerusalem as someone who led the people astray.

A Man Who Changed His Life

But there is nothing naïve about Zacchaeus's reaction either. It is incomprehensible to him that Jesus wants to spend the night in the home of one who is socially isolated, despised, and avoided. Jesus restores his lost honor to him by taking up quarters in his house and breaking bread with him and his family.

That overwhelms Zacchaeus. It releases unbelievable strengths in him. What none of the reproaches and hatred of his fellow citizens had achieved, Jesus' attention brings about. In Jesus, Zacchaeus encounters the reign of God and the new attitude that is part of it: the acceptance of one another and permission to sit together at one table because God wants to bring together all the children of Abraham—the righteous and the sinners, the strong and the weak.

Zacchaeus had gone all out in exploiting his fellow citizens. Now, in his repentance, he is equally extravagant. Arriving at home, he confesses his sin to Jesus and promises to make restitution: he will give half of his possessions to the poor and will repay fourfold the excess sums he has demanded in the past. Here again we see that this story is no idyll. Nothing remains the same. A whole life has reversed its course. For Zacchaeus it will all be extremely expensive.

It is just here that we strike our own sore point. We are all for God. We are all for Jesus. And we are also for the church. But we do not want any of that to change any part of our lives. We want both: God's cause and our own security. God's cause should succeed—and everything in our lives should remain as it is.

But that simply will not do. No one can have both: God and bourgeois contentment. The great Bernard of Clairvaux once wrote: "Whoever believes in the reign of God must be restless." Zacchaeus has met Jesus, and in Jesus the living history of God with God's people—and he has allowed himself to be disturbed by that encounter. He has set himself in motion.

At first the movement only signifies that he climbs a tree. He wants a better view. He wants to know what is going on. But then his life changes. We sense what that means: exposing his life to the new thing, transforming it for the sake of God's cause.

Now comes the decisive point: our lives are sluggish; the inertia in them is astounding. How will God manage to move the heavy weight of our lives, to set the sluggish mass of our habits in motion? The secret to God's success in doing that is joy in the story God is bringing to reality in the midst of God's people. Zacchaeus is "happy" to receive Jesus (Luke 19:6). It is not difficult for him to change his life, to be ready to turn his whole existence on its head; it is no trouble. Joy grows out of the new experience Zacchaeus encounters in Jesus, and that joy is the real driving force of his repentance.

Why Christians Are Carefree

The "Sermon on the Mount" contains the following text:

> . . . do not worry about your life, what you will eat or what you will drink, or about your body, what you will wear. Is not life more than food, and the body more than clothing?
>
> Look at the birds of the air; they neither sow nor reap nor gather into barns, and yet your heavenly Father feeds them. Are you not of more value than they? And can any of you by worrying add a single hour to your span of life?
>
> And why do you worry about clothing? Consider the lilies of the field, how they grow; they neither toil nor spin, yet I tell you, even Solomon in all his glory was not clothed like one of these. But if God so clothes the grass of the field, which is alive today and tomorrow is thrown into the oven, will he not much more clothe you—you of little faith?
>
> Therefore do not worry, saying "What will we eat?" or "What will we drink?" or "What will we wear?" For it is the Gentiles who strive for all these things; and indeed your heavenly Father knows that you need all these things.
>
> But strive first for the kingdom of God and his righteousness, and all these things will be given to you as well. So do not worry about tomorrow, for tomorrow will bring worries of its own. Today's trouble is enough for today. (Matt 6:25-34)

An Anti-Stress Program?

Such talk could initially sound as if Jesus were a wellness advisor. Why be constantly worried about oneself? Why live a life that doesn't let us sleep at night because we have a thousand worries? Why let oneself be tortured by everything that has to be done and what is still unfinished? Just don't think about it! Or better: always do only what is important at this moment! Don't let tomorrow's worries weigh you down!

Besides, doesn't the *language* of this program speak to us? How precisely Jesus observed nature: the birds who collect their food, the spring flowers that bloom almost overnight on the Galilean hills after the winter rains and light up the slopes, and even the beauty and usefulness of the grass!

We are pleasantly moved and do not even notice all the problems hidden in this seemingly comforting text, but when we start to think about it those difficulties swarm out at us.

For example: Doesn't the text recommend that we live for the day and not work? Doesn't it tell us to lie down and be lazy? No, our reason tells us: that can't be what it means. After all, one of the Pauline letters says, "Anyone unwilling to work should not eat" (2 Thess 3:10). Stop working, lay your hands in your lap: that can't be what this is about!

After all, if that were the case the images Jesus uses would not fit. The birds, for example: they work all day long. How busy they are when they are building a nest! And when the chicks are crowded in that nest—how the parents fly constantly back and forth seeking worms and insects and stuffing them into the gaping beaks of their young! You don't call that work? Even the flowers, which draw their nourishment from the soil—water, nitrogen, phosphorus, minerals—their osmosis is constantly at work.

No Forethought?

So the text cannot mean that we should be lazy. Instead, what it says is that we should not worry—about food or clothing or our lives. God cares for us, just as God cares for the birds of the air and the flowers of the field. But if the text is not talking about laziness, does it mean to say that we should not think ahead and make plans? After all, at the end we read: "do not worry about tomorrow, for tomorrow will bring worries of its own." Does that mean we shouldn't think and plan ahead?

That would mean: nothing in the refrigerator! No buying three sensible shirts at once when they are on sale! No money in the bank accumulating interest! No provision for old age and no insurance! No annual checkups from the doctor! For pastors, maybe no preparing sermons ahead of time! Let them just speak as the Spirit moves them!

But what would the consequences be? A lot of bad sermons! No concern about a good school for the children that will prepare them for their future calling! No economic system, no industry, no science! After all, entrepreneurial initiatives, scientific projects, and political activity all require planning and careful preparation, often over many years. Then the Christians would have to leave all that to the Gentiles, as we read: "it is the Gentiles who strive for all these things" (Matt 6:32).

No, that can't be right! Such an interpretation would be absurd. It can't be right, given the hunger in the world, in view of the many catastrophes caused, at least in part, by lack of planning—for example, when a school collapses on the heads of a hundred children because it was not built to withstand an earthquake, or a condominium in Florida snuffs out a hundred lives because of faulty maintenance. It can't be true in light of the many illnesses and epidemics that urgently call for medical planning and preparation!

If Jesus had meant anything like that, we Christians would have to fold our hands in our laps, stay clear of everything, and tell the sick, the poor, and the despairing: "Do not worry, saying 'What will we eat?' or 'What will we drink?' or 'What will we wear?' God knows that you need all these things." That would be nothing but a shocking cynicism. The gospel words about unconcern simply cannot mean anything like that. But what *does* the text mean? What does Jesus mean to say?

Worry Calmly?

Not long ago I read the following interpretation of our text in a church bulletin:

There is a right and a wrong way to care for ourselves. We Christians live under God's paternal kindness, and for that reason our concern has acquired a different character. Of course Jesus knows that care and planning are necessary for human existence, but the care of those who believe in the reign of God has a different character from the planning and concern of the Gentiles. For those who do not believe in God every misfortune is a catastrophe, as is every illness and, in the end, death itself. Therefore people without faith must constantly be anxious and concerned, must unceasingly try to avoid the great and small catastrophes of the world—and yet they cannot escape them. It is different for Christians. They also have concerns, but they are unperturbed by them; they are not anxious. They can approach everything with great calm and profound trust because they know they are sustained by the care and fatherly love of God.

Would that not, at last, be a serious, reasonable suggestion for resolving the problems we have with this gospel text? A Christian also has cares, but she cares calmly, without worry, unfazed, enlightened, and without fear. Still, I find that interpretation inadequate. It is not simply false, but it ignores the crucial factor. It seems to lack any experience of what Christian community is, and therefore it cannot approach the really decisive truth.

Why Christians Are Carefree

If we want to interpret the gospel of unconcern rightly we have to notice the audience to whom these words of Jesus were first spoken. Who were they? Then it becomes entirely clear: the addressees were not just some group of Gentiles, but they were also not simply Jewish listeners, the crowd that repeatedly pressed around Jesus. No, the text in question was addressed to the little group of disciples who were on the road with Jesus, wandering without rest through Israel (see the description of the addressees in Luke 12:22). This is about the situation of disciples.

Look more closely at their way of life! They have left everything: their own houses, families, work. Jesus moves with them throughout Israel, living a restless life. They are on the road with Jesus so that the coming of the reign of God may be proclaimed throughout the land. Usually Jesus and his disciples did not know in the morning where they would lodge at the end of the day (see Luke 10:5-12). Would they find people who would receive them into their homes that evening?

Still, it was not just the disciples. There were many others who did not travel with Jesus but who heard and accepted his message about the reign of God and then returned to their homes: *localized* followers of Jesus, sympathizers, friends, those who had been healed, helpers, supporters. We may think, for example, of the man who made a well-furnished upper room available to Jesus for the celebration of his last meal (Mark 14:12-16), or of people like Mary and Martha (Luke 10:38-42).

So Jesus and his disciples are not alone. They can rely on a network of friends and sympathizers throughout the land. This is precisely where we should locate the lack of concern that Jesus demands of his disciples. They can be carefree because there will always be people who will take them into their homes at evening. Then there is a mutual giving and receiving: Jesus and his disciples need people who provide them with food in the evening and shelter for the night. These localized followers, in turn, need living contact with Jesus and his disciples so that their family can enter into the new thing: the quiet revolution of the reign of God.

There is thus a give and take between the two groups: the disciples no longer live for themselves and their private interests but for the people of God—and the resident followers no longer live only for themselves and their children. Thus everywhere in Israel where Jesus comes, and people receive him and his disciples, something new occurs: a new togetherness of people, a new family extending beyond the natural one.

This makes it clear that the trust of which this gospel speaks is not a magical one that says "God will make it happen." It is by no means a romantic living-for-the-day. The carefree attitude to which Jesus refers has a very real basis: the houses of Jesus-followers throughout the land where Jesus and his disciples are received. Then round about these houses, after Jesus' death and resurrection, the first communities arose. It was in those houses that people gathered after Easter—to pray and celebrate the Eucharist.

Genuinely Christian Communities

But what does all that mean for us? What could this text tell *us*? We had to work through the theme of freedom from care to get at what Jesus is really aiming at. As we saw, the disciples could be free from care because they were not alone; they were part of a network of Jesus-followers, of people who, together with them, were expecting the coming of the reign of God. On the other hand, the people who in the evening received the disciples into their houses learned to think with Jesus and the disciples: to place the reign of God and its needs above all else. Their first concern was now "the kingdom of God and its righteousness" (Matt 6:33).

So there arose within Israel a form of society in which many engaged in mutual aid. The goal of that community, of that supporting-one-another, was to make apostolic work possible: the messengers of the Gospel were to have the time and the strength to be able to proclaim the Gospel. They were to be put in a position to devote themselves to their task of preaching. They were to be able to live entirely for the sake of the reign of God. But those touched by the Gospel likewise placed concern for the reign of God above everything else by helping the preachers—and thereby God cared for them also. God gave them the peace promised to them by Jesus' messengers (Luke 10:5).

At precisely this point we are all affected by this Gospel. Do we want community in this sense?—as a coming-together of many who live in solidarity, as a communion of sisters and brothers who are there for each other so that commitment to the Gospel can be made possible? Do we want that? Do we want to help change our parishes in that direction, so that they become communities in which there is mutual aid, mutual encouragement, mutual consolation, ongoing common repentance—and thereby the absence of worry?

I am convinced that precisely that is the background of this Gospel of freedom from care. Without that background it would not only be incomprehensible; it would also be reckless and without conscience. But read against the background of "living communities," in which many join their lives together and are there for one another, it is Good News.

The Reality of Persecuted Christians

I admit that for many Christians in the West all that is hard to grasp because our communities are for the most part far from such "togetherness." We live in a security network of insurance programs—health, life, auto, and so forth—social institutions and a great variety of organizations that aid people in need. We expect effective aid especially from the state.

But what about those for whom there is no such helpful state?—or for whom there is one, but at some point, in face of a profound catastrophe, the state itself is helpless? Or what about all the Christians who do not live in a supportive state at all but in one that exploits or even persecutes them?

Are we really aware of the fact that only a small portion of all Christians live in democratic countries that uphold religious freedom and public social programs? In many, shockingly many, of the countries on earth Christians live in the most bitter misery, are excluded, robbed of their rights, persecuted, or simply eliminated. They are literally compelled to hold together, to meet secretly in houses, and to beg us who live in secure situations to help them. We never dare forget that the words of Jesus are not only for us but, ever since his resurrection, for all his followers throughout the world. Yes, Jesus really spoke about freedom from care, but that freedom presupposes the solidarity of his sympathizers and followers.

How God Consoles

There are words that lose their luster over time, and there are others that are misused so long that no one dares use them any more. But neither of those things is true of the word "consolation."[1] It has retained its power until today. No misuse has been able to destroy it. "Who would want to live without the comfort of trees?" Günter Eich asked.[2] At the death of his father, Matthias Claudius spoke of the "soft, sweet consolation" of the resurrection.[3] The word has never worn out, probably because we cannot live without being consoled and because the world is constantly in danger of sinking into a gray, disconsolate state.

Sacred Scripture offers us consolation at many points. In the Beatitudes of the Sermon on the Mount we read: "Blessed are those who mourn, for they will be comforted" (Matt 5:4). It is good to reflect on that statement, because if we understand it we will have understood all the Beatitudes in the Sermon on the Mount.

What is most striking in Matthew 5:4 is that nothing is said about *who* will console the sorrowful; the question remains completely open, because the second clause is in the passive voice: "they will be comforted." We find such passive forms quite often in Jesus' sayings, such as "All who exalt themselves will be humbled" (Matt 23:12), or "Ask, and it will be given you" (Matt 7:7), or "Do not judge, so that you may not be judged" (Matt 7:1).

---

[1] Or "comfort."—Tr.

[2] Günter Eich, "Ende eines Sommers," in *Angina Days: Selected Poems*, trans. and introd. Michael Hofman (Princeton and Oxford: Princeton University Press, 2010), 16–17.

[3] Matthias Claudius, "Bei dem Grabe meines Vaters," may be found, *inter alia*, in George F. Comfort, *A German Reader* (New York: Harper & Bros., 1882), 105.

Biblical scholars have long been aware of these passive formulations in Jesus' way of speaking. They say that what we have here is a *passivum divinum*, that is, a passive expression for God's acting; such passive forms are said to be frequent in contemporary Jewish apocalyptic texts. Accordingly, "Do not judge, so that you may not be judged" would mean "you must not judge *others*, so that God will not judge *you*." Accordingly, Matthew 5:4 would say "Blessed are those who mourn, for God will comfort them." That interpretation does make good sense. God will eventually wipe all the tears from our eyes (see Rev 21:4). God will console us.

When we read the second beatitude in Matthew this way we see immediately that it takes up texts from Isaiah: for example, God's speech in Isaiah 51:12: "I, I am the one who comforts you," or the moving words of Isaiah 66:13: "As a mother comforts her child, so I will comfort you."

When People Are Reconciled

How wonderful, that God will comfort us! We ourselves can never really supply for the dearth of consolation in the world. Its misery breaks forth again and again. There are wounds in us that only God can heal; others are not even aware of them. There are tears on our faces that only God can wipe away. Others do not even notice them. There is guilt in us that only God can forgive. Other people do not even suspect it . . .

But is that true? Sometimes it is good to let oneself be drawn from thought to thought and expression to expression; then it can happen that we suddenly arrive at a point at which we come to a standstill and realize: None of that is true!

Saying that there is guilt only God can forgive does not match up to the New Testament. It is, in fact, in the very nature of the church that there all sin and guilt can be confessed and forgiven (John 20:23). When Christians are reconciled with one another or when in the sacrament of reconciliation the priest speaks the words of forgiveness—*in that moment, God forgives*. Therefore it must also be true that *we* can wipe away each other's tears. When we do so, God wipes away our tears. Therefore it is also wrong to say that there are wounds only God can heal. Those who follow Jesus can also heal each other's wounds. Precisely when they show one another their wounds and bandage them, God is their physician.

If all that is true, we must seek a deeper understanding of the statement that it is God, God's very self, who will console us. It is not that our starting point was wrong! It is certainly true that *God will console us*. But the real mystery of the church consists precisely in this: that in it the eschatological future has already begun, and so it is manifest there that the eternal God speaks and acts in human beings—first and most profoundly in Jesus, who is truly human and yet at the same time the full presence of God. But the same is true of all those who, in Jesus Christ, have become daughters and sons of God.

It is God who will console us. That is true. But in the present time God will and does console and comfort us through all who receive us as sisters and brothers, bind up our wounds, wipe away our tears, and are good to us in every way. That is precisely the way in which God consoles.

And the Church?

If all that is true, *one* question answers itself: namely, whether we will be consoled in the present and not only in heaven. To put it another way: then the question is whether the Beatitudes of the Sermon on the Mount are comfort only for the future beyond this life, acting like drugs because they rob those who are to be consoled of the ability to act in the present. If God consoles us now—through other people, and only through other people—indeed, if that is God's way of comforting, then we must wipe away the tears from others' eyes *now* and satisfy their hunger *now* and bind up their wounds *today*.

No matter what happens, heaven remains heaven. It is not superfluous; it is our entire hope. Only there can the ultimate and all-encompassing consolation begin. But the kingdom of heaven, Jesus says, has already begun among us. God already consoles us through our sisters and brothers. The church is meant to be the place within history where the end-time consolation that God gives in abundance is already a shining present. The church is the messianic place of God's consolation in the world.

Certainly the church can never be that in and of itself. If it were to attempt such a thing by its own strength it would have to despair in the face of the endless suffering of the world and admit its own unconsoled state. But it can do so in the messianic power of the one of whom Isaiah says:

> *The spirit of the Lord GOD is upon me, because the LORD has anointed me; he has sent me to bring good news to the oppressed, to bind up the brokenhearted, to proclaim liberty to the captives, and release to the prisoners; to proclaim the year of the LORD's favor, and the day of vengeance of our God; to comfort all who mourn; to provide for those who mourn in Zion—to give them a garland instead of ashes, the oil of gladness instead of mourning, the mantle of praise instead of a faint spirit.* (Isa 61:1-3)

This text from Isaiah that Jesus and the earliest church regarded as key to their self-understanding says that through the Messiah God consoles the sorrowing and despairing people of God so that they may become a place of joy and jubilation for the whole world. From that point of view there is also a profound reason why the second beatitude in the Sermon on the Mount leaves the person of the consoler unclear. This way of speaking holds every possibility open: God consoles. The Messiah consoles. The messianic people will become a consolation. People console. God consoles through people.

Thus we may all enter into the words: "Blessed are those who mourn, for they will be comforted." That passive formulation creates a space for the church and enables it to become a consolation in itself. "They will be comforted" is thus not merely a *passivum divinum* that speaks of God's action but also a *passivum ecclesiasticum*, a passive that refers to the action of the church—a passive that makes room for the church to become the messianic place of God's eschatological consolation.

The Grave of Johann Adam Möhler

A final affirmation that in this way the Bible is rightly interpreted is found in the text of Isaiah 66:13, quoted above: "As a mother comforts her child, so I will comfort you." It continues: "you shall be comforted in Jerusalem." The reference here is to the restored people of God, the holy city of the end-time—what, according to New Testament faith, the church has become. Thus Scripture tells us that in the church we may find the consolation we so earnestly seek. In the church, in the sisters and brothers who travel the way of faith with us, we already find the consolation with which God comforts us as a mother.

Therefore, if it takes its messianic calling seriously, the church must be such as to be our consolation. But we, too, must be a consolation to the church, as is written on the tombstone of Johann Adam Möhler, the greatest theologian of the Tübingen School: *Solamen ecclesiae.* He was a comfort for the church.

The Burden and the
Joy of Being Chosen

Many biblical scholars identify four passages in the book of Isaiah that they call "Servant Songs." These are Isaiah 42:1-4; 49:1-6; 50:4-9; 52:13–53:12. The four texts bear serious theological weight. They are about a "servant" chosen by God, one in whom God trusts absolutely and who thus becomes God's instrument in the world.

Israel as the Servant of God

This "servant" is Israel, banished to Babylon. Here we should note the following: obviously the Babylonians deported especially the intelligent, competent, and influential people from Judah—the crafts-people, the scribes, the educated, the leaders. And obviously, in the wake of the terrible catastrophe, precisely those Jews deported to Babylon asked themselves: is this the end of Israel? Will God no longer hold to the promises? Our land is desolate. Jerusalem, the holy city, has been destroyed. We no longer have a temple. We cannot even obey the Torah in all its details. So is it all over?

Then, in their exile, a prophet appeared, one whose name we no longer know but who spoke in the tradition and the power of the earlier prophet Isaiah. Biblical scholars call this prophet "Deutero-Isaiah" ("Second Isaiah"). He proclaimed to the deported people: "You have not been rejected by God. God has not forgotten you. On the contrary: you have been given a very special, indeed a crucial task. You have been chosen to carry forward the history of the people of God. You are a very special instrument in the hand of God. You are the 'servant of God.'"

Centuries later the church saw Jesus Christ himself in the figure of that servant of God. That was fully justified because everything

God intended Israel to be was concentrated in Jesus. In him all of Israel's hopes achieved their goal. He himself embodied, in his own person, the eschatological Israel.

At the beginning of the first Servant Song we find what we might call a presentation of God's servant, Israel. God points to Israel and says:

> *Here is my servant, whom I uphold, my chosen, in whom my soul delights.*
> (Isa 42:1)

The idea of Israel's being "chosen" stands out. This concept of election is characteristic of all four of the Servant Songs, running like a scarlet thread through the texts. The great theologians of the early church would then take up this idea of election, which indeed occurs in other Old Testament texts. They would call the Christians in their communities not only "saints" or "those who are called," but also "the elect," "God's chosen ones" (Rom 8:33; Col 3:12; 1 Pet 1:2, and frequently elsewhere).

However, words such as "election," "being chosen," and especially "the elect" give us a lot of problems. Many people do not like such words or what is meant by them. For me personally it was highly embarrassing for someone to say to me: "You are one of the 'chosen.'"

There is a bad odor attached today to the word "election" (in the spiritual sense). It reeks of sectarianism or at least reminds us of people who think they are better than others. A lot of people have been moved to cynical laughter at the idea that believing Jews see themselves as the "elect nation." People who claim to be chosen by God are hated. Because such problems are connected to the idea of election, we will do well to clarify what the Bible really means by it.

No Preferential Treatment

First: That God has chosen a particular people in the world does not mean that God loves only that people and not the others. God desires the happiness and salvation of all. But that salvation, that happiness must first be made visible in a clearly defined people as a way of being with God, so that the other peoples may freely choose the same path for themselves.

Election thus does *not* mean that a particular people is *preferred* by God but rather that this people is taken into service *for the others.* Israel's election is for the sake of the world; therefore, near the end of the second Servant Song it is said of Israel:

> *I will give you as a light to the nations, that my salvation may reach to the end of the earth.* (Isa 49:6)

The "that" is crucial. Ultimately it is not all about Israel, God's servant, but about the nations, the earth, the whole world.

Better Than the Others?

Second: Election also does not mean that God's elect people are better than the other nations. It is true that they should be. The people of God should be filled with "the knowledge of God," should be holy and irreproachable, and yet they also sin, they also reveal profound entanglements and guilt. The real difference between this people and other societies is instead that the people of God have been able to recognize what the world is all about and how world-society can finally find peace. Passing on that knowledge, and doing so through its whole existence: that is the task assigned to the people of God.

The Burden of Election

Third: Finally, election also does not mean that the people's lives are easier and simpler. Those who are chosen have the greater responsibility. They are to be "a light to the nations," guides for the seekers, and for that reason those who are chosen stand most particularly under God's judgment.

Besides, there is more to it than that: those whom God has chosen, in carrying out their task, repeatedly encounter deaf ears, pure lack of understanding, perhaps even a wall of resistance. Often the others simply do not want to understand. They harden themselves and go their own way, and then it may be that in such cases God's chosen, in their anguish, will say, as in the second Servant Song:

> *I have labored in vain, I have spent my strength for nothing and vanity.*
> (Isa 49:4)

Haven't we ourselves often silently thought such things? But it is not bad that such thoughts arise in us. In those cases we must only add, as does the Servant:

> . . . *yet surely my cause is with the* LORD, *and my reward with my God.*
> (Isa 49:4)

That is: the meaning of our work for God's cause cannot be measured by external success. God knows the hidden effects of our faith and efforts, and God is our reward. That suffices.

Jesus: All Alone at the End!

I think it should be clear by now that God desires the salvation of the whole world, but God's plan is not grasped by everyone. It is always a minority who recognizes and seizes it. The burden of election then lies on that minority—a heavy burden that the minority is basically unable to bear. Ultimately the whole must fall upon one who is able to bear it: Jesus.

When we consider Jesus' story we see at once that in the end he was entirely alone. One of the Twelve had betrayed him; Peter had denied him; even most of the disciples he had chosen had run away. In the end Jesus was alone and bore the whole burden of election along with his cross. Of all the elect in Israel there remained in that moment only one who had understood God and desired nothing other than to serve God's plan. Now everything—the whole future of the world—depended on that one. He bore the burden of history; he had finally and irrevocably become the "Servant of God."

But because he did not run away, because he did not shake off the burden of election, the people of God could be gathered anew and the task could be divided and laid on many shoulders. Therefore we may say that everyone who has chosen in freedom for Jesus Christ is one who is called and chosen by God.

The Joy of Election

That is indeed a burden and a constant responsibility, but it is also a great joy—the most profound joy in our lives. God responds to the Servant's lament precisely by placing something even greater before that servant's eyes: it is not only about gathering the people of God but about the salvation of all nations. Already in the first Servant Song we read: "I have put my spirit upon him; he [the Servant of God] will bring forth justice to the nations" (Isa 42:1). This text speaks primarily about Israel in exile, which has been chosen to bring to the peoples the salvation of God and the justice it creates, and for us Christians it speaks first about Jesus, the unique Elect and Bringer of Salvation. But if we allow ourselves to be called by him and "remain in him," we, too, have a share in that promise. Then we may rely on it that the almighty God is working in the world through our little services. It is not as if we were cogs in a giant machine—not at all! Rather, we work as God's friends, chosen by God as fellow workers (John 15:15).

Discipleship: Hard and Easy

The fourteenth chapter of Luke's gospel contains a text that really would terrify us if we were not all too familiar with Jesus' sayings:

> *Whoever comes to me and does not hate father and mother, wife and children, brothers and sisters, yes, and even life itself, cannot be my disciple.* (Luke 14:26)

How could Jesus say such a thing? More than that: how could he demand such behavior? To hate father and mother, spouse and children, even one's own life for his sake: what on earth does that mean? Fine; biblical scholars explain that, given Old Testament usage, "hating" here is not about aggressive emotions but "putting in second place," "putting last," "having less regard for." But that does not change the severity of Jesus' words.

Nor can we get away with saying that Jesus spoke those words at some point in a totally exceptional situation and that it by no means applies to everyone. No, this says that all who "come to Jesus" must make themselves completely available, following Jesus not by halves, not only with part of their lives, but with everything they are. After all, the gospels talk about it incessantly, and even the Old Testament says it: there, the principal commandment for *everyone* in Israel is:

> *You shall love the LORD your God with all your heart, and with all your soul, and with all your might.* (Deut 6:5)

So we cannot say that the text in Luke 14 is some kind of exception; elsewhere in the gospels everything is more moderate and civil. No! All four gospels speak this way, and it is about one of the core elements of Jesus' preaching. So the question remains: is Jesus allowed to make such a demand? Isn't it a hopelessly excessive challenge to any human being? Is anyone even capable of such a radical "totality"? With such a demand before our eyes, wouldn't we be burdened with a bad conscience to the end of our days? We need to reflect on this problem because it is one of the most important questions a Christian must face.

An Initial Reflection

I have said that the text I quoted from Luke's gospel demands everything of those who want to follow Jesus: their whole lives, their whole strength. But then I ask: does that "everything" actually exist in Christianity? Is something of the sort demanded only of Jesus' disciples?

I think, for example, of a doctor who has to be extraordinarily attentive during her office hours and completely focused, who then in the evenings and on Saturdays makes house calls, who is preoccupied with her problem cases, and who, beyond all that, is obligated to constantly update her knowledge. Can physicians allow themselves to do their work only by halves? And is that the case only for doctors? I could speak of politicians, people in business, locomotive engineers, truck drivers—or of athletes. I can quote the trainer of an internationally acclaimed basketball team who said recently in a press conference that success requires total commitment. "Basketball has to be like a religion for my players; they have to love the sport almost more than their wives. And they have to practice—four to five hours a day for ten years."

It is no different with artists. They cannot permit themselves to do anything by halves. Artists must put in everything: their whole strength, without interruption. To take three more examples: someone who attempts to ascend a cliff alone, without technical aids or security ("free solo"), must be absolutely focused or fall off the wall. A pilot in a big airliner who allowed herself to be distracted would be acting irresponsibly. Everyone who cooks has to keep eyes, hands, and nose coordinated and work in a controlled rhythm; otherwise the menu will go awry. There is no serious profession that one can do "on the side" or with one hand.

In fact it would be shameful, and we would make ourselves objects of social ridicule, if we thought we could follow the calling of a

Christian as something secondary, that one could be a Christian with half one's strength, and that an hour on Sunday, a daily morning and evening prayer, and a contribution to a good cause would suffice to support faith.

When Jesus speaks in the gospels, again and again, about the fact that his disciples must follow him with full commitment and with their whole lives—if we look closely, that is the most normal thing in the world! It is no different anywhere in our society when it is a matter of acting seriously and responsibly.

A Second Reflection

No one can be forced to be a Christian: it is a matter of freedom, of personal decision. In the short but remarkable letter to Philemon, Paul prays for the slave Onesimus, who has run away from his master, Philemon. He has fled to Paul, who is imprisoned in Ephesus. Paul has taught him in the prison and has baptized him. Now he sends him back to his master and begs him to forgive Onesimus and to receive him back into his household—but as a beloved brother in faith and no longer as one enslaved (Phlm 8-20).

What I find important here is that in this letter, written with great affection, Paul does not command anything: he *asks*. Philemon is not to act under pressure. He is asked to accept Paul's advice freely (Phlm 14). It is precisely the same with Jesus. Each person is free to follow him or not.

Just after the text in Luke 14:25-26, in fact, Jesus explicitly calls the people who follow him to consider carefully what they are about to do. He illustrates his challenge with the parable of building a tower— probably the reference is to a two- or three-story house, a so-called "residential tower" (Luke 14:28-30). At that time such a building (in contrast to a one-story, mud-brick house) called for a lot of preparation. Woe to the one who built a multistory house and did not consider the structural principles—or who ran out of money before the building was finished! Such a person would become the laughing-stock of the whole town! So Jesus warns against following him too hastily. The reign of God demands one's whole self. Discipleship in the reign of God means that God takes hold of my whole life; I am no longer in charge, nor are any of my private interests. God cannot be an afterthought.

A Third Reflection

It is true that Jesus demands of his disciples their devotion, their whole strength, their entire dedication, but he does not lay an unbearable burden on their shoulders. The devotion to the reign of God that Jesus demands does not oppress people; rather, it raises them up and for the first time gives them the dignity and freedom for which human beings are created. Here again, a glance at our normal everyday world can help us.

How is it when someone builds a house and has not only saved for it over many years but also does part of the construction work? Such a person builds late into the night; it is hard work. There are difficulties. The husband is worn out; the wife as well. But is the labor on their own house an unbearable burden to them?

That can indeed happen, but usually it is otherwise: as hard as the labor is, it is combined with a deep satisfaction because the couple see their house coming into being. They are excited at being able to live there soon. They plan how the yard should look; they see themselves sitting on the patio under the vines they will cultivate there.

So it is with the reign of God. It demands everything of us, but it is joy to work for God and to be able to gain people for God's cause. What we do out of joy becomes a light burden.

That is precisely what Jesus meant by the parable of the treasure hidden in the field (Matt 13:44). A poor day-laborer is plowing, and the plowshare strikes a treasure hoard. The laborer buries his hands in the jewels and silver coins, then swiftly reburies the treasure, *sells everything he has*, and buys the field. In that way he secures his legal right to the treasure. What is crucial in the parable is the fascination aroused by the find and the overflowing joy that fills the finder. It is not at all hard for him to invest *everything*. This is *the* deal of his life.

We have to understand that not one hour we devote to Jesus' Gospel, to the Christian community in which we live, and thus to the church as a whole, is lost! It is the most precious thing in our lives. In the end the only thing that will count will be what we have done for God's cause.

Can There Be Such a Thing as "Normal" Christians?

In all this the tasks can be quite different. In my "three reflections" I have deliberately made no distinction between "disciples" of Jesus and "normal" Christians, since each of us has her or his calling. Each has his or her own pathway in faith. Each of us has a particular way of being "totally" with Jesus.

It may be that God will demand a great deal of one or another of us. But it may also be that God asks nothing more of many of us than that we feel profoundly grateful that we belong to the church, and that we continually rejoice with all our hearts that the church exists as God's "presence." That enduring mutual joy is already infinitely much. Indeed, I am convinced that a life that is nothing other than pure gratitude for and joy in God's cause may well be the highest form of sanctity.

Overflowing Riches

We all know the story of the miraculous multiplication of loaves. This account of the feeding of a great crowd of people on "the other side of the Sea of Galilee" (John 6:1) must have been singularly important to the authors of the four gospels: they tell of it in no fewer than six different places (Mark 6:30-44; 8:1-10; Matt 14:13-21; 15:32-39; Luke 9:10-17; John 6:1-15). In John's gospel it all begins with five barley loaves and two fishes. When the remnants are collected after the meal there are twelve baskets full of bits of bread (John 6:13). The story is thus designed to show the abundance that has come into the world with Jesus Messiah. But this incredible fullness encounters us not only in this story; it appears in many other parts of the gospels.

Lavish Fullness

It meets us in Cana, at a wedding that threatens to end poorly because the wine has run out (John 2:12). We can only understand the situation if we know that at that time a wedding could last a week or even longer, and that everyone passing through the village was invited. The wedding was the high point in the life of every Israelite. Here the messianic fullness is shown in the wine miracle Jesus performs. He changes some five hundred to seven hundred liters of water into wine: thus Jesus' gift is lavish. There is no restriction, no limitation, no stinginess. The great stone jars are filled to the brim, and the wine is so good that the steward asks in astonishment why such a superior wine is only being distributed at the end of the feast (John 2:9-10).

Lavish fullness meets us also in Bethany, in the house of Simon the leper, where a woman produces an alabaster vessel filled with the most expensive oil of nard and pours it over Jesus' hair, so that the disciples are bewildered and talk about senseless waste. But Jesus defends the woman (Mark 14:3-9).

We find something similar also in Jesus' parables: the land on which wheat is sown, despite all the enemies that threaten the harvest from start to finish, produces a mighty yield. The wheat that found good soil "tillers" itself so that nearly every seed that was sown produces thirtyfold, sixtyfold, or even a hundredfold (Mark 4:1-9).

To take another example from Jesus' parables: a mustard seed, no bigger than the head of a needle, becomes a mighty bush, a world tree in whose branches the birds of the air build their nests (Matt 13:31-32).

A third example: a poor day-laborer, while plowing, comes across a buried treasure of immeasurable value, and a wholesale merchant who deals in pearls is one day offered one such as he has never seen before: huge, and with an indescribable luster (Matt 13:44-46).

Yet a fourth example: a young man who has squandered his inheritance and forfeited his rights as a son is received back into the family by his father—without a moment's hesitation. The father runs to meet him; the lost son receives a signet ring and an expensive robe; the fatted calf is killed; a feast begins (Luke 15:11-32).

Still more: a landowner treats the day-laborers he hired late in the afternoon to harvest his grapes as if they had worked all day. At evening he pays them a full day's wage (Matt 20:1-16).

And more even than that: a king releases a desperate debtor whose existence has been ruined, forgiving him the unimaginable sum of ten thousand talents (a hundred million denarii). At that time one had to work a full day to earn a single denarius. Thus the king forgives a sum of money worth a hundred million workdays (Matt 18:23-35).

But enough with examples! Wherever we look in the gospels we are met, again and again, by overflowing abundance, wealth, superfluity, and even lavish squandering.

The Law of Superfluity

Apparently that is no accident. Rather, what we see here appears to be a fundamental law of salvation history. In one of his books Joseph Ratzinger described it as "the law of excess or superfluity."[1]

---

[1] Joseph Ratzinger, *Introduction to Christianity*, trans. J. R. Foster (San Francisco: Ignatius Press, 1969), 193.

It means that God gives more than we need, more than we can dream of, even more than we can imagine. This basic law of salvation history is explicitly formulated in the gospels:

"To those who have," Jesus says—that is, those who share in the history of God with God's people—"to those who have, more will be given, and they will have an abundance" (Matt 13:12). And those who have left house, brothers, sisters, mother, father, children, or fields for Jesus' sake and that of the gospel will receive them all back "a hundredfold," and will have them now, "in this age" (Mark 10:29-30).

Superfluity, wealth, and lavish fullness are thus the signs of the age of salvation—not scarcity, stinginess, meanness, and indigence.

Why is that? It is because God is overflowing life and wants to give humans a share in that divine life. Thus the principle of superfluity and lavishness is already visible in creation. What kind of profligacy appears in buds and flowers alone! Wouldn't ten kinds of flowers have been enough? And what a huge number of seeds for producing a single living thing! What an extravagance of planets, fixed stars, and spiral nebulae! A whole universe is lavished to prepare a place for the human spirit on *one* tiny planet.[2]

At this point we may well continue (almost in shock, almost stammering): what a lavish number of human beings, of whole nations, until at last God found the *one* people in which to anchor the abundance of divine grace in the world. The book of Isaiah has God express very directly that prodigality of peoples for the sake of the one people of Israel:

> *I give Egypt as your ransom, Ethiopia and Seba in exchange for you. Because you are precious in my sight, and honored, and I love you, I give people in return for you, nations in exchange for your life.* (Isaiah 43:3-4)

The Law of Dying and Living

However: this side of divine extravagance also includes the truth that God gave, spent his only Son for the world. The death of Jesus thus also makes it clear that the overflowing fullness of salvation must not be understood as a fairy tale in which the table sets itself, the rice pot overflows, the jug of milk is never empty, and the fat

---

[2] See Ratzinger, *Introduction*, 197.

purse full of gold pieces never goes slack. Overflowing grace can reach us only when we ourselves die: that is, when we abandon our self-assertion and acknowledge our weakness, indeed, our helplessness. God can only fill empty hands.

As long as we assert ourselves, we make no space for God's action. And so long as we make no room for God, God cannot bestow on us the fullness of salvation. The brilliance that again and again lies on the church does not derive from its model efficiency and high morals but from the fact that there are so many holy people in it who admit their weakness, become entirely listeners, and desire nothing but that God may act.

"When Kindred Live Together in Unity"

Rivalries between sisters and brothers in the flesh are, alas, all too common. Siblings who no longer talk with one another but instead speak deprecatingly about each other—those things are part of the world we live in. Often siblings even quarrel; it may be that one is the aggressor and the other altogether a victim. Think of the story of Cain and Abel! And it is not necessarily always brothers who attack one another; sisters can do the same, and it is just as horrible.

Often it is a matter of pure envy. Most frequently the quarrels are about inheritances. In older cultures, therefore, it was primarily the inheriting *brothers* who quarreled. In the Ottoman Empire from the fifteenth to the seventeenth century it was practically a rule that a new sultan, on his accession, simply had his brothers and half-brothers killed—supposedly to maintain good order in the empire.

Hatred and murder between brothers are a common theme in the ancient sagas, because legends and poetry are based on the world's realities. The same is true in the Bible: it tells of Abel and Cain (Gen 4:1-16), Jacob and Esau (Gen 27:41-45), Joseph and his brothers (Genesis 37), Jephthah and his brothers (Judg 11:1-3, 7), Absalom and Amnon (2 Samuel 13).

It is obvious that Israel's wisdom teachers would have assailed enmity between brothers and condemned it, because hatred between brothers in the flesh destroyed whole families. But they not only criticized it; they contrasted it with fraternal harmony, which they praised. That seems to be the case in Psalm 133 also. It is a brief, artfully arranged psalm that praises sibling love in its first couplet:

> *How very good and pleasant it is*
> *when kindred live together in unity!*
> *It is like the precious oil on the head,*
> *running down upon the beard,*

on the beard of Aaron,
running down over the collar of his robes.
It is like the dew of Hermon,
which falls on the mountains of Zion.
For there the LORD ordained his blessing,
life forevermore.

As I have said: at first glance this seems to be about harmony between physical brothers and sisters, but if we look more closely we become suspicious. Why doesn't the psalm simply speak of "houses" in Israel, that is, the real places where the success or failure of familial life is decided? Why, instead, do "the mountains of Zion" suddenly appear? More: what does "the beard of Aaron" have to do with sibling love? We need to examine the psalm more closely.

Cascades of Fragrance

For the moment let us consider Aaron's beard! Oil dripping from a hairy head onto a beard and from there to the robe does not seem very appetizing. Many a grimace passes over the face of a housekeeper who hears this psalm verse about oil dripping on a robe. What on earth do clothes stained with oil have to do with the beauty of sibling unity?

To answer that we must first put ourselves in the context of the ancient Near East, and particularly that of a rich man's banquet. It would have included not only delicious food, vintage wines, lovely flute music, and elevated or witty conversations; at that time a proper banquet also included a whole bouquet of fine fragrances. These were achieved through lavish flower arrangements, especially including an abundance of lotuses, but also perfumes given to the guests as they arrived. The basis of these perfumes was not alcohol, as is now the case, but fine oils. Accordingly, the perfumed oil was not sprayed but poured, in thickened form, on the heads of the guests as they were greeted. Then, in the heat of the banquet, the oil thinned out again and dripped down on the guests' clothing, whereupon the banquet hall was filled with the finest odors from all the fragrant substances mixed with the oil. In other words, the result was an enduring perfume that lasted throughout the evening. Thus the one praying the psalm at that time could only associate the dripping of perfumed oil with a celebratory meal, a formal gathering—a great, expensive feast.

Festal Meals on Zion

Psalm 133 also mentions "Zion," which evokes other associations. The one praying would by no means link Zion, as the Temple Mount in Jerusalem, with feelings of affliction, hardship, or judgment, but instead with the assurance of God's help and God's abundant blessing. The image for that blessing in this psalm is dew: more precisely, a heavy fall of dew on Mount Hermon. When dew falls in southern lands and especially in desert regions, it is much more abundant than in northern climes (see Gen 27:28 and Deut 32:2). The dew can "saturate" the land. Because it is so thick it can even keep plants alive in times of drought. Obviously our psalm does not mean to say that the dew from distant Hermon will miraculously fall on Jerusalem. "Dew of Hermon" simply refers to quality. Here it is an image of superabundant blessing.

Now we need to bring the two images together: the banquet and the cascade of divine blessing like dew—all of it localized on Zion. Given such a constellation of imagery, the person praying must almost inevitably think of the three great annual pilgrimage feasts prescribed by Torah (Deut 16:16) and, more precisely, of the joyous gathering of all Israel at those festivals. For example, regarding the Feast of Booths the book of Deuteronomy prescribes:

> *You shall keep the festival of booths for seven days, when you have gathered in the produce from your threshing floor and your wine press. Rejoice during your festival, you and your sons and your daughters, your male and female slaves, as well as the Levites, the strangers, the orphans, and the widows resident in your towns. Seven days you shall keep the festival to the* Lord *your God at the place that the* Lord *will choose; for the* Lord *your God will bless you in all your produce and in all your undertakings, and you shall surely celebrate.* (Deut 16:13-15)

Clearly, at these festivals as many people as possible came from throughout Israel to gather in Jerusalem for worship and communal meals. It was absolutely necessary that people who were socially dependent, the marginalized, and even foreigners should participate, for according to the theology of the book of Deuteronomy a primary purpose of these feasts was to overcome social barriers, bring people together, and make Israel one family of sisters and brothers.

It is not only in the book of Deuteronomy that sisterhood and brotherhood in Israel take center stage. The love commandment in the Holiness Code is likewise about that sibling bond. The well-known "you shall love your neighbor as yourself" (Lev 19:17-18) demands that every Israelite expand the solidarity that should rule in every family to include the whole of Israel. "Yourself" means the whole family, which is broken open and expanded to embrace all Israel.

All that should make it clear that the high praise of brotherly and sisterly community with which Psalm 133 begins is about a great deal more than mere domestic solidarity in individual families. The praise is for sister- and brotherhood in *all of Israel*. Throughout the people of God there are to be no rivalries and sibling hatreds. Israel must be "a single people of sisters and brothers." Then God's blessing will flow over the whole nation like the dew of Hermon—and especially on the city God has chosen as a personal possession: Jerusalem.

It is also true that in the book of Deuteronomy the Levites, too, are participants in this festival of familial love (Deut 16:11, 14), and in Psalm 133:2 Aaron obviously represents all the priests in Israel. To put it in contemporary terms: the meals celebrated during the great pilgrimage feasts must include everyone, clergy and laity: the whole people. No one may be excluded.

All this shows that the acclamation, "How very good and pleasant it is when kindred live together in unity!" refers not only to relationships within individual families; it regards all Israel as a single family that again "lives together" at the festivals on Zion. That is why Psalm 133 is quite correctly included, within the Psalter, in the group of so-called "Pilgrimage Songs" (Pss 120–134).

Jesus and the "New Family" of His Disciples

This radical expansion of the natural family was then taken up by Jesus. At some point, probably near the beginning of his public work, his own family wanted to take him "by force" (Mark 3:21) and confine him at home. His brothers are convinced that what people are saying is true: "he has gone out of his mind."

Today's readers, when they see that, get a faint notion of the family pressures to which every individual in ancient cultures was subjected. But Jesus resists his brothers; not only that, he creates a "new family." Mark tells it this way:

Then his mother and his brothers came; and standing outside [in front of the house in which Jesus was teaching], they sent to him and called him. A crowd was sitting around him; and they said to him, "Your mother and your brothers and sisters are outside, asking for you." And he replied, "Who are my mother and my brothers?" And looking at those who sat around him, he said, "Here are my mother and my brothers! Whoever does the will of God is my brother and sister and mother." (Mark 3:31-35)

Because Jesus would not let himself be distracted from his task, not even by his own family, he had to free himself from them quite formally by asking "Who are my mother and my brothers?" But he does not stop there. He creates—and here that is a juridical act—a "new family." In doing so he fulfills and completes exactly what the love commandment in Leviticus 19:18, the theology of the book of Deuteronomy, and Psalm 133 are aiming at.

Now, in conclusion, I have to speak of one final striking detail in Psalm 133. In verse 3, that is, at the very end of the psalm, it speaks of "the mountains of Zion." Two things about that expression are noteworthy: first, we have here a rare and solemn plural form of the Hebrew word for "mountain." Second: as applied to the surface geological formations of Jerusalem the word "mountains" is a huge exaggeration. Everyone who has been in Jerusalem knows that it is hard to call Zion a "mountain," and that it certainly does not have multiple summits.

It is true that in the Bible "Mount Zion" is a mythical or, better said, an inflated theological term. It is, so to speak, the "eternal, primal mountain." But that still does not explain the plural "mountains." Could it be that there is a theology in the background here according to which the *one* Mount Zion with its saving, precious blessing arises anew *everywhere* that Jews in the Diaspora assemble as sisters and brothers to praise God? Then the plural would have a real significance, and then Psalm 133 would reflect a kind of Diaspora theology such as we find in Psalm 87. There, too, the text speaks of the "holy mountains" of Zion (Ps 87:2), and the many nations become citizens of the Holy City.

If these observations are accurate we would have here, as in many other texts, a marvelous interplay of Old Testament and New Testament theology, for then the holy city Jerusalem, with Mount Zion, would arise wherever Christian communities assemble to praise

God—dispensing blessing and binding nations together in unity to form the one international people of God. That, at least, is what we read in the letter to the Hebrews:

> . . . *you have come to Mount Zion*
> *and to the city of the living God,*
> . . . *and to innumerable angels in festal gathering*
> . . . *and to the [festal] assembly . . .*
> *and to Jesus, the mediator of a new covenant.* (Heb 12:22-24)

Then every celebration of the Eucharist is a festive gathering on Mount Zion—an assembly that makes people of many classes and origins into one people of sisters and brothers.

Table Arrangements in the Reign of God

The gospels rather frequently describe Jesus' being invited to a meal. At one of those meals this happened: Jesus saw how the guests were seeking, unobtrusively but eagerly, to acquire the best seats. He said:

> *"When you are invited by someone to a wedding banquet, do not sit down at the place of honor, in case someone more distinguished than you has been invited by your host; and the host who invited both of you may come and say to you, 'Give this person your place,' and then in disgrace you would start to take the lowest place. But when you are invited, go and sit down at the lowest place, so that when your host comes, he may say to you, 'Friend, move up higher'; then you will be honored in the presence of all who sit at the table with you. For all who exalt themselves will be humbled, and those who humble themselves will be exalted."* (Luke 14:8-11)

Status Symbols

So the invited guests want the best places. Jesus is very familiar with that social game and he rightly condemns it. Of course, he also puts his finger on us because there is scarcely any drive within us as elementary as protecting our reputation and honor.

Every society has developed rituals and symbols meant to ensure that the place occupied by individuals in society is visibly documented. In Europe, in the Middle Ages and long afterward, there were official rules for clothing that marked the different classes. Their purpose was also to show the rank of each individual. The lower orders wore clothing made of hemp and sheep's wool; the upper classes wore expensive imported materials such as silk and velvet. Color also played an important role. The poor wore clothing in natural colors, especially grey and brown. The rich, in contrast, were permitted to wear materials dyed with precious imported hues. Purple was reserved for the upper nobility, and gold adornment was likewise permitted to them alone. Bourgeois women were not allowed to wear gold, even if they had it.

Those are examples from the past, but we have no need to travel back in time; nothing has changed. Social differences are still demonstratively marked. We have status symbols as obvious as those in the Middle Ages: an SUV limousine next to the smaller sedan, a second home in Portugal, a sailboat on the shore of Lake Champlain, a Rolex, a personal attorney. Even if we do not own a luxurious limousine or a second home—woe to anyone who attacks the position in which we see ourselves located.

It is true that we smirk at frantic attempts to make others aware of one's own status, and yet—perhaps in a more dignified way—we do exactly the same thing. We are careful to keep our weaknesses hidden and see to it that our achievements are honored. We long to be praised, even though we skillfully qualify the praise we receive. We refuse to accept help because we think we do not need it. We constantly compare ourselves with others around us and all too often we delicately disparage them—with the unacknowledged intention to advance ourselves. Basically, we do just what Jesus criticizes: we keep our eye on the best seats.

A Painful Text

What does Jesus advise us, then? What does he suggest we do instead? He tells us not to seek out the highest places, next to the host or at least close by. Instead, we should sit down in the lowest place; then the host will come and lead us to a better one.

But isn't Jesus advising us to play a game of false modesty that is all too transparent? Isn't he saying that we should choose a bad place in order to get a better one? Isn't that a *calculating* modesty that is not modest at all but aims at nothing but enhancing our own reputation? Isn't it pure strategy that has nothing to do with real humility?

We could read the text that way, but Jesus thought differently. He judges here with an eye to practical wisdom, or better, in the sense of the Old Testament's counsel for living. He simply speaks of what an experienced person would do: hold back, by no means choose the best place. He would do exactly what the biblical book of Proverbs advises the wise to do:

> *Do not put yourself forward in the king's presence or stand in the place of the great; for it is better to be told, "Come up here," than to be put lower in the presence of a noble.* (Prov 25:6-7)

Jesus applies this wisdom, already suggested by reason and possible of execution without any kind of background considerations, to shed light on relationships in the reign of God. The model behind his words is: if it is this way among experienced people in the normal world, then it will certainly and all the more be true in the reign of God. So Jesus makes an observation on real relationships among the guests into a parable about right behavior in the reign of God.

We are sadly in need of this parable, with its climactic statement: "all who exalt themselves will be humbled, and those who humble themselves will be exalted" (Luke 14:11). That tells us that God determines each one's worth, not we ourselves. It is a restatement of what Mary says in the Magnificat: "He has brought down the powerful from their thrones, and lifted up the lowly" (Luke 1:52).

Table Manners in the Reign of God

Where the reign of God is appearing there are different, altogether new possibilities for behavior. Where the reign of God is in bloom we no longer need to fight for places; we may allow them to be shown to us. Where the new life under the rule of God is beginning, we no longer have to "make a name" for ourselves because our names are written in heaven (Luke 10:20).

When we live together in the sight of God we no longer need to hide our weaknesses because there it is obvious that all are weak. We ourselves are the poor, the disabled, the blind, and the lame of whom the Gospel speaks (Luke 14:13). We can show our wounds because now all wounds can be healed.

Thus what Jesus says about right behavior at a festive banquet, what at first glance appears to be a somewhat unfortunate rule for politeness, overflows into a parable speech. The concrete behavior of the guests becomes an occasion for Jesus to make a fundamental statement about life in the reign of God. If Christians were living according to these table manners in the reign of God the world would no longer be recognizable. A revolution would have begun; everything would have been turned on its head.

So it would be a mistake to conclude from the social rule in Luke 14:8-10: "fine, it all depends on our improving our manners—not talking with our mouth full and not starting to eat until the lady of the house has begun, using our napkin correctly and not interrupting others, all of us being a little better behaved, a little more polite, a little more gracious. . . ."

The new thing Jesus began in Israel is not to be had that cheaply. The "new table arrangements in the reign of God" have entered the world in a different way. They are realized in that Jesus washed his disciples' feet at the Last Supper, doing what no one wants to do: the work of a slave (John 13:1-17).

However, that statement also has to be guarded against misunderstanding. It is not difficult, now and then, in festive moments, to offer noble gestures—embracing one another, carrying others' luggage, devoting an hour of our own precious time to them. We must not put the foot washing in the supper room on that level. Something greater happened there.

Jesus, in his own person, put an end to the constant battle between "master and slave"—the endless strife between "above and below," the eternal rivalry between the powerful and the weak. He brought an end to all that by living no longer for himself but fully and completely for God's cause—and thereby totally for others.

That was so monstrous and revolutionary that even the pious rebelled against him and killed him. It was only his death that uncovered our real situation, gave us new companionship at one table, made possible community in which those who serve and those who are served rejoice equally so that God's banquet can begin today. Since then, we are all participants in God's wedding with God's people and in what the book of Deuteronomy so longed for: the feast in the Holy City at which everyone, even the poor and strangers, can rejoice before God (Deut 16:9-12, 13-15). This feast has been made possible by Jesus' self-surrender, by him who chose the path to the lowest place.

Thus it is not a matter of showing a little more empathy but of understanding what has been given to us: a new life in the "city of the living God," the approach to the "festal gathering" that extends to eternity, participation in the eschatological meal that is beginning even today (Heb 12:18-29).

Since Jesus, "humbling oneself" does not mean a cramped, demeaning lowering of oneself before the other but the humble admission: "I did not deserve to be invited, but I was. I can be there, and the joy of the meal will never end. In that joy it does not matter to me in the least where I am seated."

Does Faith Produce Violence?

We in Europe have nearly forgotten that on September 11, 2001, Islamist terrorists flew two passenger planes into the two towers of the World Trade Center in New York. The twin towers completely collapsed, and 2,753 people were killed.

Since then an accusation has been circulating around the world; it had existed previously, but now it is growing louder: namely, that the most horrible violence in the world is the product of the religions. Because they are fixed and obstinate in their ideas, it is said, they are immovable and intolerant, dogmatic and ready to resort to violence. Now that willingness to exercise violence is all too easily converted into blind and aggressive rage. Therefore religions are dangerous, and the most dangerous of all are the monotheistic religions, because in them the dogmatic rigidity is most pronounced.

The English author Dick Francis, in one of his best mysteries (entitled *Straight*), writes almost as an aside and therefore all the more effectively: "Historically, more people have died of religion than cancer." I vehemently reject that infamous sentence. It cannot be proven. It is much more likely that humanity would long since have succumbed to depression without the consolation and joy of the religions. But I will not go into that here.

I do not deny that in the history of Christianity there have been intolerance, hatred, oppression, violence, and in many cases murder—carried out by Christians. What I do firmly dispute is that intolerance and violence are part of the nature of Christian faith. The exact opposite is the case. That is: when Christians have been intolerant, when they have hated, defamed, oppressed, excluded, and murdered, they were acting contrary to the New Testament, contrary to their origins, and against their own doctrine.

The Sermon on the Mount

As far as the New Testament is concerned, that is all completely clear. Ultimately, the Sermon on the Mount contains those incredible statements that strike all weapons from Christians' hands and obligate them to nonviolence:

> *Do not resist an evildoer. But if anyone strikes you on the right cheek, turn the other also; and if anyone wants to sue you and take your coat, give your cloak as well.* (Matt 5:39-40)

> *Love your enemies and pray for those who persecute you, so that you may be children of your Father in heaven; for he makes his sun rise on the evil and on the good, and sends rain on the righteous and on the unrighteous.* (Matt 5:44-45)

The church has been endowed with those statements, and they cannot be circumvented. They are altogether clear. They cannot be eliminated. They have an incredible power. They have changed the course of world history. They have been lived by countless Christians, not just by martyrs and saints. The failure of many Christians—indeed, the failure of whole Christian generations in the face of those sayings—cannot dismiss the Sermon on the Mount from the world or eliminate the history of its influence.

The Objection

Certainly I must, of course, immediately address the objection one always hears at this point: "Yes," someone says, "those statements in the Sermon on the Mount are very clear, but the New Testament and the Old are a single book, and the Old Testament does present a God of violence, a jealous, intolerant, fanatical, and cruel God who calls for hatred and destruction. That makes Christians' 'sacred scripture' *as a whole* just as conflicted as the Qu'ran."

What shall we say to this objection, which is not only hammered into Christians' ears from outside but also lurks in the minds of many believers?

The objection has no notion of the real Bible because it does not comprehend the relationship between Old and New Testaments. That is, the New Testament, with its demands for nonviolence and love of enemies, is not an accidental and random appendix to the Old Testament; it is its definitive interpretation and clarification. From a formal point of view the New Testament is for Christians the "final redaction" of the Old. Because the New Testament excludes violence and intolerance, all the violent texts in the Old Testament are placed within a new context. They must now be read in light of the New Testament—where they must be critiqued and perhaps understood at greater depth in light of this "final redaction." The Old Testament does not yet contain the unique voice that clarifies the whole: the voice of Jesus Christ.

Many voices speak in the Old Testament, because it is on a journey out of the religions to the one, true God. The theologians and prophets of biblical Israel led their own people along that road in a way that is truly revolutionary. That did not happen without advancing knowledge, massive opposition, and a good many setbacks. Hence the many voices! At first glance they seem to be shouting at each other in chaotic confusion.

This is especially clear when the subject is violence. The Old Testament does, in fact, contain texts that assume violence as a matter of course or even call for it. To that extent the critics are correct. But what they overlook is that in the Old Testament itself, quite without reference to the New Testament, there is a steadily increasing critique of violence. That growing critique is apparent especially in postexilic texts in which Israel looks back at its own history—a history brimming with violence from without and also within and among the people of God itself.

Critique of Violence in the Old Testament

Consider, for example, the first chapters of Genesis, the primal history that makes up the beginning of the Torah. In those chapters God looks at creation and sees that the world has not become what, according to the divine will, it ought to be. World society is full of violence. Genesis 6:11-13 says explicitly:

> *Now the earth was corrupt in God's sight, and the earth was filled with violence. And God saw that the earth was corrupt; for all flesh had corrupted its ways upon the earth. And God said to Noah, "I have determined to make an end of all flesh, for the earth is filled with violence because of them. . . ."*

This text and the story of the great flood that follows are meant to tell readers and hearers that God does not approve of violence in the world. God wants a different world: one without intimidation, without threats, without corruption, without misuse of power, and without violence. God wants a world society that lives in justice and peace.

But how can such peace be established in the world? The Old Testament gives an astounding answer: not by means of a nation in the world that is stronger than all the others—a nation that will strike down every emerging source of violence with still greater violence and so play the role of a world police force. The temptation to think that way is great, because there are also advantages to having a world police. It is even necessary, just as police and courts of justice are needed in individual countries. And yet in its authoritative prophetic texts, in which the multiple experiences and hopes of Israel are concentrated, the Old Testament does not anticipate the end of violence through counterviolence.

Swords into Plowshares

I am thinking here, for example, of Isaiah 2:2-5. Here world peace is not established through a people that is better armed and more powerful than all others but through the people of God, which listens to the instruction of its God and lives as a just society. In precisely that way Israel will become a city on a hill to which all nations look, indeed make pilgrimage, to learn how a right society is constructed.

It is still a vision. According to Isaiah 2 that state of the world has not yet been achieved, but the people of God must begin to live as God's longed-for society. Then it will come to the whole world. This incredibly audacious text reads:

> *In days to come*
> *the mountain of the Lord's house*
> *shall be established as the highest of the mountains,*
> *and shall be raised above the hills;*
> *all the nations shall stream to it.*
> *Many peoples shall come and say,*
> *"Come, let us go up to the mountain of the Lord,*
> *to the house of the God of Jacob;*
> *that he may teach us his ways*
> *and that we may walk in his paths."*

> *For out of Zion shall go forth instruction,*
> *and the word of the* Lord *from Jerusalem.*
> *He shall judge between the nations,*
> *and shall arbitrate for many peoples;*
> *they shall beat their swords into plowshares,*
> *and their spears into pruning hooks;*
> *nation shall not lift up sword against nation,*
> *neither shall they learn war any more.*
> *O house of Jacob,*
> *come, let us walk*
> *in the light of the* Lord*!* (Isa 2:2-5)

This text thus asserts that world peace will only be achieved through
nonviolence, by the destruction of all weapons. But the new peaceful
world order is not founded on the insight of the nations—in modern
terms, on their enlightened reason, their dialogues and conferences.
It comes from the instruction of Israel's God. This God proclaims a
new social order, and that new order must first of all be lived—by
the people of God themselves, who will make the instruction and
nonviolence of its God a reality in its own midst. Only when that
happens will peace be possible for the other nations as well. Hence
the appeal to Israel at the end of the vision: "O house of Jacob, come,
let us walk in the light of the Lord!" (Isa 2:5).

Now let each judge for herself or himself: Is the God behind Isaiah
2 a God of violence, a God of aggression, a God who rages and destroys? But the Old Testament goes much further. It knows from its
people's own history that the one who eschews violence must often
then suffer violence and be ruthlessly trodden down by those who
rely on power alone. So the authors who created Isaiah 40–55 (so-
called Deutero-Isaiah) fashioned the four Servant Songs out of the
experience of Israel, oppressed and trodden down by the nations. In
the symbolic figure of the "Servant of God" they speak of disempow-
ered and exiled Israel.

God's Servant

Against this "servant of God," that is, tiny Israel, whose representative figures have already been exiled to Babylon, the nations have
come together. They crush the servant of God, but he remains faithful
to his God and seeks refuge in God alone. He does not strike back

against the violence concentrated on him, nor does he avoid it. In just this way the servant of God astonishes the world of the nations. In Isaiah 53 we suddenly hear a confession by the powerful who have raged against the servant of God. The nations and their kings realize what this outcast was and what God wills through him. Now they must confess:

> . . . *we accounted him stricken,*
> *struck down by God, and afflicted.*
> *But he was wounded for our transgressions,*
> *crushed for our iniquities . . .* (vv. 4b-5)

With this theology of the book of Isaiah, the Scripture has reached a point that cannot be superseded. It is a revolution in thought, one that overturns everything—and it is found in the Old Testament itself. It is the insight that it is better to be a victim than a violent victor. It is the realization that true peace in the world can only be created by the victims, never by the victors.

Certainly interpreters have never been able to agree about whether the Servant of God in Isaiah is simply the embodiment of defeated Israel or is an individual in whose life Israel's fate is reflected. There is, indeed, much in favor of the idea that the Servant of God in the book of Isaiah represents Israel living in Babylonian exile. But here we can leave the question open.

The King of Peace for Israel

After all, in the text toward which I have been pressing all this while, the question is clearly decided in favor of an individual. In the book of the prophet Zechariah, which offers one of the latest but also most important texts on the subject of violence, the Messiah—that is, the figure of an individual—brings peace to Israel and to the world.

The background here may be one of Israel's most profound experiences: it is better to be a victim than a violent victor—yes, but to be purely a victim is something that a whole people cannot manage and certainly cannot sustain. Better: the people of God can only do that if an individual will precede it on the path of absolute nonviolence.

That is precisely the theme of Zechariah 9:9-10. The Messiah, about whom all Jerusalem is erupting here in joy, comes on a donkey, the mount of the poor. It is impossible to make war while riding on a donkey. So the Messiah-king comes as a nonviolent person, pacific and bringing peace. The Messiah will destroy the chariots of Ephraim and expel the steeds of Jerusalem. Note: it is not the weapons of Israel's enemies that are destroyed; the people of God themselves lay down their arms. Thus this late text restates what Isaiah 2 had already said, but now interprets it in terms of the Messiah who is to come.

As I have said: the text of Zechariah 9 is late. When it was written, Alexander the Great had already established a world empire extending from Egypt to India with his Macedonian military tactics. The Messiah on the donkey is most probably a deliberately contrasting image to the world ruler Alexander on his war steed. This Jewish Messiah-king has no power—or, better, his only powers are meekness and humility. And yet that kind of power is greater than that of Alexander.

Thus we find concentrated in Zechariah 9:9-10 a long line of Old Testament teaching. We could summarize it this way: God does not want a world full of violence, and God's means for healing such a world is a people that lives nonviolence. That means, however, that this people must become a victim. And because a whole nation cannot do that, there must be one who precedes it on the path of absolute nonviolence so that, then, as many members of the people of God as possible can follow in those footsteps.

Jesus: Epitome of Peace

That is the breadth and depth of Old Testament thought. The New Testament could not say more; it could only add that this *One* has, in fact, come. He experienced everything the Old Testament had already seen, and now all that remains is that he win over his people to prefer being victim rather than being perpetrator of violence. Against that background Jesus says:

> *"Come to me,*
> *all you that are weary and are carrying heavy burdens,*
> *and I will give you rest.*
> *Take my yoke upon you, and learn from me;*
> *for I am gentle and humble in heart,*
> *and you will find rest for your souls."* (Matt 11:28-30)

The "rest" Jesus speaks of so urgently here is not primarily the soul's sweet rest of interiority but also and above all rest in the land, relief from enemies, the repose in which, at evening, each can sit before her house and under his fig tree. This Jesus saying, like many of his other words, is primarily intended in a social sense. Jesus is thinking of the peace that comes from nonviolence; he means the peace of the people of God that the prophets of Israel desired for the whole world. With an incredible instinct and unheard-of certainty Jesus takes up the best texts of the Old Testament. He lives entirely out of the Old Testament, and he brings it to fulfillment.

After all this, can we still say that the Old Testament proclaims a violent God, a God of aggression and intolerance? No, in contrast to the Qu'ran, the Bible is clear about the question of violence, and not only through the New Testament. In the Old Testament itself the criticism of violence grows ever louder, and the Old Testament already accomplished the gigantic revolution in thought, the idea that it is better to be a victim than a violent victor.

We should be proud of this peace tradition that began with Abraham, blazes forth again and again in the Old Testament, is definitively finalized in Jesus, and into which, through faith and baptism, we have been received.

Cursing, Then and Now

In the year 1967, during excavations at Tel Dēr ʿAllā, an Aramaic text that speaks of a seer named Balaam was discovered on plaster remnants of a wall. The text comes from the end of the ninth century BCE and is therefore very old. Unfortunately, it consists only of fragments. Still, the fragments show that this Balaam was regarded at the time as a famous seer. His homeland was most probably in Mesopotamia.

Curses Were Not Empty Words

Israel was not alone in having seers and prophets; they were found among other peoples as well. They interpreted the present and the future, but they were also summoned to bless and curse, and psychologists and cultural historians today tell us, correctly, that at that time curses were anything but harmless. They worked on all those who believed they did, and such belief was universal in the ancient Near East. In many cultures today as well, the evil eye and cursing are seen as so effective that people use a variety of countermeasures to try to shield themselves.

We have to read the biblical story of the seer Balaam in Numbers 22–24 against that background. When the King of Moab employs Balaam, for a high price, to curse Israel, the curse is supposed to weaken Abraham's people so much that its vitality will be destroyed. Given the contemporary mentality, that was a serious danger for Israel, even though in the middle of the story a theological reflection assures us that "surely there is no enchantment against Jacob, no divination against Israel" (Num 23:23).

The text now found in the Bible has a long prehistory, as we can see when we examine it. Some of its lines even seem to contradict others. But the overall direction of the narrative is quite clear: Balaam is supposed to curse Israel, but he cannot. He can only bless this people; more precisely, as soon as he tries to curse them he has to recognize that the power of the true God stands behind Israel. He must recognize that Israel is abundantly blessed by its God, and so his attempt to curse them is suddenly transformed into a blessing. Nevertheless, the king of Moab doesn't surrender so easily. He tries again and again, using different setups, to get Balaam to curse them. Instead, his stubbornness only magnifies the blessings on Israel.

"How Fair Are Your Tents, O Jacob!"

Most profound theologically and most beautiful in its wording is Balaam's third blessing (Num 24:5-9):

> *"How fair are your tents, O Jacob,*
> *your encampments, O Israel!*
> *Like palm groves that stretch far away,*
> *like gardens beside a river,*
> *like aloes that the* Lord *has planted,*
> *like cedar trees beside the waters.*
> *Water shall flow from his buckets,*
> *and his seed shall have abundant water . . ."* (Num 24:5-7)

But it is not only Balaam's blessings that are elevated poetic texts. Another masterwork is the narrative, using motifs from fable, that describes Baalam's comical battle with his donkey (Num 22:21-35). We must read the story as a text within a text. It intends to show, in its own way, that under no circumstances will God allow Israel to be cursed. At the same time, with hefty irony, it shows how even an ass can be wiser than a prophet who does not follow the way of God.

However, the episode with the she-ass is only a delaying element in the resolute forward march of the action. Israel has been chosen by God and therefore is blessed by God and indestructible. Those who seek its destruction will never reach their goal. In this way the text inaugurates a powerful theological line of thought that began already in Genesis 12:3, where God says to Abraham:

> *"I will bless those who bless you, and the one who curses you I will curse;*
> *and in you all the families of the earth shall be blessed."*

Balaam's third speech takes up that promise:

> "*Blessed is everyone who blesses you,*
> *and cursed is everyone who curses you.*" (Num 24:9)

In the great Matthean text about the judgment of the world (Matt 25:31-46), where the "blessed" and the "cursed" stand over against one another, this biblical theme then receives its Jesus-form as he says to those blessed by God: "just as you did it to one of the least of these who are members of my family, you did it to me" (Matt 25:40).

In recent decades that statement has become a favorite preaching text. The "least of these who are members of my family" (or: "the least of my sisters and brothers") are almost always equated with all those who suffer throughout the world. Jesus meets us in those poor, those people in need. As lovely and correct as the thought is, Matthew 25:31-46 is referring to something else.

Here the least in Jesus' family are not the poor of this earth but Jesus' persecuted and suffering disciples—that is, eschatological Israel (see only Matt 10:40, 42). Anyone who comes to the aid of Jesus' disciples is helping Jesus' cause and therefore belongs to those who are "blessed" by his Father.

God has tied the salvation of the world to what God began with Abraham and what continues in the persecuted communities of Jesus. They are infinitely precious to God, who comes to the aid of anyone who supports them. Those who do not support them, who even persecute them, destroy their own lives. As much as God is on the side of all the poor, what is most important in the world for God is the existence of God's people, because in the long run it is only through this people that the misery of the world can really be relieved.

Are There Curses in Our Day?

As we have seen, in the ancient Near East a curse was not innocuous. It had effective power. But isn't that magical thinking? Aren't we far beyond such strategies for dealing with the world?

By no means! In reality that is all much closer to us than we think. After all, a curse was not intended to destroy; its purpose was to drain the life force from the world in which the accursed lived—from their tribe, their people, the community of nations, or even the people of God. It was meant not only to kill but to extinguish the memory of the accursed. In the Old Testament, Psalm 109 gives us a striking example of such an attempt to ruin people. In it a faithful Israelite is cursed with all proper ceremony, thus:

> *When he is tried, let him be found guilty;*
> *let his prayer be counted as sin.*
> *May his days be few;*
> *may another seize his position.*
> *May his children be orphans,*
> *and his wife a widow.*
> *May his children wander about and beg;*
> *may they be driven out of the ruins they inhabit.*
> *May the creditor seize all that he has;*
> *may strangers plunder the fruits of his toil.*
> *May there be no one to do him a kindness,*
> *nor anyone to pity his orphaned children.*
> *May his posterity be cut off;*
> *may his name be blotted out in the second generation.*
> *May the iniquity of his father be remembered before the* LORD,
> *and do not let the sin of his mother be blotted out.*
> *Let them be before the* LORD *continually,*
> *and may his memory be cut off from the earth.*
> . . .
> *He clothed himself with cursing as his coat,*
> *may it soak into his body like water,*
> *like oil into his bones.* (Ps 109:7-15, 18)

This great curse is thus intended to have someone in Israel declared guilty before a judge, but not only that! The person's life is to be so corrupted that even his prayer, the most profound expression of his faith, will be sin. And not only that! Her existence and that of her family are to be destroyed. Even the memory of him, or her, with spouse and children, is to be extinguished.

What is so horrifying in all this is that this life-destroying curse is uttered in the name of God and in the name of piety and humanity. Those who want here, quite literally, to eliminate an entire family appeal explicitly to God, and they accuse their opponent of having violated the love-commandment (v. 16: "For he did not remember to show kindness, but pursued the poor and needy and the broken-hearted to their death").

The Old Testament contains no other cursing text that is as broadly conceived or as aggressively formulated as the one just quoted. But the one uttering the curse is not the speaker of the psalm; it only quotes the curses of the opponent, directed against the one praying the psalm. The extended curse at the center (vv. 7-18), in which the opponents' charges are grouped together, is in fact a parenthesis surrounded by the prayer of the one being cursed (vv. 1-5; 20-31). This framing shows what is really happening here. Those who, in the name of faith, want to destroy the presence and the memory of a person with her or his whole family from the midst of the people of God "speak with lying tongues" (v. 2) and "reward . . . evil for good" (v. 5).

Thus Psalm 109 illustrates, shatteringly, that it is not only pagans (as in the story of Balaam) who want to destroy the people of God, but that there was something comparable within the people of God itself: those who preen themselves as pious and faithful want to destroy their own sisters and brothers in the faith.

The same thing happens today, as it did then, though with other means and mechanisms. Cursing technique today takes the form of "fake news," that is, false information deliberately promulgated to the world, and—most dangerous of all—in the form of "facts" that are distorted and interpreted one-sidedly. What did Georg Christoph Lichtenberg (1742–1799), the great master of physics, mathematics, and aphorisms, say on this subject?

> *The most dangerous of all falsehoods*
> *is a slightly distorted truth.*[1]

Character assassination of this type is found not only in the popular press and social media; it is often practiced in serious media as well—even in Christian media. And no one should say that this modern style of cursing is ineffective. It can be as efficient and evil as ancient magic—when it is believed.

---

[1] Georg Christoph Lichtenberg, *Notebook H (1784–1788)*, 7, at https://www.goodreads.com/quotes/428551.

A Battle in the Wilderness

The story of Israel's time in the wilderness contains an episode that is highly instructive. It is the story of the battle with the Amalekites in Exodus 17:8-16. As late as the time of Saul, that Bedouin tribe, which controlled important caravan routes in the Sinai peninsula, remained one of Israel's bitterest enemies.

The battle itself is not described in detail. The crucial feature of the narrative is the role played by Moses. While Israel's army is fighting, led by Joshua, Moses stands on a hill, visible to all those fighting. In one hand he holds the staff of God (see Exod 4:1-5, 17, 20) and the other hand is extended over Israel's fighters (Exod 17:9-11). As long as Moses holds up his hands, Israel is stronger; whenever he lowers them because of his exhaustion, Amalek's strength increases. As Moses' hands become heavier and heavier his companions give him a rock to sit on, and they support his arms from both sides so they can remain aloft until sundown. So Israel conquers.

How Can the People of God Survive?

For the moment let us forget the question whether the people of God may make war at all, as other peoples do, and most certainly let us set aside the question whether the motif of lifted hands that make victory possible may represent magical thinking. Instead, let us simply accept the narrative as an image that tells us how the people of God can survive.

Joshua and his army have to fight, but it is not only their courage, and most certainly not their numbers, that make them victorious over the enemies. It is only Moses' lifted hands that bring victory, as the subsequent story featuring Jethro, Moses' father-in-law, shows: Moses "represents the people before God" and "brings their cases before God," and God teaches Israel "the way they are to go and the things they are to do" (Exod 18:19-20). So in our story Moses represents the helping, saving action of God that empowers Israel, showing it the way.

On the other hand, in spite of Moses' lifted hands Israel could not defeat Amalek unless its army staked its life on fighting the whole day long. So God's action does not replace human action; Israel's survival is God's work and at the same time the work of Israel itself. What the God of Abraham, Isaac, and Jacob desires to have happen in the world can only be done through people who understand God's thoughts, take on God's work, and make it their own.

Certainly it would be altogether wrong and would discount Israel's religious-critical discernment to interpret this mutuality between God and God's people according to the model of a "cooperative" division of labor: God does half by intervening at critical points in history and people do the other half, allowing God to help at points where their strength runs out. No, Israel's survival is wholly and entirely God's work: Moses' hands must remain outstretched from morning till evening. But at the same time, the survival of the people of God is wholly and entirely the work of human beings: Joshua and his army have to fight from morning till evening.

The People of God Needs a Center

The theology of our narrative, however, extends much further: Moses not only represents God's uninterrupted action; he is also the representative of Israel, its intercessor, its advocate before God. So the narrative makes a further statement, this time in the sense of genuine cooperation.

Israel needs warriors like Joshua who stick out their necks and risk their lives, but it also needs a Moses it can look up to. The power that comes from Moses is certainly not the power to wage war, but it is just as important: the people of God cannot live without orientation, without a central figure who points the way. It needs a figure who is widely recognizable and whose faith is consolation and support for Israel. It needs a visible sign of unanimity. Only with the two together—the role of Joshua and that of Moses—can the people of God survive in the long term.

The narrative even offers a further refinement: Israel needs not only battling Joshua and strength-giving Moses. Moses himself needs help: his two companions have to support him so that he can hold his arms aloft and not let them sink.

This tense combination of very different charisms receives still further consideration in the subsequent narrative in Exodus 18:13-26 as Moses is visited by his Midianite father-in-law, Jethro. Jethro is an experienced man. He knows how to rule. When he sees how Moses gives judgment "from morning till evening" (note the repetition of the motif!) and then is completely exhausted by nightfall, he advises him to delegate duties and install chiefs over thousands, hundreds, fifties, and tens. They can help him in carrying out his office; otherwise "you will surely wear yourself out, both you and these people with you" (Exod 18:18). Moses takes his father-in-law's advice and shares responsibility.

A Center That Enables Unanimity

So also the following chapter, Exodus 18, reflects on the community within the people of God. It is a mutual willingness to help and to be helped, and for Moses it means that he need not try to do everything himself. However: the people of God needs a broadly recognizable, judging, and inspiring center such as Moses. That center makes unanimity possible and represents the hidden center that God is within Israel.

If we consider the lines of this very subtle theology, the question whether the people of God may fight with the sword ceases to be so troubling. There are clear answers to that question in other Old Testament texts, and it is then definitively decided by Jesus when he tells Peter: "Put your sword back into its place, for all [among the people of God] who take the sword will perish by the sword" (Matt 26:52).

We need not burden our narrative with the question of nonviolence. The subject here is different. This story is about what makes it possible for the people of God to survive, portraying a repeated experience in Israel: namely, that God does everything and at the same time God's people must do everything—and then it also speaks of the community of believers within the people of God that, gifted with a variety of charisms and offices, goes its way in a unity fashioned around a single center.

Elijah Wants to Die

The first book of Kings tells how, one day, the prophet Elijah wishes he were dead (1 Kgs 19:1-5). He has fled to the place where, at that time, every Israelite went when hunted and persecuted: the wilderness. It was possible to hide in the maze of countless gorges and wadis; there were cracks and caves in the chalk cliffs where no one could find you. One problem: there was no food to be had, and worse still, there was no water. You would die of thirst.

Against the Cult of Ba'al

So Elijah is on the run. He is being sought by the royal police forces of King Ahab and Queen Jezebel. Ahab ruled the Northern Kingdom (Israel), and he had married the Canaanite woman Jezebel, daughter of the king of Sidon. It was a political marriage. Jezebel brought her gods with her to Samaria, above all Ba'al, the weather god who controlled rain and fertility. Thus the cult of Ba'al was now officially sanctioned in Israel alongside that of YHWH. The king himself built a temple to Ba'al in Samaria and established an official cult for Ba'al there (1 Kgs 16:29-33).

Evidently a good many people in Israel found that quite attractive. Elijah was the only one who raised a public protest and thereby attracted the deadly hatred of the queen. She sent word to him that she would have him killed (1 Kgs 19:2).

Elijah's very name was programmatic. "Eli-Jah" means "My God is Y(a)H[WH]," and of course in this case it meant "*My* God is YHWH and no other." Elijah's mission was to make sure that in Israel only YHWH would be worshiped. He was convinced that the God whom Israel had experienced in its history must not be dragged into the world of the Ba'als and thus placed on the same level with them. If YHWH were worshiped alongside other gods, that was apostasy from the ancestral faith. Therefore Elijah confronted the people with the question:

> *"How long will you go limping with two different opinions [at the same time]?*
> *If YHWH is God, follow him; but if Ba'al, then follow him."* (1 Kgs 18:21)

That is probably an allusion to the cultic hopping dance of the priests of Ba'al (1 Kgs 18:26). They danced before Ba'al, incorporating complicated contortions first in one direction and then immediately in the other. Israel is twisting itself in the same way: now toward YHWH, now toward Ba'al, depending on which is more useful at any given time.

Elijah's Lament

"How long will you go limping in two directions?" was Elijah's literal question. But the people were stubbornly silent and gave Elijah no answer (1 Kgs 18:21). They did not want to give up their worship of Ba'al. The final text, as it presently reads, then tells of God's powerful judgment on Mount Carmel, causing the people to fall on their faces and confess the true God of Israel (1 Kgs 18:30-40), but in the very next chapter the crisis is renewed by the isolation of Elijah, brought about not only by Queen Jezebel's threats but even more by the absence of faith in Israel. Have the people already forgotten their confession of YHWH on Mount Carmel? In any case, Elijah is still socially ostracized and in deadly danger, so he flees into the wilderness and hopes for death. He expresses his anguish to God with a lament:

> *"I have been very zealous for YHWH, the God of hosts; for the Israelites have*
> *forsaken your covenant, thrown down your altars, and killed your prophets*
> *with the sword. I alone am left, and they are seeking my life, to take it away."*
> (1 Kgs 19:10)

It is true that, as the narrative continues, Elijah's lament receives correction. God tells the prophet:

> *"I will leave seven thousand in Israel, all the knees that have not bowed to*
> *Baal, and every mouth that has not kissed him."* (1 Kgs 19:18)

So Elijah is not alone. There are many more than Elijah knows who have remained faithful to Israel's God. Still, his lament touches something essential: In this moment the history of God with God's people really depends on his own passionate zeal. The seven thousand silent Israelites in the land would not be enough, no matter how important they are.

What Makes the Difference

"I alone am left." If we see Israel's faith as mere religion and the history of that faith as nothing more than the history of a religion, we can only see this lament by Elijah as a massive overstatement. The "religious" sentiment is deeply rooted in human beings and can never be eliminated because it takes its starting point from human needs. The "religious" never depends on the fidelity of an individual. This is clear in light of the free-floating forms of religion that have arisen with the retreat of Christianity: they all relate to natural elements, to the well-being of the individual ego, to self-discovery and powers of self-healing. Salvation lies in the self.

Israel's faith, however, is far beyond what the religions find essential. It is not primarily about human needs but rather about the will of God, that is, God's plan for the world. Likewise, Israel's faith is not about what has always been lovely and has moved human beings, but about what God began anew with Abraham, contrary to all human possibilities. In a world that only revolves around its own concerns and therefore unceasingly hops back and forth, that faith is in acute danger. The new thing always hung by a thin thread; day by day it depends on the faith of a few and whether those few continue to find followers.

We have to keep this background in mind if we want to understand the stories about Elijah in 1 Kings in their full import. Elijah, far out in the wilderness; Elijah, under a broom tree; Elijah, in profound resignation; Elijah, wishing to die. We understand his resignation. Even today many in the church say bitterly: "There is no point to any of it. My work is useless. Unbelief is growing, and along with contempt for God society is increasingly adopting as its guiding principle that the individual ego is the measure of all things. Who can possibly change that?"

It is in precisely this situation, though, that an angel comes to strengthen Elijah. The angel says to him:

> *"Get up and eat." He looked, and there at his head was a cake baked on hot stones, and a jar of water. He ate and drank, and lay down again. The angel of the* Lord *came a second time, touched him, and said, "Get up and eat, otherwise the journey will be too much for you." He got up, and ate and drank; then he went in the strength of that food forty days and forty nights to Horeb the mount of God.* (1 Kgs 19:5-8)

Making the Origin Present

Thus Elijah receives help. He gets sufficient food to enable him to walk to the mountain of God, the place where God was first revealed to the people and gave them a social order. Elijah is led to the origin. This bringing of the origin into the present is the real help for the people of God. Not nostalgia, not a false romanticism about the origin, not *return* to the origin, but *making it present*! Elijah receives enough bread, enough strength and aid, to make it possible for him to make the origin present.

In this way God provides in order that the imperiled threads of salvation history will not break. For a moment in the history of the people of God everything depended on a single person: Elijah. But God strengthened him. God saw to it that he was provided with bread so that he might go on living.

The liturgy links these stories about Elijah with our own story, with that of the church that again and again gathers around the table of the Eucharist. In this way it means to tell us that what is at stake is the continuation of God's history. That depends on every one of us. God does not leave us helpless but gives us the bread of the Eucharist that joins us, each time, to our origin: namely, the preaching of Jesus, his death, and his resurrection.

A Cloak Flies Through the Air

When God comes, all too often there is no place left. We have already made our arrangements. All the rooms in the house of our life are full. We have our own ideas, our own wishes, our longings, our dreams. We have already accepted all kinds of duties. We know what we want. There is no space left for God—and after all, does God have any right to intrude on our private lives?

"I have to care for my parents," says one. "I have a family, after all," says another. "My job demands all the strength I have," says a third. "I am building a house," says a fourth. "I don't have time."

"I have bought a piece of land, and I must go out and see it; please accept my regrets," says one. "I have bought five yoke of oxen, and I am going to try them out; please accept my regrets," another apologizes. "I have just been married, and therefore I cannot come," says the third of the invitees in Jesus' parable of the great dinner (Luke 14:18-20)!

Those are certainly not idle excuses! All the reasons are valid! But we always have valid reasons, and God always comes last. Given all that, God's cause in the world should have been finished by now; we have constructed our lives in such a way that there is not much time left for God. When God calls us, we are as busy as can be. Still . . . it could be altogether different, and that would be a real miracle. It is from such miracles that Israel lived and the church lives.

A Cloak Flies Through the Air

The prophet Elijah lived in the Northern Kingdom of Israel during the royal period. As more and more Israelites fell away from the true God and turned to the much more convenient and attractive gods of the land, Elijah was almost alone in standing for YHWH's cause. Elijah complained about being so alone; he was mortally weary (1 Kgs 19:4-5).

Then God said to him (we are simply following the biblical narrative): You already have a successor. I have someone in mind who will continue your work (1 Kgs 19:16). Soon after, Elijah meets Elisha (1 Kgs 19:19-21), who is engaged in plowing. He has not been educated as a prophet; he is a farmer and the son of a rich landowner, for his fields are not on the barren slopes of the mountains but in the fruitful lowlands where it is possible to plow with several pairs of oxen. Elisha is working with no fewer than twelve spans, and he himself is working behind *one* of them.

Elijah passes by and throws his prophet's mantle over Elisha as he is plowing. It is a prophetic symbolic action that means: now you are my helper. You belong to me, and thereby you are also God's helper in carrying out the great plan God has made for bringing salvation to the world. God needs people for that: you, in particular. Come and help!

Elisha is profoundly moved. He understands that this is about God's cause, which is more important than his own, more important than the twelve span of oxen and all the broad acres of his parental farm. Elisha's heart is burning. He wants to follow Elijah.

But then the "serious reasons" we all know make themselves heard. The matter is not so simple. In any case he must first take leave of his parents. Literally, the text of 1 Kings 19:20 says he must "kiss them again." Above all, he has to discuss the whole situation with his parents. A lot of arrangements will be necessary; there are important matters to consider. Leaving everything behind—that is not so simple.

Elijah understands what is happening in Elisha's mind. He says: "What have I done to you?" (1 Kgs 19:20). That means: certainly, go to your parents! You are altogether free. No one is compelled to serve God, and in case you don't want to, pretend that nothing has happened between us. You can go your own way.

In the Middle of the Field

The narrative does not tell us what happened within the wealthy heir in that moment of liberation; it only says how he acted: he did not return home. He did not even take the time to collect wood and meat for a farewell meal with his workers. He is so moved by God's cause that he loses no time. He simply has the servants chop up the wooden yokes, make a fire, and slaughter two of the oxen. Then he holds a farewell feast with his workers in the middle of the field, and after that he follows Elijah (1 Kgs 19:21).

So God does find a place in the world. God again and again finds people who allow their lives to be overturned for the sake of God's cause. God even finds people who hear that divine voice and act immediately where they are. The Bible is full of such stories.

Jesus calls the fishermen Simon and Andrew, who are casting their nets: "Come, follow me," and they follow (Mark 1:16-18). He says one day to another: "Follow me!" and that one says: "Lord, first let me go and bury my father." The situation is not altogether clear to us; either the father had just died, or the person called is asking for time to care for his elderly parent until his death so that he may fulfill the requirement of respect for parents written in the fourth commandment. To him Jesus says the shocking words: "Let the dead bury their own dead; but as for you, go and proclaim the kingdom of God" (Luke 9:59-60). Still another comes to Jesus because he is deeply moved by him. He says he wants to follow Jesus, but first he must take leave of his family. Jesus says to him: "No one who puts a hand to the plow and looks back is fit for the kingdom of God" (Luke 9:61-62).

All those stories clash with our bourgeois reason. But what does that bourgeois reason do? It has never really solved a single problem in this world. The poor are still hungry. The world is full of refugees. Wars and threats of war are unceasing. Hope for the world depends solely on God's repeatedly finding people for the salvation God wants to create—people who allow themselves to be moved, who make room for God, who do not say: "Soon!" or "Next year!" or "If I may just take care of this and that . . ."

Yes, God finds people. Because we are all afraid of such a thing this is probably the greatest miracle that happens in the world. It is pardonable that we first defend ourselves within and say: "That can't happen; why me?" That would be completely normal. What is important, however, is that we do not close ourselves off, but instead let the miracle of obedience to God happen to us.

Many Kinds of Calling

The stories of how Jesus calls disciples are in many ways similar to the narrative of the calling of Elisha. Those called recognize immediately: "I am the one, I myself. And it is about the most important thing in the world." In the face of such a cause it is impossible to delay answering. One cannot say "maybe" or "later" or "only under such and such conditions." One can only say "yes" immediately, as Elisha did, as Peter and Andrew and all the apostles did.

Still, there is another method for avoiding such a calling; it is to say: "a calling for the reign of God—that is only for priests or for men and women who enter a religious order. It is only for people who make vows, putting their whole lives at God's disposal. That is not for me. I am a 'normal' Christian. I do not have that kind of calling, so the stories of Elisha or those about how the apostles were called have nothing to do with me."

Such arguments avoid the issue; they are evasions, an effort to avoid God. Everyone who has been baptized and received the Holy Spirit is called, and in the church there are many callings.

For example, there is the call to poverty but also the call to wealth, which means using one's property in a way that serves God's cause. There is the calling to celibacy for the sake of the kingdom of heaven but there is also the calling to marriage for the sake of the heavenly reign. That means opening one's marriage and family to God's cause, as many married couples have done throughout the church's history. I think, for example, of Prisca and Aquila, who received Paul into their house, gave him a job, and supported his missionary work. It may well be that without the help of that couple Paul would have been unable to accomplish quite a few things (Acts 18:1-4).

There are countless different callings in the church. Every baptized person has her or his own; each has an opportunity to serve God's cause that is appropriate to that person. For each it is only a matter of listening carefully to what God wants of one, and then saying "yes" without hesitation—like Elisha, like Simon and Andrew, and like countless Christians in the course of the church's history.

Mary and Martha

Again and again the evangelist Luke surprises us with narratives that are not to be found in the other three gospels. But after all, he says in the introduction to his gospel that he has "investigated everything carefully from the very first" (Luke 1:3). One of the accounts that Luke probably obtained from reliable sources and "servants of the Word" tells of the two sisters Mary and Martha. Luke relates how one day the two were visited by Jesus and his disciples (Luke 10:38-42). Martha, evidently the head of the household, "welcomed him into her home" (Luke 10:38).

Martha and Mary

So we are to picture Jesus in the house, in conversation with others, surrounded by his disciples (Luke 10:23, 38) and perhaps some of the neighbors. But at his feet sits Mary, gazing at Jesus, doing nothing but listening and looking and forgetting everything else. Also present is her sister Martha, who is depicted as the counterimage to Mary. She is fully engaged in caring for her guests. Probably she is preparing the evening meal besides making all sorts of arrangements for the crowd that has suddenly invaded her house.

We can imagine how busy she is, how she tries to bring some order out of the chaos that, she believes, would erupt if she does not keep a tight grip on everything. We can also imagine how from time to time she casts an annoyed glance at her sister, who is not lifting a finger to help her.

At some point she can't stand it any longer. Her annoyance explodes and she makes a little scene before Jesus—although with some skill, clothing her speech in polite language:

> *"Lord, do you not care that my sister has left me to do all the work by myself? Tell her then to help me."* (Luke 10:40)

She thus not only shames her sister publicly but also makes a mild accusation against Jesus: ". . . do you not care . . . ?" Jesus comes to Mary's defense against Martha:

> *"Martha, Martha, you are worried and distracted by many things; there is need of only one thing. Mary has chosen the better part, which will not be taken away from her."* (Luke 10:41-42)

A Bit of Church History

The church has considered this gospel passage for centuries, seeing in Martha and Mary the embodiment of two different ways of life: Martha became the symbol of the active life, Mary representing the tranquil, contemplative life. Doesn't this gospel passage show that one is choosing the better part by abandoning the busyness of life and sinking into contemplation of God and the mysteries of the life of Jesus, so as to be wholly with Jesus and living in the presence of God?

Still, the duty to act in the world could not be repressed. In spite of this gospel, was it not more Christian to feed the hungry, clothe the naked, free the prisoners, build roads for pilgrimage, establish schools and hospitals, and care for the elderly and the sick instead of constantly singing psalms and meditating on Sacred Scripture?

Thus the choice: active, busy life or tranquil, contemplative living? Both the ancient and the medieval church struggled enormously with this problem. The medieval church even produced orders of knights who set forth, sword in hand, in order (as was the fatal belief) to do "the will of God," and also contemplative orders that withdrew altogether into the cloister. It also established orders that tried to balance praise of God and work to improve the world.

Prayer or Action?

The subject is still current today; the old questions arise in newer and newer forms. Should we pray that God will feed the hungry in the world, or should we act instead of praying? If we put the question that way, of course, we see right away that something is wrong with it.

In fact, if we look more closely at the story of Martha and Mary, we quickly observe that it is the *finale* to a longer composition, beginning with a kind of prelude in Luke 10:23-24. There Jesus calls his disciples blessed, saying:

> *"Blessed are the eyes that see what you see! For I tell you that many prophets and kings desired to see what you see, but did not see it, and to hear what you hear, but did not hear it."*

That is: the ancient promises are being fulfilled in the *now*. What prophets and kings longed for, what was not yet given to them, is now present: the reign of God and with it the new family, God's new society. Now, at last, the new thing can be seen and heard. The leading ideas in this little prelude are "see" and "hear."

In the *finale* to the whole literary composition of Luke 10:23-42, then, Mary sits at Jesus' feet—and *sees* and *hears*. So Luke pictures her for us as a disciple of Jesus who is receiving and honoring the blessing promised in the beatitude spoken previously. She can do nothing other than sit at Jesus' feet, looking at him and listening to him.

So is "doing" thus set aside and devalued? So that no one should come to such a nonsensical conclusion Luke inserts a long middle section between prelude and finale, namely, the story of the merciful Samaritan (Luke 10:25-37), one who binds up the wounds of the victim, places him on his own mount, brings him to an inn, and pays the host for the costs, while a priest and a Levite simply pass by the beaten man. That whole narrative is about right "action." The verb "do" appears no fewer than four times in the story of the merciful Samaritan (see Luke 10:25, 28, 37b, 37d). The narrative ends with the emphatic command: "Go and *do* likewise!"

Thus the overall composition, with its three sections, makes it clear that right *doing* is decisive, but for the church to do what is right it must first listen to the words of Jesus. The church must see and hear. It must learn to see the world through God's eyes, and it must look to the new messianic thing that has begun in the world with Jesus. Only then can it discover its *real* need and do what is right.

A Fundamental Question

In the Western church at present there are any number of interest groups fighting for changes in the church. They say the church must reconsider a variety of things. It must eliminate outdated traditions, change outmoded structures, do *this* and *that* and act, at last, with regard to *this point* and *that point*, and all in all it must do a great many things differently.

It is not easy to judge these kinds of initiatives, because at the beginning of the third millennium the church is in great distress. The world and society have changed in unfathomable ways; many things are perceived quite differently. Much needs to be seen anew and considered at greater depth. Cannot traditions also become atrophied? Must they not be made fluid again in order to attain their true aims? We may, indeed we *must*, raise such questions.

However, we also need to ask ourselves which has more weight: what is to be demanded in terms of society's concerns and what is required of us by the Gospel? Must we look first and primarily to society, or to Jesus? Must we listen primarily to society's interruptions or first of all to Jesus? The answer is not as simple as it might seem at first glance, because it is precisely a sober awareness of the society in which we live that might possibly give us the ability to hear and be alert to what Jesus wants to say to us.

In this situation the composition in Luke 10:23-42 may give us an answer: first of all we have to do what Mary, Martha's sister, did in that happy hour. Obviously the church requires our action because it must constantly repent and because we all must do likewise, again and again. But first we must consider how Jesus acted, and we have to listen to Jesus—and we can only do that if we take time for it.

In short: the church needs people who again and again look to Jesus and listen to him; they are primary. Then right action will follow, almost of itself. Listening and doing are thus not opposites. Mary and Martha can be reconciled. Mary can learn from Martha, but Martha can, above all, learn from her sister Mary.

The Leper's Plea

We find it hard to understand what leprosy meant in previous ages, and to empathize with those who suffered from it. Leprosy was a hideous and ruinous illness. It is true that experts now say that leprosy in the Bible was not identical with the forms of lepra bacteria that kill nerves, block blood vessels, and cause whole limbs to atrophy. Instead, leprosy in the Bible refers to a whole variety of skin diseases such as vitiligo, psoriasis, scabies, or eczema.

That, of course, does not alter in the slightest the horror then aroused by "leprosy," because the key factor was the social isolation connected with such skin anomalies. Lepers had to live far from villages and towns, and if a healthy person came near them they had to shout a warning: "Unclean! Unclean!" (Lev 13:45-46). They were really "outsiders." They were socially dead.

Untouchable

Consider for a moment what that kind of social isolation meant in concrete terms. Lepers were not to touch healthy people, and they themselves were "untouchable." Fear of infection was profoundly rooted and affected one's relatives in particular. No one got near a leper; at most one might wave at them from a distance. In this way the sick person was cut off, far away from the living and from life, someone who had to feel like a failure and a loser.

To some degree we can, after all, conceive of what life felt like for lepers in the time of Jesus, because the sense of being cut off exists among us too. The COVID crisis gives us at least some sense of what it means to be suddenly isolated or constantly put at a distance from others, but, above all, those who are attacked by a deadly disease experience something of the situation of the lepers of that day.

Consider, for example, a person who has just heard from the doctor that she has cancer. She shudders involuntarily from elementary fear: "How can that be? Why this? Now it has struck me, not somebody else. Why me?" The cancer victim feels herself isolated from the healthy, suddenly alone.

But the healthy are also affected. They are unsure how they should relate to the sick person. They feel awkward and helpless. Of course, they encourage the sufferer. They say: "You'll soon be better! You'll survive it! Cancer treatment has made enormous strides." But in their hearts they feel differently. Suddenly there is something that will separate them. Every healthy person will try to banish the thought— but it is something that simply has to be faced and overcome.

I remember clearly how oddly I behaved when I visited a leper colony in Africa. It was admirably administered by a Christian religious order. The sick were well housed and received effective medical treatment. For most of them the progress of the disease had already been arrested. They loved receiving visitors; they looked at me expectantly. But I was oddly self-conscious and reserved. I was secretly afraid to shake hands with a sick person. Oh, how ashamed I felt afterward!

But for lepers in Israel at that time there was another factor besides social isolation that we should not overlook: They felt themselves stricken and punished by God. They were convinced that their illness had something to do with profound guilt: that of their parents or their own (Pss 31:11; 38:2-5; cf. John 9:2). The faults of their family or their own sins had now—so they believed—revealed themselves in their own body, visible to everyone. They had been struck by God.

Touchable

In that light we must see the healing of lepers in the New Testament with new eyes. These people were often without hope either of being healthy again or of escaping their social isolation. Still worse: they must have felt abandoned by God. It is in just that situation that they meet Jesus, and he immediately breaks all the rules for relating to them. Mark tells of it in the very first chapter of his gospel:

> *A leper came to him begging him, and kneeling he said to him, "If you choose, you can make me clean." Moved with pity, Jesus stretched out his hand and*

touched him, and said to him, "I do choose. Be made clean!" Immediately the
leprosy left him, and he was made clean. (Mark 1:40-42)

Thus Jesus did not heal the leper from an appropriate distance; no, he touched him! He grasped him. And in doing so he broke through a barrier. "Jesus stretched out his hand and touched him" is not an ornament, an embellishment of the narrative. It is an elementary act—contrary to hygiene, contrary to proper behavior, contrary to Torah (see Lev 13–14).

Why does Jesus touch the leper? It has to do with his proclamation of the reign of God. When the reign of God comes—Jesus is deeply convinced of this—in Israel and in the whole world beyond Israel all creation will be renewed. It will be as it was intended to be and should be: unspoiled, fresh as a morning, beautiful, free from the "leprosy of the earth." Therefore Jesus *had to* heal the sick, make lepers clean, free the possessed, drive out the demons of society; he *had to* touch the sick because it also belongs to a liberated and healed world that community is restored and all social isolation is tangibly at an end.

The Plea of the Leper

What is significant here is not only what *Jesus* does; it is just as important to see what the *leper* does before Jesus touches him: he does not remain at a distance. He approaches Jesus. He begs for help. He falls on his knees before Jesus. He says: "If you choose, you can make me clean."

The striking aspect of what he says is "if you choose." Thus the healing depends solely on Jesus' will. That is uncanny, for every Jew who knew Scripture had to think, in the presence of this event or in hearing it reported, of an incident in 2 Kings (5:1-27). There we find a very exciting story about a healing from which I will take a single detail:

The Syrian general Naaman from Damascus, the general in charge of all Syrian troops, suffers from leprosy. No physician can help him. At the suggestion of an enslaved Israelite woman, he is sent by his king to Samaria to be healed by the prophet Elisha.

It is true that the Syrian king does not send his general directly to Elisha but first of all to the king reigning in Samaria, the ruler of the Northern Kingdom of Israel, and gives him a letter for the king that reads: "When this letter reaches you, know that I have sent to you my servant Naaman, that you may cure him of his leprosy" (2 Kgs 5:6).

Obviously the Syrian king wanted his general to be healed by the prophet Elisha, but because Elisha was working within the territory under the jurisdiction of the king of Israel he sends Naaman first to the king of Israel, in accord with diplomatic custom. The latter, however, misunderstands the case and the polite language of the letter; he becomes angry, tears his garments, and cries out:

> *"Am I God, to give death or life, that this man sends word to me to cure a man of his leprosy? Just look and see how he is trying to pick a quarrel with me!"* (2 Kgs 5:7)

This cry of the king of Israel is so revealing because it shows that leprosy was a matter of life and death. One who was a leper passed out of the sphere of life into that of death. Social isolation was like a living death.

However, the incident reveals a great deal more. Only God can bring someone out of such a death ("Am I God?"). Only God can heal leprosy. So when the leper says to Jesus, "If you choose, you can make me clean," he attributes to Jesus a power that only God has. He is filled with an ultimate trust. He believes that God acts personally in Jesus. He entrusts himself to Jesus, expecting everything from him.

And We?

Would we pray as the leper does? Would we beg with the same trust? Do we cry out to Jesus when we are in trouble? Do we fall on our knees before him? Do we tell him all the troubles of our lives? Do we expect, with boundless trust, that he will help us and draw us out of our distress?

Maybe we do; maybe we do not, and if we do not, there may be many reasons. *One* reason that quite often plays a role in the minds of believers may be that they do not dare to ask God for personal aid. May they really appeal to God for help with all their personal problems? Must one's prayer not be about great and universal things: the crises of the world, the misery of nations, the cause of the church—the reign of God? A believer may think just that way, and then she no longer dares to appeal to Jesus in her personal need.

Is that right? I think not. It would only be right if one's personal crises and personal burdens had nothing at all to do with the *reign of God*. And that would indeed be the case if one were to live *only for oneself*, having only oneself in mind, thinking only of one's own happiness and well-being.

But if one's life is instead fundamentally oriented to God and God's will, then one may pray for everything; then one may ask great things for oneself and even appeal to Jesus to overcome the little crises in one's life. Then one is really "seeking first the reign of God," and then one may expect that "all these things will be given as well" (Matt 6:33).

Sickness and Guilt

Breaking through the roof to bring a sick person into the living room is, to say the least, unusual. Of course, it is somewhat easier in a Near Eastern house with a flat roof of clay and woven reed matting than with our officially approved concrete structures. But even in Capernaum it must have created quite a stir. We can almost see the chunks of clay falling from the ceiling. That is why the story of the sick person who came through the roof because people were crowding around the door so thickly that no one could get into the house that way must have made such an impression on those present (Mark 2:1-12). That was something worth retelling, and no one would have easily forgotten it.

So a paralyzed man is let down through the roof to reach Jesus. What confidence on the part of the sick man as well as those who lowered him! Jesus turns to the sick person, and all the people hold their breath, awaiting a new miraculous healing. But Jesus says something no one expected: "Son, your sins are forgiven."

That statement shocked the scribes who were present because a human being was claiming the right to forgive sins. Forgiving sins, they rightly supposed, is something only God can do. For us, Jesus' statement is shocking because we are no longer used to seeing a link between sin and sickness.

Only a Breakdown of the System?

For people today illness is a disruption of the system that requires repairing; that in turn demands the correct diagnosis and the proper treatment—the appropriate pharmaceuticals and the newest devices, in some cases an operation followed by rehab. Certainly in the meantime insightful persons are clear that there is also a connection between *soul* and health, but then it is a matter of a *spiritual* breakdown that must be appropriately repaired. For that, psychiatrists or psycho-therapists are the ones to call.

It is a somewhat foreign idea to people today, however, that there is such a thing as guilt: deep-seated guilt, and that such guilt can poison lives and cause illness. Certainly it is not common to suppose that guilt cannot be argued away but requires forgiveness.

Television series show us every evening how foreign the notion of guilt feelings has become. Their regular programming sources include, among many other things, breaches of various taboos, but especially adultery. Whenever, following the climactic scenes, the husband accuses his wife, or the wife her husband, the series proceeds according to fixed rituals. The man usually says: "I can explain it all. It had nothing to do with the two of us," and the woman says: "It just happened; it didn't mean anything." With such formulae both husband and wife absolve themselves of any guilt—and that, indeed, is what the television series want to convey: "It doesn't mean anything. That's the way people live nowadays. We media people are always close to life; we are realistic." They are, of course, silent about the fact that their aim is to impose a new image of humanity.

Have we Christians grasped that in our consumption of media we are uninterruptedly injected with models of behavior that not only call the Jewish-Christian tradition into question on *certain points* but construct an *overall interpretation of the world*, indeed a *world* as such, that cannot be our own? In that world, oddly enough, despite its overpowering moralism, there is no longer any genuine guilt.

As believing Christians we take sin into account. But do we also consider the possibility of a *power of sin* that is not content to occupy a single room in the house that is our life? Do we not live with a somewhat naïve idea that sin can be sharply and clearly defined, as a kind of ugly fleck on a clean life, so to speak? In that case an occasional betrayal is indeed a betrayal, but otherwise everything is fine with us. Then a deliberately nurtured hatred is, of course, an unpleasant story, but apart from it everything in our lives is utterly respectable. Setting God aside over a long period of time is, indeed, somewhat disturbing, but otherwise we are upstanding folk.

The Span of Sin

In reality sin is something that does not work cleanly, within limits, at a single point in our lives and relationships. Every sin *goes all out;*

each is an attack on God and on the world—simply because it is an assault on God's order of creation.

With every sin we attack God, but we do so by attacking what God has created: the *world*, which should have been a mirror of God's beauty and goodness, and God's *people*, in whom God's plan for the world should be visible. When I violate God's commandments, I deprive the world and the people of God of the brilliance they should have.

To put it more simply: sin mars not just a part of my life but the whole of it, and not just my life but those of the others around me. Because of my greed or laziness, my false ambition or resignation, others suffer. Besides, sin focuses my attention on myself so that I cannot perceive the needs of others. I am so wrapped up in myself that I simply can no longer see where I am really needed.

Even a single individual can poison the atmosphere in a community and destroy its cohesion, but if there are many such, then the demon solidifies. A world that should be a paradise becomes a "vale of tears," as an old prayer has it.

In such a poisoned atmosphere sicknesses multiply. Often they emerge first among the weakest, those who are least able to resist, those with thin skins. Sickness can certainly be connected with sin: obviously not necessarily the sin of those affected. It could be the sin of a person's ancestors, of his or her surroundings, of society, of failure to offer aid.

Clearly we must not associate sickness first and only with human guilt; that would not do justice to the complexity of creation and evolution. Disruption of organic functions, collapse of the immune system, signs of wear and tear, the weaknesses of age, and many manifestations of illness are simply part of creation—as is death itself, the most radical and comprehensive failure of our life-functions. This caution is certainly important, but it does not change the fact that all too often there is a connection between sickness and guilt.

With Watchful Eyes

In John 9:3 Jesus says of a man born blind: "Neither this man nor his parents sinned." Still, it can also happen that he does not simply heal a disabled person without saying to the one healed: "Your sins are forgiven." In any case he must have observed the possible connection between sickness and guilt with incredibly acute eyes.

Jesus encounters a person who is lame and he sees how sin can cripple people, making them unable to move. So first and foremost he bestows forgiveness of sin on the disabled person, almost as representative of the crippling of the whole people of God. The disabled person entrusts his whole existence to him—and is healed. Everything that has bound him, because of his own sins or those of others, falls away. He stands up, takes his cot, and goes home, healed.

Similar healings occur everywhere Jesus goes. There must have been an atmosphere of wholeness around him. In his vicinity illnesses vanish, demons flee, minds become clear. People begin to trust one another and to view their lives in the light of God. Out of joy in the reign of God and trust in the coming Messiah, wellness grows. From now on what happened in the house at Capernaum can take place every day.

The same can happen here among us. Capernaum has no advantage over us. Messianic salvation and wholeness are given to us, too, and it all depends on whether we attend to each other as God has attended to us. Everything depends on whether, following Jesus' bidding, we accept one another, help one another, and continually forgive one another.

There are many kinds of disabilities, but there is also the promise that we can be freed from every one of them—not only for the sake of our own wholeness but also for that of others.

The Basis of the Biblical Ethos

Paul had an especially warm relationship with the community in Philippi. It was the only one he allowed to give him financial support (Phil 4:14-18). The letter to the Philippians was probably written in Ephesus while Paul was in a Roman prison there. That letter to the community in Philippi contains the following statement:

> . . . *whatever is true, whatever is honorable, whatever is just, whatever is pure, whatever is pleasing, whatever is commendable, if there is any excellence and if there is anything worthy of praise, think about these things!* (Phil 4:8)

What is striking about this sentence is that in it Paul uses a whole list of adjectives that had a singular and stellar sound in the ancient world, above all in the ethics of the Stoa. Translation can scarcely do them justice. The words Paul chooses echo like such terms in modern usage as "respectable," "upright," "cultivated," "enlightened," "humane." Paul wanted his communities to match their pagan contemporaries in universally respected virtue.

A Rational Ethos

Must we, then, conclude that Christian ethics were identical to those that moral reasoning, including that of non-Christians, regarded as appropriate and human? We should not be too hasty in saying "no, Christian ethics is more, much more than what common moral reason sees as appropriate." The answer might not be that easy!

To approach a solution we can go farther back to the time of the Old Testament and take a brief look at the Ten Commandments. It is undisputed that those commandments also, for the most part, formulate an ethos we find everywhere in the ancient Near East: care for elderly parents (fourth commandment); prohibition of killing without legal reason (fifth commandment); prohibition of disrupting another's marriage (sixth commandment); prohibition of kidnapping (the original sense of the seventh commandment); forbidding the giving of false witness in court (eighth commandment); forbidding the acquisition of others' property (ninth and tenth commandments). None of that was proper to Israel alone; it was a tribal ethos and wisdom teaching found throughout the Near East.

Then what is the biblical ethos? Is it only a summary of what was regarded everywhere as proper? Is it only a melting pot of all that is rational, the human experience that regulates social life?

It is correct, in any case, that Israel's moral norms and, with them, those of the church are fundamentally rational—more precisely, that they agree with what one might call the logic and reason of creation. To that extent the ethos of the Bible has a great deal in common with the moral reasoning of all peoples—and yet there is a profound difference. My listing of the Ten Commandments omitted the beginning:

> *I am the* LORD *your God, who brought you out of the land of Egypt, out of the house of slavery; you shall have no other gods before me. . . . You shall not make wrongful use of the name of the* LORD *your God. . . . Remember the sabbath day, and keep it holy.* (Exod 20:2-8)

The beginning of the Ten Commandments thus formulates an historical experience that is fundamental to the whole biblical ethos: God has a people in the world that belongs to God (the "thou" of the address in the Ten Commandments refers first and above all to the people of Israel as a whole). God has led this people out of slavery in Egypt into freedom. In this way God was proved to be Israel's true and only God, and therefore God's people must not have any other gods besides this One, no matter who (first commandment).

This is the absolute LORD, a God whom Israel cannot control as the religions in Israel's neighborhood continually try to do to their gods through magical formulae, incantations, and a variety of other religious practices (second commandment).

After all, everything belongs to Israel's God: every day and every year, everyone's whole life. To make this palpable there must be, at the latest after every sixth day, a single day in which the monotony of life is disrupted, when people and animals rest, a day that belongs entirely to God (third commandment).

Ethos Drawn from History

In this way Israel became a space of historical experience with its God—more precisely, a space for distinction, for decision. This ability to distinguish enabled Israel to adopt everything right, reasonable, and enlightened from the peoples around it, but also to reject everything that proved incompatible with its image of God and its own special experience of God. Thus from Abraham to Jesus a constant process of distinguishing continued. This gave Israel the ability to recognize what was good in other peoples but also to criticize, indeed to reject what was contrary to God's plan for creating just and free societies in the world.

This unique experience of God, surpassing all the rational resources in Israel's environment, produced an ethos that surpassed the ethical rules of the nations. I am thinking here especially of love of enemies, not only demanded in the Sermon on the Mount (Matt 5:43-48) but clearly traceable in the Old Testament as well. The Torah already says with full clarity how those in Israel were to act toward an "enemy":

> *When you come upon your enemy's ox or donkey going astray, you shall bring it back. When you see the donkey of one who hates you lying under its burden and you would hold back from setting it free, you must help to set it free.* (Exod 23:4-5)

While the word "love" does not appear in this text, the principle is there. In the Bible love is not primarily a great feeling and overpowering emotion but active assistance, support, solidarity. Here, out of the unique experience of God in Israel, even love for enemies is demanded—and that is highly unusual. It was the common ethos of the nations that one should help one's friends and harm one's enemies, and one could hate one's enemies with one's whole soul and strength.

Thus it is not only that Israel tests everything and adopts what is good. Beyond that it develops its own ethos, which presupposes a community created by God as a space of unceasing historical experience with the true God. Within that experiential space the rationality of creation can develop fully, and there it is also insightful. Without that space of experience it can go astray and even be perverted, and then it often ceases to be plausible.

For example: Christians find it comprehensible that one may not end one's own life because they know that God is the one from whom all life comes, and human dignity consists precisely in the fact that one must respect one's life (and those of others) as God's gift. For modern pagans, on the contrary, that is no longer thought reasonable because they regard themselves as in charge of their own lives. All too often they see self-chosen death as the summit of their freedom, self-determination, and human dignity. That suicide—along with its milieu and accompanying phenomena—is in fact a blow inflicted on human dignity is an idea completely excluded by many of our contemporaries. They live far from God and also far from the knowledge of how a Christian death may look.

It was necessary for me to go on at such length because that is the only way to make clear what Paul is really doing in Philippians 4:8. He is taking ideas from contemporary ethics, speaking of dignity and honor. He does not want the Christians in his communities to fall short of what educated and serious people of his time have discovered about moral truth—and yet for Paul there is a precondition for it all that makes it possible for him to locate himself within the ethos of his thoughtful contemporaries. That precondition is clear in a sentence that immediately precedes the imperatives I cited in the beginning:

> . . . *the peace of God, which surpasses all understanding, will guard your hearts and your minds in Christ Jesus.* (Phil 4:7)

The Peace of God

As with the Ten Commandments, so also here, in advance of all rational ethics, there is a naming of the space that secures and constantly clarifies that ethos. In the Ten Commandments it was the space of Israel's experience; here it is the space of experience of the eschatological Israel, namely, life "in Christ Jesus." There, in the Christian communities, a space has been created for *shalôm*, the peace that brings wholeness and salvation. It is a peace that comes from God and from Jesus Christ. It is actualized in the concrete community life of the congregation in Philippi and in the communion of all the congregations.

The baptized have become one in "the Body of Christ," the church. Now, finally, here is what the Torah of Israel desired: a holy people. In the body of that people one can continually see what is true, honorable, just, pure, pleasing, commendable, and human.

The Heart of Torah

In the first century BCE there lived in Israel a renowned Jewish rabbi who is still lauded today for his wisdom, broad-mindedness, and patience. He was called Rabbi Hillel. The following story is told of him:

> One day a Gentile came to him. He wanted very much to become a Jew, but the great many commandments in Jewish law and their subtle distinctions were simply too much for him. He did not want to learn them all by heart. So he said to Rabbi Hillel: "I am ready to become a Jew if you can summarize the whole Law, the whole Torah, while I am standing on one foot." Hillel commanded him: "Stand on one foot!" The Gentile did so. Then Hillel said to him: "What is hateful to yourself, do not do to another. That is the whole Torah; the rest is just commentary. Go and study it." (Cf. Talmud Shabbat 31a)

Obviously the wise and faithful Hillel knew that the Torah was more, and much more profound, than this so-called "Golden Rule," but he wanted to build a bridge to the rationality and humanity of Jewish faith for the Gentile.

Jesus Formulates the Center of All Commandments

In a story Mark's gospel tells (12:28-34), Jesus is in a similar situation: it is not a Gentile who comes to him but a Jewish rabbi, a scribe, and he asks Jesus what is the "first," that is, the most important commandment in Torah. Jesus gives him an answer that is still better and more precise than Hillel's. It is so brief that the rabbi could likewise have been standing on one foot. Jesus says:

> "The first is, 'Hear, O Israel: the Lord our God, the Lord is one; you shall love the Lord your God with all your heart, and with all your soul [or: life], and

with all your mind, and with all your strength.' The second is this, 'You shall love your neighbor as yourself.' There is no other commandment greater than these." (Mark 12:29-31)

Clearly, Jesus did not invent the two commandments. Both come from the Old Testament, though there they appear in very different places. The first, the beginning of the *Shema Israel*, "Hear, O Israel," is in Deuteronomy 6:4-5. The second ("You shall love your neighbor as yourself") is in Leviticus 19:18. What is new is that Jesus joins those two widely separated texts, makes them a twofold commandment, and summarizes and anchors the whole Torah in it.

Love Must Be Rational

If we listen more closely, though, we notice that another concept has entered into the form in which Jesus quotes the "Hear, O Israel," one that is not found in the Old Testament text: You shall love the LORD your God—not only with your whole heart, your whole life, and your whole strength but also (this is the addition) "with all your mind," which refers to critical thinking: "your whole rationality."

Hence love for God must also be rational: that is, it must be objective, enlightened, bringing blessing to the world. Therefore love for God cannot stand alone. It must be linked to love of neighbor. All forms of loving God that do not include the neighbor and the world are far distant from the Bible. They are not rational and therefore have nothing—nothing at all—in common with biblical faith and with Jesus.

To this point all this may seem fairly enlightening, even though the concentration of all biblical commandments in two sentences is rather bold. But what am I saying with it? Is the double commandment to love God and neighbor really enlightening? No, it is anything but. Enlightening would be, for example, "One should love one's friends and hate one's enemies." That was the normal, usual way of thinking in the ancient world. The commandment to love God and neighbor is revolutionary; it is by no means a matter of course. It presupposes the history of Israel, and Jesus also. It first came into the world with Israel and with Jesus. There is no religion in the world apart from and independent of Israel and of a Christianity that centers on a linked commandment to love God and love one's fellow believers.

If the people of God, if the church repeatedly fails in deplorable ways, still it upholds this double commandment, will not allow it to collapse, and makes it clear that the future of the world depends on this commandment.

In the twentieth century we experienced what hatred can do to the world. Hitler and his helpers' helpers slaughtered six million Jewish men, women, and children—because they wanted to eliminate that people. And today, in the twenty-first century, we are experiencing the return of such hatred. New nationalisms are arising. Political parties are beginning to hate each other. Whole rivers of hatred and hostility against individuals, groups, and other nations flow through social media. Evidently those who seek to destroy their opponents with words no longer realize that destruction with words is all too often followed by *bloody* destruction. Apparently they know nothing of the fear of God and most certainly nothing about love of God and neighbor. What Jesus formulates as the center of the Law is not only the center of the biblical message: It is the center of the world. Without that double commandment our world will be consumed.

The Twofold Love Commandment Needs the People of God

Now, however, I need to add something that is necessarily linked to the commandment of love of God and neighbor, something that is embedded, so to speak, in that commandment and without which the twofold commandment cannot function. Sacred Scripture says— and Jesus says with it—that the human being is an egoist; each thinks primarily of himself or herself and each would prefer to be her or his own god. Therefore, self-centered as we are, we cannot love either God or our neighbor in isolation. That is why the Old Testament says: "Hear, O Israel." It is not individuals who are addressed, no matter how well-disposed they each may be, but it is Israel, the people of God, the community that belongs to God.

But that means that the twofold commandment to love God and neighbor needs mutuality: the mutuality of those who are ready, in full freedom, to live according to those two commandments. The individual needs to be grounded in the people of God. Only there, where many know it to be true of each other that what *I* will is what the other also wills, that what *I* live for is what the other also lives for, that it is not *I myself* who is dedicating my life to God's cause, that my sister or brother in faith is doing the same: only where this kind of togetherness exists can there be a closely woven net, a sustaining basis on which we are able to love God and neighbor. So the commandment of love of God and neighbor is not free-floating, somewhere in the air above us. Ultimately, without community in the people of God it cannot be lived.

Without Any Hedging

It is also true, however, that people are mistrustful. That is why each of us hesitates at first and thinks: "I will join in, but only if the others do it first. If the others plunge in, I will too. Only if the others are good to me will I be good to them. Otherwise I will be the dummy in the end."

Of course, if everyone had thought that way the people of God could never have begun. There would have been no Abraham, no Moses, no Isaiah, no Mary, no Jesus. And if everyone thinks that way now, there can be no people of God today.

Jesus—and many others in Israel before him—thought differently. They lived for God and the people of God without reservation. Jesus took the path of self-forgetting love—and it cost him his life. It is only because HE fulfilled everything and because many individuals have followed his path that there is a basis of "love of God and neighbor" for us all. Only because of that is there a people of God, a church, a community.

We therefore have every reason to thank God because, through others who preceded us, God has made it possible to live in love for our neighbor and in the peace that comes from that. Moreover, we have every reason to beg God that we may forever remain in that love that we ourselves could never create but that is given us by our God—in this love that is always bound up with profound peace in our hearts and is already an anticipation of the eternal Easter joy.

How the Reign of God Happens

Let us for the moment imagine ourselves in the situation of the many Jews who were exiled to Babylon after the conquest of Jerusalem in 586 BCE and the demise of the kingdom of Judah that accompanied it.

They are living in a foreign place, a land where a foreign language is spoken. They are scattered. They no longer have a temple in which they can bow down before God. Is this people forever abandoned by its God? Is there any future for Israel? Depression spreads like a cancer of the soul. There is little courage left; eyes are dim, ears are deaf. Hands are weak and legs feel lame. Even the garrulous have fallen silent.

On the One Hand

Yet in the midst of this crippling situation the deportees hear something revolutionary: "They shall see the glory of the LORD, the majesty of our God" (Isa 35:2). Moreover, with this revelation of God something unimaginable will happen, says the prophet behind Isaiah 35 to the exiles. It will happen very soon; everything will be changed.

> *Then the eyes of the blind shall be opened,*
> *and the ears of the deaf unstopped;*
> *then the lame shall leap like a deer,*
> *and the tongue of the speechless sing for joy.* (Isa 35:5-6)

Those set free by the Lord will return to Zion. The overturning of all things will extend so far that even the environment will be involved: the way back to Jerusalem that seems so arduous and endless will be smoothed; there will be a highway that will open to the returnees. Springs will break forth in the wilderness, streams in the desert, pools will form in the sandy wastes, and the bare land will begin to bloom.

Most precious of all: everything is pure—hearts, hands, the world around—with the purity required by Torah (Isa 35:7-10).

Everything will be as it should have been from the beginning. Everything will be straightened out. Justice will at last be established. What is coming is not God's "vengeance," the ham-fisted translation in many versions,[1] but God's justice that creates well-being and puts an end to injustice. And all this will happen not as a culmination that quickly collapses again, not as an episode, not as an interlude, but as "eternal joy." The thirty-fifth chapter of the book of Isaiah—what a text!

We should understand Jesus' preaching of the reign of God against the background of this kind of prophecy. The reign of God that Jesus proclaims comes not only within hearts; it is the coming of the power and glory of God—and that glory will change everything. Things will find their identity. Relationships will be restored. Sinners will repent and turn back. Chaos will be transformed into beauty; sick people will be made whole; the blind will see; those deprived of speech will begin to speak again.

Again it is so that all this takes place not in some gray future or on the distant island of Utopia but here and now, in the midst of God's people. The gospels report how the reign of God comes and the weary world is changed:

> *The blind receive their sight,*
> *the lame walk,*
> *the lepers are cleansed,*
> *the deaf hear,*
> *the dead are raised,*
> *the poor have good news brought to them.* (Luke 7:22)

On the Other Hand

Everything I have just described, however—with Isaiah and with Jesus—is only one side of the coin. There is also the other side, namely, all the darkness that reveals itself with the same force in real history:

The exiles whom the edict of King Cyrus of Persia allowed to return home, those of whom the text says "everlasting joy shall be upon

---

[1] Including the AV, NIV, NRSV; but see NABRE, "recompense," "vindication"—Tr.

their heads" (Isa 35:10), came into a Judah that was in a very bad state. What they found were impassable roads, desiccated vineyards, a Jerusalem in ruins—its walls torn down, its gates burned; they experienced the ridicule of foreign tribes that had infiltrated the land. The poor had to sell their own children into slavery in order to be able to buy grain (Neh 5:1-5).

Was it any different for Jesus? The "Galilean spring" came to a rapid end as Jesus' opponents grouped together, resistance grew, and even some of his disciples left him. In the end he hung on a cross and died a hideous death.

So were the fascinating prophetic texts wrong? Was Isaiah 35, with the many other biblical promises, nothing but dreams and fairy tales? Was Jesus just one of those who have baseless notions of utopias—the kind that delude people and seduce them into abandoning reality?

No, most certainly not! For if we open our eyes and look closely we immediately see that the "beautiful" texts of the prophets, full of promise and intuitive as they are, are accompanied by very different ones that present a direct counterpoint.

Take Isaiah, for example! We have seen that Isaiah 35 prophesies the miraculous gathering of Israel and its return from Babylon, but other texts in the same book describe how Israel, the servant of God, is stricken. He is despised, defiled, and mistreated. He is "counted among the wicked." He is "a man of sorrows, acquainted with infirmity." He is like a "lamb that is led to the slaughter." This servant of God, this Lamb, is Israel sent into exile. It is silenced, "cut off from the land of the living." And it is only in this way that the world can be changed and the plan of God can succeed (Isa 52:13–53:12).

What about Jesus himself, in whom the whole fate of Israel was thus concentrated? Was he a dreamer who imagined a whole new world for himself? No, he also spoke of thorns that threaten to choke the seed (Mark 4:7), of the cup he must drink (Mark 10:38), of the baptism of death with which he must be baptized (Luke 12:50), of the road to Jerusalem he must travel, and of his life that would be given as ransom for many (Mark 10:45).

Incognito

What then? How does the reign of God come? Is it to be as Isaiah 35 describes or does it come in the way that Isaiah 53 puts before us?

Does it come as a "Galilean spring" or on a cross? Does it appear in marvelous times of worship when our hearts are lifted up, or in daily dying?

I think it comes in all those ways. Both sides are true. Neither can be omitted, and the interflow of sickness and healing, sorrow and bliss, failure and success, mourning and consolation is to be lived day by day without retouching or prettifying. It is an indissoluble dialectic. The reign of God is coming and cannot be halted. Jesus was completely justified in his proclamation of the reign of God. He was not fooled. But the coming of the reign of God is not something that can be observed (Luke 17:20). The moments in which its beauty appears before our eyes are rare and therefore precious. Normally it comes in hidden ways.

Joseph Ratzinger, later Pope Benedict XVI, speaks in what may well be the best book he wrote, his *Introduction to Christianity*, about "structures of what is Christian." He lists a number of such structures that appear everywhere. One of them he calls the "law of disguise." He says: God is not only the Wholly Other but also the invisible, the hidden, the unknowable. When God reveals himself it is in such lowliness as to be unnoticeable, almost unrecognizable. God is only revealed by seeming to vanish into the trivial. Literally:

> *First there is the Earth, a mere nothing in the cosmos, which was to be the point of divine activity in the cosmos. Then comes Israel, a cipher among the powers, which was to be the point of his appearance in the world. Then comes Nazareth, again a cipher within Israel, which was to be the point of his definitive arrival. Then at the end there is the Cross, on which a man was to hang, a man whose life had been a failure; yet this was to be the point at which one can actually touch God. Finally there is the Church, the questionable shape of our history, which claims to be the abiding site of his revelation.*[2]

Thus according to Joseph Ratzinger the church is subject to the law of God's disguise ("Incognito"). In the church—and so also in the transformation of the world through the church—God is also invisible, hidden, almost unrecognizable, and self-revealed only in lowliness.

---

[2] Joseph Ratzinger, *Introduction to Christianity*, trans. J. R. Foster (San Francisco: Ignatius Press, 1969), 256.

That, however, means that God does act. It means that God wants to transform the world into "the majesty of Carmel and Sharon" (Isa 35:2)—and to do so through us, poor beggars that we are. It is still true that God's reign is steadily coming. But in all this God is revealed only in lowliness, in apparent failures, in distress, even in nameless suffering, so that we may never fall into the temptation to attribute the coming of God's reign to our own power and glory.

The Biology of the Reign of God

The title of this essay could be off-putting. Biology of the reign of God? What is that supposed to mean? What does the reign of God have to do with biology? But the irritation disappears when we see clearly that Jesus used a whole series of parables about agriculture: the sower (Mark 4:3-9), the seed growing by itself (Mark 4:26-29), the fig tree putting forth branches (Mark 13:28-29), the weeds among the wheat (Matt 13:24-30), the mustard seed (Luke 13:18-19), the grain of wheat that dies (John 12:24), the vine and the branches (John 15:1-8), and the barren fig tree (Luke 13:6-9).

In the Wheat Field and in the Vineyard

Biological processes play a crucial role in all these parables. I will choose just three examples: once Jesus tells of a wheat field (Mark 4:3-9). There are thorns growing amid the wheat. They choke the grain, depriving it of light and air, and the ground is tough. In many parts of the field the topsoil is dry because it is so thin. Limestone lies close beneath the soil. Then there are the flocks of birds that snap up some of the seeds as soon as they are sown. The poor farmer! Wasn't all his hard work for nothing?

Not at all! His field produces an abundant harvest, because there are also parts with a good base, and the seeds that were sown have produced not just individual stalks: the basal nodes just below the surface have brought forth more than one stalk. Side-growths have resulted in the production of a whole bushel of stalks from each seed that was sown. In biological terms: the sprouts from the individual seeds have "tillered" themselves, and so each seed that was sown has produced thirtyfold, sixtyfold, or a hundredfold (Mark 4:8). Jesus is a careful observer. He knows how wheat grows. He knows the phenomenon of "tillering" that is so crucial for grain-growing.

Jesus also knows how a correct fertilization can affect the yield. In the parable of the barren fig tree (Luke 13:6-9) a landowner is visiting his vineyard, examining the trees and the vines. Fruit trees were always planted in Palestine's vineyards, and the vines were not tied on trellises; they lay on the ground or climbed the trees.

The landowner examines everything and sees a fig tree that has produced nothing in three years. He orders one of his workers to cut down the tree; it is just leaching nourishment from the soil. But the worker says:

> *"Sir, let it alone for one more year, until I dig around it and put manure on it. If it bears fruit next year, well and good; but if not, you can cut it down."* (Luke 13:8-9)

In the Vegetable Garden

One final example: a parable not from the wheat field or the vineyard but from the vegetable garden near the houses. Probably the disciples had irritated Jesus with their concerns and skepticism. Maybe they had said to him: "We have so many enemies, there are all too many in the land who are indifferent, and the number of our real followers is terribly small. Where is this all going? Where is this reign of God you are always talking about?"

Then Jesus shows them a mustard seed. It disappears between thumb and finger; it is no larger than the head of a pin. He shows it to them and says: "It is with the reign of God as with a mustard seed. You put it in the ground and it becomes a bush so huge that the birds nest in its shade" (cf. Mark 4:30-32). Around Lake Gennesareth, in fact, mustard bushes of the species *Brassica nigra* could grow to a height of ten feet.

Jesus must often have reflected on this wonder. Can the reign of God be compared with a mustard seed—first so tiny, then in the end so gigantic? This simple plant became an image, a symbol for him. It became a "world tree" in whose branches "the birds of the air" build their nests (Luke 13:19). Thus a "biological" observation becomes a parable of the reign of God.

In comparison to the task before it, Jesus' group of disciples was ridiculously small. Jesus had to tell them: "Fear not, little flock!" (Luke 12:32), and yet, a few decades later, there were communities of disciples everywhere around the Mediterranean; one day the church became so obvious that the Roman emperors who had long despised and persecuted them came to acknowledge them and even came to their aid as a means of knitting together the Roman world empire that was threatening to fall apart.

Our concerns are similar to those of Jesus' disciples in the past. There is little to be seen of the reign of God. Explosions of violence are increasing throughout the world. Weapons are more and more deadly, the powerful more skillful. The numbers of citizens driven by hatred and anger are increasing. Christians appear helpless. In many countries they are even persecuted, and often they are despondent. Many simply accommodate; many others are in danger of succumbing to resignation.

That is why the parable of the tiny mustard seed that grows into a bush a dozen feet high and in whose shadow the birds of the air dwell applies to us in particular. Jesus tells us in this parable: When people trust God and let themselves sink into the soil of the field God is tilling, the tiniest beginnings can become God's new world.

Of the Stuff of the World

We have seen how closely Jesus holds to reality in his agricultural parables: that is, he knows and takes seriously the rules of biology. Consequently I will dare to push this matter of the biology of the reign of God a little further.

We have the earth with its nutrients, moisture, and warmth; we have tilled the soil. The seed is sown under those conditions. Then something happens that seems amazing to us: the seed germinates and grows—and it all happens because chemicals in the earth surrounding the seed are absorbed through thin membranes. Biologists call it osmosis. The genes within the seed's cells bring about a grouping of many elements around the seed and produce a completely different relationship, so that a stem grows up, and then a head, and then grain in the head.

It is just the same with the reign of God. It is not something absolutely new, separate from what existed before, cut off from the history of the world. No, the reign of God takes up the material of the world and of our lives, regroups it, places it in a new context, organizes and transforms it. The reality toward which everything in us and around us is directed is God. It is the old things, the old material of the world, and yet everything is made new. When God has finally become the meaning and measure of all history, the reign of God, the rule of God, is present.

Thus the "biology" of the reign of God also has its basic structures and rules! These include the fact that, while we can do a great deal—breaking ground, fertilizing the earth, sowing the seed, to use the familiar imagery—we cannot create the miracle of growth. The fact that someone turns back, dares to believe, and becomes a living member of the church is something we cannot bring about on our own.

If we speak that way, however, there is danger of misunderstanding. We might put it this way: *we* do part of the work and *God* does the rest. *We* do the sowing, and everything else is *God's* business. Where we reach our limits, God takes over and does the rest.

But the biology of the reign of God is not like that! In that case God would only be a kind of stopgap. In fact, we have to do everything ourselves. If a church hall is not cleaned and accumulates dust, God does not take over. The church will only get dirtier and more repulsive. If a sound system is of poor quality, God does not perform a miracle: the older people will simply not be able to hear what the preacher is saying. And if we sing badly because we haven't practiced our hymns or our hearts are not in it, no choir of angels takes over the singing. We ourselves have to do it all—from beginning to end.

And at the same time God does it all—from beginning to end. Not even a wisp of belief would be possible for us if it were not given by God. The beginnings of brotherly and sisterly love would not exist among us if God did not give it. Where the reign of God grows, it is entirely God's work and at the same time altogether human work, so here also we must say—as we say of Jesus Christ—"fully divine and fully human, without confusion or separation!"

But how can it be that something can be the work both of God and of humans? How does it happen that the coming of God's realm can be God's very own doing and simultaneously our own work, our service, our deed? It can only happen when we let God act, when we are entirely transparent to what God wants to do through us. Again and again we have to pray that *God's* will be done and not what *we ourselves* want. We absolutely must not pray: "Dear God, make my wishes your own! Make it so that *you* will what *I* will!" We have to keep always before our eyes the truth that God must fulfill the divine promises, not our desires.

In Front of Our Faces

The parables spoken of here have something special about them that I want to mention in closing: all those who originally heard these parables had their material directly in front of them: mustard was growing in the vegetable garden. Fruit trees were blooming at the door or nearby in the village, and all over the Galilean hills there were fields of wheat and barley. Certainly Jesus could tell other kinds of parables: from the worlds of merchant capitalists, great landowners, and the powerful in general. But it is precisely here, in his "parables of growth," that he speaks of a world that was directly before his hearers' eyes.

Why? So that it would be clear that the reign of God is not somewhere far away. It is not above the clouds. It is not "somewhere." No, it is in our midst. It happens in our everyday lives. It happens where already today, through our faith, hope, and patience, God is acting among us and making the world an Easter place.

The Strangeness of the Our Father

The Our Father is the best-known prayer of Christianity. Countless people pray it, many of them daily. But it is not only the best-known Christian prayer, it also seems self-explanatory to those who pray it—and that is usually deception. If we look more closely, the Our Father is a resistant prayer. It is by no means transparent. Basically it is even strange to us, and we have to overcome its strangeness. Then, indeed, it will really lead us to Jesus and, through Jesus, to the Father in heaven to whom it is addressed.

The Form of the Our Father

We are already somewhat alienated by the fact that this prayer is so brief. The prayers of all religions tend to be lengthy, but the Our Father is characterized by extreme *brevity*. We could argue that it was probably intended only as a kind of catechetical model: Jesus simply wanted to show his disciples what the content of a prayer should be. Against that, however, is that Jesus explicitly urges brevity in prayer. His disciples are not supposed to babble when they are praying, as the Gentiles do. The latter use many words in order to ensure they will be heard by their gods (Matt 6:7-8). But it is not to be that way with Jesus' followers: the Father in heaven already knows what they need (Matt 6:32).

It must also be somewhat off-putting that the Our Father is pure *petition*. In Matthew's version it ends with the desperate cry: "Rescue us from the Evil One!" (Matt 6:13). At the latest by the end of the first century CE that conclusion was found so strange, even improper, that a doxology was added: "For thine is the power and the glory forever." That doxology (later augmented by a third member, "the kingdom") is not original; it is missing from the oldest manuscripts of the New Testament.

Why is the Our Father pure petition? Obviously Jesus was also familiar with lament before God, thanksgiving, praise. But the unbelief that confronted him and his preaching from the beginning was so great that at first the prayer of Jesus' followers had to be primarily an urgent plea.

Finally, the *form* of the first three petitions is also alienating. Why the peculiar passive, "Hallowed be Thy name"? Which of us speaks that way in normal life? Who among us would say "Swept be the stairs"? But in the first part of the Our Father the grammar that Jesus uses is *indirect* (above all, passive), so that it remains open *who* the agent is. God is asked to hallow the divine name, but so should the disciples. God must bring about the sovereign reign of God, but so should the disciples. God must make the divine will present in the world, but the disciples themselves are supposed to put it into practice.

The Content of the Our Father

Thus far we have only made some formal observations, but the content of the Our Father is just as strange to us, starting right away with the first petition: How is God's name to be hallowed? This must mean more than that we are not to "take God's name in vain," as in the Authorized (King James) version of the Ten Commandments.

In the ancient Near East the "name" referred to a person's reputation, authority, dignity, honor, character, and the respect due to her or him. "Blotting out someone's name" in the Psalms meant destroying someone's reputation forever and in that way eliminating that person (Ps 109:13). When the people of God acted rebelliously, God's good "name" was defiled, even destroyed. Then God could no longer be respected by the pagan nations; then they would say: "Where is your God?" (Pss 79:9-10; 115:2).

How else could the name of God be great in the world if not through a "treasured possession out of all the peoples" (Exod 19:5-6) that by its way of living shows that God alone is Lord? That is precisely what chapter 36 of the book of Ezekiel says, in the primary passage to which Jesus' petition for the hallowing of God's name refers. There God says to Israel: I myself will bring you back from among the nations, will gather and cleanse you so that my Name, which you have profaned among the nations, will again be holy—that is, it can no longer be insulted and slandered (Ezek 36:19-28).

The petition for the coming of God's reign, God's "kingdom," has also become strange to us, because in speaking of the reign of God we all too quickly think of heaven. The way for that was prepared by a false understanding of Matthew's expression, "the kingdom of heaven." At that time "kingdom of heaven" was synonymous with "kingdom of God" or "reign of God," and was used because a Jew, out of reverence, avoided saying the word "God," speaking instead of "the Holy One," the "Name," or the "heavens." The coming of the reign refers to the relationships in which we live now. It means this world, this history, this misery we ourselves have created. The reign of God is to come into it—and not only in some distant future but already now, in this hour—today, here!

"Thy will be done!" What about that? Most Christians understand this petition individualistically, applying it to their own lives and asking for strength to constantly seek the will of God and then do it. That understanding, of course, is not false; Jesus, too, struggled to understand God's will when he prayed in the Garden of Olives (Luke 22:42). Should he really stay in Jerusalem? Would it not be better to flee? Wasn't it God's will that he should go on living and proclaiming the reign of God in Galilee, far from the dangerous capital city?

As I have said, an individualistic understanding of the will of God is not false, but here again it is easy to sidestep the strangeness of biblical thinking. A look at the letter to the Ephesians (1:5-11), the book of Isaiah (55:6-11), or especially the extra-biblical Jewish theology of the period reveals that the "will" of God means God's "plan for history," what God desires of the world, what God dreams, what God intends, all the greatness and beauty God wants to create in the world and has long since determined to do. What has long been decided by God "in heaven" is to be made reality "on earth." But this "will" of God respects human freedom. Will people enter into the plan of God?

Thus the first three petitions all speak of the same thing, though from different points of view: namely, God's care for this world. These petitions ask that God's rule, which is completely different from the rule of human beings over each other, may break into history (second petition), may change history—*through Israel.* The people of God are to be a place of faith and holiness in the world so that God's holy Name may be recognized and respected by the nations (first petition). In just this way, we ask, may the plan of history that has lived forever in the heart of God be realized (third petition).

Only in its second part, then, does the Our Father turn to human beings. While the first part was about God's concerns, the second is about human affairs. But we have to be more precise: it is not about human cares in general but about those of the disciples. That is abundantly clear, right away, in the fourth petition. Contemporary interpreters of the Our Father think all too hastily in universal terms. They speak of "help for hungry peoples" and "bread for the world." That is well intended, but the Our Father is a disciples' prayer (Luke 11:1). Its second part is, first of all, about Jesus' disciples and their needs.

These disciples are on the road with Jesus, traveling through Galilee to proclaim the reign of God. In the morning they do not know where, at evening, they will find a roof to cover them. They do not know whether anyone will give them a meal. Therefore they have to pray for "bread for the day to come" that, in the way of reckoning time in those days, began in the evening.

Certainly an explanation of the language is necessary at this point. The wording that is current in our churches, "give us this day our daily bread," is a combination of Matthew 6:11 ("today" or "this day") and Luke 11:3 ("each day . . . day by day"). The Greek word *epiousios* is the source of the difficulty in both Matthew and Luke. Apart from the Our Father we do not find that word anywhere in ancient literature. Most probably it is derived from the Greek verb *epienai*, "approach," "follow." Matthew 6:11 should thus be translated "give us today our bread for tomorrow"!

That fits the disciples' situation exactly. They should not plan, worry, carry supplies with them, be fearful about the future; they should concern themselves only with "today" (Matt 6:34), for the disciples can trust in their *abba*, their Father in heaven, who has taken the place of their earthly father. They can be as carefree as the "birds of the air" and the "lilies of the field" (Matt 6:25-34).

Of course, this absolute trust in the heavenly Father is not an irresponsible and irrational "drifting." As we have seen, it has a fixed foundation: namely, the local followers of Jesus everywhere throughout the land who in the evening receive the disciples into their houses and give them something to eat (Matt 10:11-13; Luke 10:5-7; Mark 6:10). The fourth petition of the Our Father counts on solidarity and mutuality within the Jesus movement. People help each other. The disciples, who have left their own families to follow Jesus, need the aid of the "houses," that is, the families of local disciples of Jesus. The families, in turn, need the help of Jesus and his followers so that they can believe in the coming of the reign of God. How strange that original meaning of the fourth petition of the Our Father now seems to us!

Something similar is true of the fifth petition. It is not about reconciliation in the broadest sense, most certainly not about "the brotherhood/sisterhood of humanity." It is about forgiveness within the group of disciples and those linked to them. Where people have to deal with each other every day, at close quarters, with no escape available, daily mutual forgiveness and constant reconciliation are indispensable necessities.

Strangest of all to us praying today, then, is the sixth petition in the Our Father. How can God lead us into temptation? I constantly receive letters from Christians who pray the Our Father gladly and frequently but simply cannot understand this petition. Often they propose better expressions such as "Guide us when we are tempted!" In fact, the author of the letter of James had already reinterpreted this petition (Jas 1:13-14). Even then the Old Testament background was unfamiliar to that author's fellow Christians.

What it means is simply: God can lead people into a situation in which they are tested in order to reveal, clarify, and strengthen their faith. So God once did to Abraham (Gen 22:1); so God tested Israel in the wilderness (Deut 8:2). So must all who want to follow Jesus guard their faith (Rom 5:3-5). But let God not lead us into a testing, so says the sixth petition, that would be beyond our strength and in which we would inevitably fail (cf. 1 Cor 10:13).

How Alien Ground Can Become Homeland

I have spoken repeatedly about the alienness of the Our Father—a strangeness we must not downplay, smooth out, or pass over. We must first place ourselves in the situation of the disciples to whom the Our Father was first taught if the meaning of the Lord's Prayer is to open to us. We have to go back to the starting point!

But is that possible? Are we to walk barefoot through a hot, dry land in the hope that someone will receive us at evening? Should we preach the reign of God in the public squares of our cities? Are we to heal the sick and lepers in the name of Jesus? We live in different circumstances, in another cultural world, in another time.

The two worlds, after all, have much in common. We only need, for once, to look away from ourselves and think of our Christian sisters and brothers in China, North Korea, Afghanistan, Iraq, Iran, Syria, Somalia, Sudan, or Egypt. These are people who believe in the Gospel of Jesus and who are often under great pressures. For that very reason they depend on one another—for mutual help between households, for solidarity among themselves, for mutual support in faith. There the differences between disciples and people in general, between Christians who have "decided" and those "less certain," have long since become fluid. There it appears very clearly what is meant by a discipleship that continues even under persecution and discrimination—or at any rate in surroundings that are far removed from Christian faith.

There are many other countries where Christians will soon be living in similar situations—not that they will be persecuted everywhere, but they will have to exist in a milieu in which Christianity and most certainly the Gospel of Jesus are absolutely foreign and, basically, a matter of indifference. Then Christians will have to separate themselves not only in the firmness of their faith but also in their *way of life* much more sharply from their surroundings than they do today.

In each of its petitions the Our Father presumes discipleship, but a discipleship lived in a Jesus movement that is both widely scattered and filled with life. That is especially obvious in the bread petition. It is truly horrific when people immediately spiritualize it. But the petition for forgiveness also presumes real conditions of discipleship. Finally, there is the petition that those who pray it be protected against temptation. This petition is not about the usual bourgeois temptations but addresses the danger of losing faith in Jesus and his mission, abandoning one's own call and adapting oneself wholly to society.

Likewise, the first three petitions are not about humanity in general, a world ethos, or the development of a richer and more conventionally settled individual existence. Against the background of Ezekiel 36:19-28 this is about the people of God, which is nothing other than the instrument of divine action in the world. The name of God, the coming of God's reign, God's plan with the world—according to the Bible, all these depend fundamentally on the presence in the world of a people that mirrors God's love, justice, and mercy: the love, justice, and mercy of the God of Abraham, Isaac, and Jacob.

It is true that Vatican Council II gave a new emphasis to the theme "people of God," but we are still strangers to that basic biblical theme. The Our Father—rightly understood—could free us from our forgetfulness of God and lead us back to what the reign of God, the people of God, and faith in Jesus mean. To put it another way: it could bring us an insight into the true way of life in the reign of God.

But may we pray it at all? May we "dare" to speak it as in the liturgical introduction to the Our Father? ("As our Lord Jesus Christ has taught us, we dare to say . . .") We should not be too confident. The Our Father is not by any means a universal prayer. It is dangerous, for it presupposes that our concerns are identical with those of Jesus: the coming of the reign of God, which is to say the healing and salvation of the world—a making-holy that comes entirely from God and yet demands our entire commitment.

The Our Father presupposes that we live from the same root as Jesus: the root that is Israel. It presumes that we want the same thing Jesus wanted: the gathering and uniting of the people of God so that, through the people of God, the world can be changed. It presupposes that we live our faith not in isolation but in mutuality, in community. It presumes that we live with the same radicality as Jesus and his disciples—or at least that we long for that radical life.

So if our lives are about the honoring of God and the coming of God's reign, the authenticity of God's people—then, *then* we may pray the Our Father, and then this prayer Jesus entrusted to his disciples will become our cherished home.

An Aid to Prayer

In order that all this need not remain mere theory, I once tried to paraphrase the original Jesus-sense of the Our Father:

> *Father in heaven, we are your disciples, your community, your church. Together with Jesus, and listening to his words, we are permitted to speak to you as our father.*—Abba, dear Father!

> *Gather your scattered and strife-torn people. Make it to be the true people of God, so that your name may be honored before all the world. Give us the strength to gather people in your name, to bring them together and make them one.*—Hallowed be your name!

> *Let your reign, your rule come into the world. Be our only Master. We no longer want to serve our self-made gods. Give us the strength to live truly human lives as your people, without violence or hatred, in your peace.*—Your kingdom come!

Bring your plan to completion, the plan for the world you have conceived from all eternity. Let it come from heaven to earth, from your heart to ours. Give us the strength, together with our communities, to be your instrument, your sacrament for the world.—Your will be done, on earth as it is in heaven!

Because you are our dear Father, give us today as much of the essentials as are necessary for our service. Let our first concern be for your reign, and let it be more important to us than everything else. Let us be so filled with the need to bear witness to it that we have no time at all to plan and constantly to think only of ourselves. Give us the strength, in all this, to help one another and provide for one another.—Give us the bread we need for this one day!

We can never repay all the debts we have incurred before you, and to which we continually add. We always fall short in love. Therefore: forgive us all our indebtedness, all our guilt! We know that we dare not utter such a prayer unless we also forgive our brothers and sisters all their debts to us.—Forgive us our debts as we forgive our debtors!

It is because your reign is to break into our miserable history that we are so threatened by temptation: the temptation to fall away, to abandon our discipleship, to despair of your church and no longer believe in your plan for the world. Do not lead us into a situation in which this temptation will overcome us. Let us not fall victim to it, but deliver us from the deadly power of evil!— Lead us not into temptation, but deliver us from evil!

Obviously such a paraphrase cannot replace the Our Father. Jesus' prayer is better. It does not require many words. It is brief and incisive. Its vividness comes from the very fact that there is no need to say many words to God. God knows what we need, even before we ask.

We should pray the Our Father every day, as Jesus taught it and the church has handed it down to us—pray it slowly, thoughtfully, and reverently. We should protect it as we would a costly treasure. It not only leads us to the center of our Christian existence; it also shows us who Jesus really was, because it draws us to the heart of his heart.

Unceasing Prayer

"Rejoice always!" says 1 Thessalonians 5:16. That sounds good. We like it. We are "with it." But what kind of joy is it? It doesn't mean "Always be in a good mood!" or "Always be cheerful!" or "Be sure to have fun!" Paul was not inclined to offer such suggestions for "wellness."

"Rejoice always!" This is about a much deeper joy. It can even be mixed with sorrow, but repeatedly overcomes it because it transforms all sadness. For Paul the joy of which he speaks is a fruit of the Holy Spirit (Gal 5:22). It is not something we can produce on our own; we can only be open to it. It is God's gift.

All the same: even if we understand the command to "rejoice always" rightly, because we read it in a Christian sense, the saying is illuminating. It sounds wonderful.

But then Paul immediately adds a second command that is quite similar in form—and it does not enlighten us; it doesn't sound so good; we really don't like it. This call to continual joy is followed, without interruption, by a call to continual prayer: "Pray without ceasing!" (1 Thess 5:17). We should not only live always in the joy of God but also pray without interruption. What does that mean?

Is it a command to recite prayers all the time, without interruption? Or is Paul urging the community in Thessalonica to hold regular prayer meetings or thinking, in visionary form, of something like the later "perpetual adoration" in which the parishes and monastic houses within a diocese form a chain?

Four Examples

"Pray without ceasing!" What could that mean? Let me try to access it with four examples from daily life.

First: here is a married couple. They are not beginners at married life; they have already overcome their first marital crises and in doing so they have learned to respect the "otherness" of the partner. They no longer try to educate the partner and shape her or him according to their own ideas. What a miracle! They still love each other: even more, in fact, than at the beginning.

They talk together. They laugh and chuckle. They wish one another "good morning." They say "good night" at bedtime. They say "enjoy!" before they begin a meal. *He* does not say: "These are *not* the best dumplings you've ever made!" but instead "This mushroom sauce is truly delicious!" "Yes," she says with satisfaction, "this time I put in some white wine and a clove of garlic."

I won't go on describing the days and nights of this couple: all the little polite gestures like "Thank you!" and "Please!" and "I'm sorry!" and "Oh, you did that well!"—the many little signs of their companionship. Sometimes it is a loving glance, sometimes only a small gesture, but often a great deal more!

Of course they are not speaking with each other all the time. Each has her or his own work, but somehow they are always present to each other. It may be that one calls the other late in the afternoon: "Things are a little chaotic at the office. I'll probably be home an hour later than usual." They realize how close they are when one of them has to go on a trip, and especially when one or the other is in the hospital for an operation.

It is all a constant communication: often quiet, often reserved, sometimes almost imperceptible, often impatient, or hot, or passionate. There are certainly spaces in this communication, times when outsiders cannot perceive it—yet it is still there and never ceases.

Oh, if only it were that way in every marriage! Unfortunately, we know how often it is the reverse, which brings me to my second example: no more "good morning" or "good night," no "please" and "thank you," no seeking the face of the other, no yearning, no conversation, no sign. One can predict that unless a miracle happens the two will soon separate. In reality they are already parted.

A third example: the world of children! Here no description is really necessary: we all know, mothers especially, how children seek communication (I am speaking of "normal" children)—how they continually want to touch, see, hear, express themselves, talk.

My last example: not long ago a fifteen-year-old told me how he suffered. He lived with his parents and a brother two years older than he in an apartment. Because he supposedly had insulted his brother at some time or other, it had been years since his brother had spoken to him. The elder brother completely ignored the younger one, paid no attention to him, consistently and literally looked past him.

All that is creepy. The parents were helpless. I found the whole thing unimaginable, but it was true, and I would say it is a crime, because in this way the younger brother was made an un-person. He was no longer even an object. His existence was denied.

What can we learn from these four examples? People who are in community express that community with one another. They look at one another, nod to each other, speak together and tell each other many things. They used to send each other letters when they were apart; now they use their smartphones. They exchange thanks and requests, kudos and complaints, questions and answers, seeking and repeatedly finding each other—all of it not as a burden but as a matter of course.

Prayer: An Unceasing Conversation

Everything I have just tried to describe is true also of our relationship to God. If there is no living conversation between us and God, no thanking and asking, no lamenting and praising, God will never be a person for us—and thus in the long run nonexistent.

But for those who pray, God is a living person, a conversation partner, the "God of my life" (Ps 42:9). Those who pray experience that God is looking at them, signaling in a thousand ways the new joy that is being put into their hearts—and that for them nothing is "in vain." They have fixed themselves in God.

They tell God everything that moves them, complain to God about their miseries, pray to God for help. They are attentive to God's favors and are always thankful. They learn more and more how to connect everything to God.

This fixing-oneself-in-God and living-with-God cannot be limited to one hour a week; it can only be an unceasing conversation. Those experienced in prayer know that this ongoing conversation is very concrete—as tangible as when lovers talk to one another. They tell each other everything; they want to be always close to one another.

I hear the objection: that is sheer nonsense! Laughing and giggling with God? You can't treat God that way! It demeans God's greatness, doesn't take God's hiddenness and the incomprehensible mystery of

God seriously. — Answer: In that case Jesus, too, demeaned his heavenly Father and failed to take him seriously, because he addressed God with the familiar expression *Abba*, "dear father" (Mark 14:36).

I can hear the next objection: That is all private devotion, religious individualism, "God and the soul, the soul and its God!" — Answer: No, that is not at all what it is. If the ongoing conversation with God is genuine it includes everything: the neighbor in need, the community that sustains us, the church into which we are baptized, the world that presses on us every day. We only need to read Paul's letters to see what "pray without ceasing" meant concretely for Paul. For example, at the beginning of First Thessalonians he writes:

> *We* [this "we" refers to Paul and his coworkers Silas and Timothy] *always give thanks to God for all of you and mention you in our prayers, constantly remembering before our God and Father your work of faith and labor of love and steadfastness of hope in our Lord Jesus Christ.* (1 Thess 1:2-3)

That is just one example. Paul's letters are full of passages that show, again and again, that Paul's constant prayer is not an isolated gyration around God and his own soul, but that all his praying is knotted with and woven into the happiness and neediness of his congregations and their common work of building community.

I can hear a final objection: "I work all day long. My job has to be done properly and it occupies my whole attention. If it is done correctly, it is service to God. Nothing more is required. It is enough for me to bring the whole week's happenings before God on Sunday, in the common prayer and praise of the congregation." — Answer: anyone who does not complain, beg, thank, and give praise to God all through the week cannot do it on Sunday, either. Obviously Sunday is the climax, the high point of the week when everyone and everything come together. But in order to be gathered it has to grow beforehand.

Think again of the two people who love each other deeply. Obviously there are hours when they celebrate their love. But that could not happen if, in the time between, they were not engaged in that silent, often scarcely perceptible, and yet unceasing conversation with one another: sometimes in words, sometimes without words, sometimes very seriously, but often with smiles on their faces.

Inattentive

He really should have been listening, especially because it was a good sermon. But in the pew in front of him was a man (whom he knew) with his four-year-old daughter (whom he also knew) on his lap. The child was very still, not disturbing anyone, and seemed to be listening like the adults around her. But she had leaned her head against her father's head, and he had very black hair and his daughter had blond hair that shone in the sunlight that was pouring through one of the big, bright windows of the church, with dust motes floating in it. The light fell directly on the child's head. Black and gold.

Suddenly his own head was busy with biology, with genes and their unalterable laws and implacable play. His thoughts wandered from the mother's hair (brown) to the grandmother's hair (ash blond), and then on and on—and suddenly it was no longer about hair but expanded to the infinite combinations of earth's matter, the cascades of cellular neurotransmitters, and finally the incomprehensible history of evolution, the arduous journey of more than four billion years from the first blue algae to the earliest amphibians that dared to move from water to land, to the earliest mammals, to human beings—finally even to the father with black hair, his blond daughter, and the preacher, who was still at work with well-chosen words, with refreshing intelligence and turns of phrase that he skillfully wove from time to time into his interpretation of the Gospel.

Those wordplays gave another boost to his imagination—far, far into the past. He heard the grunting cries of our apelike ancestors who moved through the forest seeking berries and insects, and he imagined how language developed over millions of years out of this mixture of grunts and shrill cries, language that the pastor in the pulpit was now shaping with refined organs of speech, this language that had developed a whole realm of concepts that could speak of God and God's creation, of the redemption and perfection of humanity.

And he found that the evolution of language was a phenomenon as unimaginable as the evolution of human beings out of cyano-bacteria—and at the moment when, in the swift movements of his fantasy, he had come to just the point at which he sorrowed for all the Christian fundamentalists who cling to the idea that the earth was created in a relatively short time as a completed product, and he said to himself, not for the first time, that a Creator who worked by allowing the world to evolve—out of the dust of stars through primitive one-celled beings to the enchanting child in the pew in front of him—that such a Creator was infinitely greater than the God of the fundamentalists—

At that moment the preacher said "Amen," and the child smiled at her father, and he himself was not at all sure what he should think about his inattention.

The Wealth of the Poor Widow

Among the most spacious new features of the Jerusalem temple begun by Herod the Great was the "court of the women." There, behind the columned ambulatories, was a hall devoted to receiving contributions for maintaining the temple and the regular presentation of animals for sacrifice. That hall was called the "treasury." In it people presented their gifts, naming the amount and the purpose for which they were to be used. Temple officials sat at the various containers for coins, with their trumpet-shaped mouths, checking that the money was in the prescribed form or whether it was sufficient for the purpose named.

Thus everyone in the vicinity could hear what was donated. Some of those who gave a lot of money would have made the size of their sacrifice known very loudly and clearly.

Jesus is near the treasury and hears how contributions are stated and their purpose announced. There is constant coming and going. Mark writes (12:41) that "many rich people put in large sums." We can imagine all the people going and coming: Jews from the homeland and from the Diaspora, men and women, rich and poor. Their class and origins can be seen from their clothing and often also heard in their language or dialect.

Two Copper Coins

Jesus continues to watch and listen. He sees how a poor woman enters the treasury. Her clothing shows that she is poor and her style of dress that she is a widow. She thus lives in twofold misery: she is not only poor, but she has no helper and no legal protection through a husband.

Jesus sees her handing her gift to the priest and hears that she is donating two copper coins. A copper coin was the smallest amount there was. Jesus is deeply moved by what he sees. It is a severe contrast: first the rich, now the poor! First silver coins, often in large amounts, now two "coppers"!

Jesus also sees the background: the rich for whom donating a few silver shekels doesn't pinch at all and the poor widow who gives everything she has. The two copper coins could have assured her something to eat for the next day. They were literally life-support. But of this desperately needed sum she gives not half—she could, after all, have given the priest just one coin—but all.

Jesus sees the whole scope of the event, and he is also certain why the woman has given her all: she wants to make her little contribution to give brilliance to the temple. She believes in the promise that rests on the house of God.

Jesus calls his disciples together, points to the woman who is already leaving the hall, and tells what he has seen. He also interprets it: the widow has given more than all the others, because they have only donated a small part of their property while the poor woman has given everything, all she had to live on (Mark 12:43-44).

Evidently Jesus sees the widow's sacrifice in the context of his proclamation of the reign of God. The meaning of the reign of God is that God turns entirely to human beings in tender, loving care, without reservation, in order to bring the divine glory into the world. God's turning to humanity is an historical event: it takes place in Israel (and through Israel for the whole world), and it is manifest in the new community spirit Jesus creates. The reign of God entices those who are able to experience God's overflowing care, so that they in turn give everything they have: their whole heart, their whole existence. The poor widow who gave her two copper coins becomes for Jesus the real symbol of this "everything."

The evangelist Mark deliberately placed the scene with the widow immediately before the great eschatological discourse and the beginning of the passion story proper. The widow's gift already reflects for him the "totality" of Jesus' surrender of his life. But the widow's act also illustrates the scriptural saying Jesus had quoted shortly before:

> You shall love the Lord your God with all your heart, and with all your soul, and with all your mind, and with all your strength. (Mark 12:30)

The story of the poor widow's sacrifice shows how that fourfold "all" appears concretely: it is beyond all beautiful words. It is easy to say to God: "I belong entirely to you," but whether that phrase matches one's own reality is shown in concrete deeds. In the case of the widow it appears in the fact that she gives not just one copper coin, but both. Decisions in favor of the reign of God are just that real. They are about money, time, and substance. They cut into our lives. God wants everything and will not settle for part of us. God wants us whole and entire.

Can Such a Thing Be?

The objections come immediately, and loudly: Isn't a God who makes such demands a horrible god, one who devours human beings, flesh and bone? One who demands human sacrifice? A god who deprives widows of their last pennies and envies the lucky ones their good fortune? What is the woman supposed to eat the next day, if she has given everything away?

At precisely this point we see that the story of the widow's sacrifice—like all stories in the Bible—demands that we ask about the right "place" and the right "space." The reign of God is not something nebulous, located in the transcendent or only buried deep in the human soul.

Rather, the reign of God demands concrete "space," that is, concrete society. The reign of God begins where people live the new togetherness given by God and dedicate everything they have to that common life. Then the poor widow is no longer alone. Then there are many who offer her shelter, share their meal with her, and console her in her sorrow. In this togetherness given by God people are not devoured, flesh and bone, or deprived of their freedom; instead, it is precisely here that they find their freedom and life.

The Flour Crock and the Oil Jug

This is shown—in the concentrated form of a legendary story about a prophet—from a different angle in a tale that also involves a poor widow. It is in 1 Kings 17:8-16. The lives of this widow and her son are threatened by famine because it has not rained for a very long time—but even so, she gives the last of her food to the prophet Elijah so that he can survive and God's history with Israel can continue through him. And in that very way, it happens that her own life and that of her son are saved.

Here the flour crock that is never empty and the oil jug that is always full are in no way symbolic of a lotusland in which people do not need to do anything. Rather, they are symbols of the abundance that comes about when people give everything they have for God's sake. This fundamental law of the reign of God "functions" only in the presence of the vessel or form that ensures that nothing given by the individual members of the people of God goes missing. That form, indeed, is the church community that has become reality since Jesus' death and resurrection. Mark can tell the story about the poor widow who gives her all without comment because it reflects his own experience of community.

We are fairly well informed about the importance of the state of widowhood in the early church: widows who placed their whole lives—often also their whole estates, if they were wealthy—at the service of the church. They did not remain alone; they were part of community life. On the other hand, the early church saw it as one of its most important duties to provide its own poor, and often those outside also, with the necessities of life. So there came into the world a new thing: a network of Christian communities living in solidarity. In that sense the little story about the widow's offering represents a silent revolution.

At the close of this reflection it needs also to be said that none of this is a *cheap* recipe for improving the world. Anyone who thinks that the phrase "solidary community" represents, at last, a simple formula for creating equality, helping the poor, and changing the world is mistaken. Solidary community is not a given. Sacred Scripture says that Jesus had to die so that community could exist at all. Only those who are ready to follow him can give away everything they have. Only where there are people who die daily with Christ and rise with him can community come about. Then, however, the truth of what community is, what church is, sheds its shining light.

How the Church Grows

Chapter 6 of the Acts of the Apostles begins a new section. We could also say that the sixth chapter opens a new epoch in the narrative course of Acts. Everything Luke has reported thus far was characterized by a profound unanimity in the young community, but now, at this point, something different suddenly appears: a tone not heard before.

The Hellenists' Complaining

Luke writes: "Now during those days . . . the Hellenists complained against the Hebrews" (Acts 6:1). It is no accident that the author chooses the word "complain." In using that word Luke wants to hint that the Jerusalem community is experiencing exactly what is told of Israel during its journey in the wilderness: rejection, revolt, rebellion (cf. especially Exodus 15–17).

Probably the word "complain" is somewhat too soft for what Luke really means here. This is something like a rebellion. The Hebrew equivalent (*tlnt*) of the Greek word Luke uses in Acts 6:1 (*gongysmos*) can also describe the low growls of dogs just before they attack (Ps 59:16). It is possible that Hebrew speakers thought of something like that when they spoke of "complaining" or "murmuring."[1]

Quite a few exegetes believe that Luke romanticized the early Jerusalem community. Evidently they have not read Acts very carefully, because the beginning of chapter 6 reveals no such glorifying romanticism. The young Jerusalem community repeats the sins that the Old Testament attributes to the Exodus generation: mistrust, complaining, rebellion.

---

[1] The AV reads "there arose a murmuring of the Grecians against the Hebrews." —Tr.

But what is the concrete reason for this misery that falls on the community? Luke says that the Hellenists' widows were being neglected in the daily distribution to the poor (Acts 6:1).

And who are the "Hellenists"? They are Greek-speaking Jews from the Diaspora who have settled in Jerusalem in order to live and die in the Holy Land. Evidently some of these Greek-speaking Diaspora Jews had joined the community of disciples in Jerusalem.

Conflicts arose between them and the Aramaic-speaking part of the community, whom Luke calls "Hebrews," over care for the Hellenist widows. That stands to reason. Financial problems in a community can quickly lead to conflict. The Jews from the Diaspora—those who, for example, had moved to Jerusalem from Italy, Greece, or Asia Minor—no longer had the support of their relatives and their home synagogue. They were much more socially exposed than people who had always lived in Israel, and so they were quicker than others to need support from the community. If the women among them became widows they were most certainly dependent on the aid of the Aramaic-speaking part of the congregation. It was all too easy for mistrust to arise and quickly lead to a feeling of being neglected or even disadvantaged.

It seems, however, that there were other reasons for the tensions within the community. Luke does not name them, but his description of the situation gives us abundant clues: two different languages were spoken in the Jerusalem community: Aramaic and Greek. Language is always more than an external garment. A different language always means different feelings, different thoughts, a different culture. Evidently this division in thought and perceptions of reality extended even to theology.

From the great speech given by Stephen before the Council (Acts 7:1-53), we see immediately that the "Hellenists" could speak much more critically about the temple and the Torah than the "Hebrews" (Acts 7:51-53; cf. 6:13-14). Then, when after Stephen's martyrdom a persecution arose over the Jerusalem community, it seems that only the Hellenists were pursued, not the Hebrews. This shows that the tensions depicted in Acts 6:1 were not merely a matter of social conflict. They were also divisions over theology and the question of how radically the young community should appear and speak in public.

We find it difficult to decide in retrospect which theology was better: that of the Hellenists or that of the Hebrews. The Hellenists had set in motion a mission among the Gentiles. When Luke writes in Acts 8:1 that after the death of the Hellenist Stephen a great persecution of the church in Jerusalem broke out, and that all the members "except the apostles" were scattered through the regions of Judea and Samaria, we can only interpret that historically to mean that it was the Hellenists who had to flee Jerusalem while the Hebrews (here represented by the figure of the Twelve) could remain in the city. Immediately thereafter we have a description of the missionary work of Philip, who most certainly did not devote himself solely to "waiting on tables" (Acts 8:4-40). Philip was a Hellenist. Thus it was the persecuted Greeks who began the mission outside Jerusalem and continued ultimately into Syria to work among the Gentiles (see Acts 11:19-20). It was the Hellenists who made the little congregation of Jewish disciples of Jesus into an international people of God. They unswervingly turned the new thing that had come with Jesus into actual fact.

However, they were also in part responsible for the fact that the church's connection to Israel became more and more fragile. On precisely this point the Hebrews were more conservative. They held fast to the temple and they kept the whole Torah. At the same time, they insisted that *the church is Israel*. That was later forgotten by many in the purely Gentile Christian church (see Rom 11:17-20). So ultimately the quarrel between the Hellenists and the Hebrews represented a crossroads—with serious consequences.

The Initiative of the Twelve

Hence the situation of the community was serious: there was a threat of division—or we may say it had already arrived, for social reasons but for theological ones as well. How would the young church deal with this situation? That is precisely Luke's interest, so we must pay close attention to the text.

The Twelve take the initiative. They do so because they are the center of the community and one of their principal duties was to be a symbolic representation of the unanimity of the community and to continually make it a reality. They gather the whole congregation. The text says literally that they "call them together" (Acts 6:2). That is: this is not just *any* gathering; it is a meeting before the face of God of the "*ekklēsia*," the community called by God.

Now the Twelve make a suggestion to the community called together, a proposal for alleviating the division and dealing with the crisis. The proposal is accepted and put into action by the whole assembly. There are three things about this suggestion that are interesting and are of great importance for us as well:

First: The proposal gives the community a new form. A new category of service is created, and thus the form of the community is altered. Seven men are chosen from within the community and all of them are Hellenists, as we can see immediately from their Greek names: Stephen, Philip, Prochorus, Nicanor, Timon, Parmenas, and Nicolaus (Acts 6:5). The seven are chosen by all, and then the Twelve install them in their office with prayer and the laying on of hands.

People of a "charismatic" bent are often resistant to forms, structures, and institutions. They prefer that everything happen spontaneously—with full conviction and an infinite quantity of good will. They tend to forget that there can be no faith and certainly no living without fixed forms. Even love needs law. We cannot avoid the fact that according to Acts 6 the community is rescued because the Twelve and the assembly itself—the growing community—give it a new form.

Second: This new form is supposed to make it possible for the common table to be free from restrictions, tensions, or any "neglect of the widows." We can translate that to today by saying that "service at table" should make it possible for there to be *convivium* and *convivere* in the community again, eating together and living together with all that implies, up to and including economic matters.

Third: The particular goal of this newly possible togetherness is that the community can do justice to its missionary task, what Luke calls "service of the word" (Acts 6:4). Obviously, one cannot exist without the other. The community can only be missionary if all work together in such a way that mission can go forth. The missionary "service of the word" of part of the community presupposes the solidarity and support of the whole. At the end of the section in Acts 6:1-7, then, we read—and this was the purpose, for Luke, of his whole depiction of the conflict:

> *The word of God continued to spread; the number of the disciples increased greatly in Jerusalem.* (Acts 6:7)

Crisis Helps the Church to Grow

Luke means to say that it is especially in crisis, in the profound distress of the young community and the response forced by that distress, that the community is able to grow. The strife between the Hellenists and the Hebrews was not eliminated by people softening their feelings and speaking politely to each other but by all joining together in taking a new step.

So we need not lose heart when the church falls into profound crisis. Not that the distress is not what it is: it is always sad and even frightening. But that crisis can lead to a new step in the church's growth if only it listens to what the crisis wants to tell it and if all those within it join together to find the answer—namely, what God's will is. Certainly this new step in growth presupposes something more than structural change. It also requires self-surrender and discipleship of Jesus on the part of those who serve the word and who allow themselves to be led by the Holy Spirit (Acts 6:3). Luke makes that clear in the person of Stephen, and then of Philip.

Aloof and Immovable?

When we hear mention of Greek philosophy we immediately think of Plato and Aristotle. In fact, those two great philosophers exercised an enduring influence on the thought and culture of the West. But there was a philosophical trend whose influence was still greater in antiquity: that of the Stoa. When Paul wrote the letter to the Romans the philosophy of the Stoa was much better known and more influential than the teachings of Plato or Aristotle because the Stoics asked primarily: How should people live in the world so that their lives will be successful?

The Stoics were realists. They saw the world's misery, the hollowness of society, and the people's greed. They saw the powers and authorities to whom people are subjected. They knew how people are driven by their passions and their fear of sickness and death.

In view of this world of greed, uncertainty, and fear, every good Stoic teacher taught his students to withdraw into themselves. Purify yourselves, they said, so that no passions will rage within you. Allow no desire to reign over you. Your masters must be nothing but moral reason and your conscience. Fight for inner freedom, detachment, so that nothing can disturb you. Then you will find peace in your innermost self. When you have achieved that detachment of the soul you have no need to fear death any longer, because what is terrible is not death but the *idea* of dying; that alone causes you to fear. Once you have done away with that fear-inducing idea, nothing else can disturb you. Then you will be victor over all worldly powers; they will no longer be able to touch you. Therefore wise persons do not permit themselves to be guided by any kinds of ideas or opinions, but only by their own reason. It alone makes them independent and free.

At first glance one might think that Paul, too, was influenced by the Stoa, because in the eighth chapter of his letter to the community in Rome he writes, in a gorgeous passage, that nothing any longer has control over us—hardship, distress, persecution, famine, nakedness, peril, or sword. We overcome all those things (see Rom 8:35-37).

If we look more closely, however, we can see the profound difference between Paul and Stoic philosophy. I will describe it in three ways.

The First Difference

Paul is far from propagating the idea of the enlightened and imperturbable human being; to know that, one only has to read his letters. Paul thinks and acts with enormous passion. He has much about him of the prophets' impetuosity and of divine passion. He allows himself to be shaken by the situation of his people (Rom 9:1-3), the conditions in his congregations (for example, see 1 Cor 6:1-11), the suffering of creation, saying that it is groaning as if in labor pains (Rom 8:18-23). It is true that Paul also speaks of the heart's peace, but it is not the peace of the Stoics who have withdrawn into the "self." It is the peace that comes from following Jesus Christ. It is the peace of the Holy Spirit.

The Second Difference

Paul does not use philosophy to downplay suffering and death. What is terrible about death is not only the *idea* of it, he says, but death itself. As Jesus became angry when he encountered the reality of death in that of his friend Lazarus (John 11:33), and as Jesus himself died a horrible and merciless death, so also for Paul death is an inscrutable power that may not be waved away with clever words. Paul looks at the reality of his apostolic life and says, in the words of Psalm 44:22:

> For your sake we are being killed all day long; we are accounted as sheep to be slaughtered. (Rom 8:36)

One needs to have seen how animals are led to slaughter, how they fight with all their strength because they sense what is about to happen to them—to have seen how their throats are cut and their blood spurts . . . at any rate, that is the image with which Israel describes its existence, and Paul chooses the same image for Christians' existence in the Roman Empire. No, it is impossible for him to minimize the inexorable power of death as the Stoics do. Only when death remains death does God's power—the victorious power of God that raises the dead— have its full weight.

The Third Difference

As Paul sees it, rescue from hardship, distress, persecution, and peril comes not from the tranquility of the soul but from the love of God that has seized us in Jesus Christ. Romans 8 speaks of that at a crucial point: namely, at the climax of the passage from which I have just quoted:

> *I am convinced that neither death, nor life, nor angels, nor rulers, nor things present, nor things to come, nor powers, nor height, nor depth, nor anything else in all creation, will be able to separate us from the love of God in Christ Jesus our Lord.* (Rom 8:38-39)

For Paul this love of God that surrounds and sustains believers is precisely *not* something distant, invisible, and unimaginable that rests only in the heart of God. The love of God has entered into history— visible, perceptible, physical—for Paul defines the love of God as the love that has reached us "in Christ Jesus." Here again we have to see precisely what that means. When Paul says "in Christ," he means the church, the community, the mutuality of those who accept one another and are present for one another—because they are "in Christ."

So we may and must understand the conclusion of the text this way: Nothing in the world can separate us from the love of God that encounters us in the church and in the sacraments, as physically as it took form in Jesus Christ. Nothing can separate us from that love.

We have no need to obscure the "sufferings of this present time" (Rom 8:18), to explain them away or suppress them. We can let sickness be sickness, dying be dying, death be death. We may call all our fears by name and express them. We may accept reality with the same sobriety by which Israel accepted the realities of the world.

Only then will sickness no longer be sickness and dying no longer be dying and death no longer be death, for all these powers, even the powers of fear, worry, and lust for life, are already robbed of their power and can be transformed into resurrection. This does not happen through retreat into the self, by means of Stoic imperturbability, but through the love of the one who rescued Jesus from death. That love is not a beautiful philosophical idea but a reality of history.

Baptism as Death and Resurrection

In Romans 6:3-14 Paul speaks of the central event in the life of every Christian: baptism. This is the most important New Testament text for an appropriate understanding of this great sacrament. At the beginning of the passage Paul writes:

> Do you not know that all of us who have been baptized into Christ Jesus were baptized into his death? Therefore we have been buried with him by baptism into death, so that, just as Christ was raised from the dead by the glory of the Father, so we too might walk in newness of life. (Rom 6:3-4)

The meaning of this text is not clear at first glance. Why is Paul talking about death here? More than that: why is he talking about being buried? What does all that have to do with baptism? Parents bringing their child for baptism do not want in that very moment to be thinking about death and burial. How did such a baptismal theology come about?

The Earliest Baptismal Practice

At first the answer seems simple. In the earliest church, whenever possible, baptisms took place in flowing waters. The baptizer and baptizand walked into a river and the baptizand was immersed, thus being simultaneously buried in the water (see Acts 8:36-39). The model was John the Baptizer's baptizing in the Jordan.

The background, however, was the rescue of Israel from the power of Pharaoh. Paul had already connected Christian baptism with the passage of the Israelites through the Reed Sea (1 Cor 10:1-4). It is true that the Exodus narrative says that Israel passed through the sea on dry ground (Exod 14:22, 29). For Paul, however, the Israelites had to "pass through the sea" (1 Cor 10:1), and for him that was the precise connection to Christian baptism.

Thus in the earliest days of the church baptism was a real immersion, a burial in water—but at the same time a rescue from the waters, a passage through death to life.

At this point we modern Christians have some difficulty: the immersion in early Christian baptismal practice has long since become a gentle pouring of water. When a few drops of baptismal water run over the forehead of the baptizand we sense nothing of the symbolism of being immersed and buried. We no longer even need baptismal fonts or stone basins: decorative christening bowls suffice. We can still associate baptism with washing and cleansing, but no longer with dying and being raised from the floods of the deep, the waters of chaos and death.

All that brings us closer to the theme of "death" and "the grave" in Pauline baptismal theology, but we have still not approached Paul's train of thought. We can only understand this when we realize that Romans 6:3-14 has a background that shapes and structures the text, and that background is nothing other than one of the oldest Christian creeds.

An Early Confession of Faith

Paul quotes it in 1 Corinthians 15:3-5, and explicitly as the decisive confession of faith that he himself received soon after Christ was revealed to him and that he now hands on to his communities:

> Christ <u>died</u> for our sins in accordance with the scriptures, and . . . was <u>buried</u>, and . . . was <u>raised</u> on the third day in accordance with the scriptures, and . . . appeared to Cephas, then to the twelve. (1 Cor 15:3-5)

This confession of the early church's faith names not only the Easter appearances but three crucial mysteries in the life of Jesus: his dying for our sins, being buried, and being raised from the dead. These three events are the precise substance of Paul's baptismal theology in Romans 6: Christians are baptized into Jesus' death, are buried with him, and pass with Christ "from death to life" (Rom 6:13).

Now it is clear what baptism ultimately has to do with death and burial: the baptizand is baptized "into Christ Jesus," that is, the Messiah Jesus. This means being baptized, in this sacrament, into the fate of Jesus, his life, and above all, its ultimate culmination. That in turn means dying with him, being buried with him, rising with him to new life. Were it any less, then the baptizand would not really become one with Christ.

Real Rescue

But what, exactly, does it mean that the baptized die with Christ? Is it only on the symbolic level? That would be too little. Their dying and being buried with Christ must also become a lived reality; otherwise the sacrament would be nothing but a mystery-action like those performed in myriad mystery cults in antiquity. Dying with Christ, in contrast, relates to real history: the history of Jesus Christ. Must not "dying with" Christ then be likewise historically and socially visible? Paul gives us the answer to that question especially near the end of the whole section when he writes:

> *So you must also consider yourselves dead to sin and alive to God in Christ Jesus.* (Rom 6:11)

Thus in baptism we die to sin. That is simply decisive for Pauline baptismal theology. However, Paul is not referring to personal sins that the baptizands (who at that time were primarily adults) had already committed at previous times and against which they would battle in future. Beyond that Paul means, above all, the *power of sin* that has embedded itself in the world because of the ever-repeating disobedience of humans, the power that dominates society, that robs people of freedom, darkens their minds, and perverts their actions.

It is obvious that this power of sin has played a fearful role in history: a glance at the newspaper or ten minutes of television news suffices. It is clear to every thoughtful person that here we are encountering not just single, isolated crimes—such as the murder of a politician or the rape of a woman—but beyond them a set of *evil powers* that saturate history: misuses of power over generations, webs of lies that prove altogether impenetrable, national prejudices that cannot be eliminated, models of hostility to life that dominate society and are regarded as obvious truths, injustice that constantly produces more injustice.

In his death Christ broke through that *realm of power* because he had lived truth and nonviolence, entirely and transparently. It is true that the powers of evil in the world killed him, but they could not block his surrender to God, his fidelity to his duty, his love even in death. Therefore his death created a space of freedom such as there had never been before: a space of freedom for God, freedom from evil, freedom for mutual love.

For Paul and the whole New Testament that space of freedom is the church. In baptism the baptizand is received into the church, into the realm of God, into salvation from the possibilities for evil in the world. This, incidentally, is also the reason for baptizing infants: even the helpless child has the right to be brought into this space of salvation and freedom. It is not as if the church is immune to invasions of evil—disobedience to God, sin, afflictions—but the possibility of freedom lies open. Sin has lost its sinister power to estrange people from God and to dominate everything.

New Society

In fact, the men and women of the early church experienced baptism as a profound turning point. They knew that in accepting the faith and the gift of baptism they were entering into a new creation, a new form of society. They experienced baptism as a change of allegiance—turning away from the gods and demons of pagan society and entry into a new life. What the early church called *agapē*, living no longer for oneself but for God and others, was experienced as a radical change in one's life, a transition from previous pagan existence, from death, into genuine life.

Those who have understood Romans 6 will not speak thoughtlessly of church reform. They will know that church reform is only genuine reform when the fundamental experience of the early Christians I have just described takes on new life in our congregations—as an exodus from the many life-destroying models of society and an entry into a new form of life, an experience of a life newly given.

The child over whose forehead the baptismal water flows knows nothing of all that, and yet it is already part of the Christian community that does know. It is placed back in the arms of its parents, who know—that is, who know that they are empowered to show their child that space for life in freedom and faith.

Active Waiting

At some point in the second half of the second millennium BCE, perhaps around the year 1250, a little group of foreign workers broke out of an Egyptian labor camp. They were oppressed people, without rights. The group fled through the lines of Egyptian border guards, eastward into the wilderness. They trusted in their god, the god of their ancestors. They were looking to establish a new society, one in which there would finally be justice and no oppression.

The exodus of that little group took place in the margins of history. Apart from the border guards no one gave them a thought, but the refugees breathed a sigh of relief when they no longer felt the rods of their overseers on their backs. By the time the Old Testament told of this exodus, centuries later, the story had long since become a "type," that is, the model and concretion of all of Israel's experiences of liberation.

A Look Back at the Book of Wisdom

The Old Testament book of Wisdom also uses this kind of compressed narrative technique in looking back at the exodus from Egypt. For the Egyptians—says the wisdom teacher who wrote this book—the night of the exodus was one of dreadful fears that arose like phantoms out of the depths of their souls (Wis 17:9-20). For the Israelites, in contrast, it was a night of liberation because they trusted in God's promises.

In this one night of exodus the author of Wisdom gathers together all Israel's subsequent Passover nights, during which all Israel watches and waits. The songs in praise of the ancestors are sung (Wis 18:9) and, as profound silence has enveloped everything and night is half gone, God's all-powerful word leaps down from heaven to rescue Israel and free it from its enemies (Wis 18:14-15).

Israel waits with full confidence in this night. It is not a passive, inactive waiting. Those who wait obligate themselves to share their property and their whole lives with one another, including the dangers that may come (Wis 18:9).

The Christian Community's Waiting

Thus the book of Wisdom provides us with a key for better understanding particular passages in the gospels: for example, Luke 12:32-48. There Luke has shaped a composition made up of a number of Jesus' parables and images. What unites these pieces of tradition is the waiting of the Christian community for their returning Lord.

As with the historical exodus from Egypt, this is a tiny group in the midst of a superpower society, a group that endures and hopes: "Do not be afraid, little flock, for it is your Father's good pleasure to give you the kingdom" (Luke 12:32). The future does not lie with the powerful, the rich and satisfied, but with these little, humble people who count for nothing. It is they who are chosen for the new thing God has long prepared and that is God's whole joy and longing: namely, that God's new world (the New Testament calls it "the kingdom of God" or "the reign of God") is breaking into the old world and transforming it.

In the communities Luke has in mind this new world of God's has already begun: the rich share with the poor. They do not just extend alms out of their abundance. Instead, they seek to create solidarity within the community: justice and mutual aid.

Such an overwhelming social process is possible because the heart—that is, the whole desire of these people—is not where money and power exercise dominion but where the reign of God is at stake (Luke 12:13-21). They are dressed for action and they have burning lamps in their hands (Luke 12:35). Long Near Eastern robes had to be belted high for running and for labor, and no one could simply switch on a light. Ancient lamps were difficult and tricky to ignite; anyone who was waiting for something or someone was well advised to leave all the lamps burning. So the image of the high-belted robes and burning lamps also speaks of waiting—but a waiting that is alert to spring up and willing to accept a task.

This thinking-with, caring-with waiting is then illustrated in a parable. We see a landed estate with an inner court and a large gate leading to the outside. The owner has been invited to a wedding feast somewhere in the neighborhood. Thus the gate is closed, the beam that serves as a bar has been lowered—but no one is sleeping. Everyone in the house is awake, ready to throw open the gate and receive their master when he returns—even though wedding feasts could last a long time and the corps of servants did not know when the master would return (Luke 12:36-38).

In the early church such "servant parables" were interpreted as referring to Christ's return. The Christian communities saw their role as that of the waiting servants who longed for their master to come back. However, by Luke's time it was already clear that Christ's return might be delayed. There were already servants who said "the master is delayed in coming" (Luke 12:45) and acted accordingly. And there was already reason enough for the communities to emphasize the Lord's words: "You must be ready, for the Son of Man is coming at an unexpected hour" (Luke 12:40). Had "imminent expectation" already changed to a kind of "constant expectation"?

The Coming of the Lord in the Eucharist

For us today the question of the so-called "delay" of the parousia is again different, because in the meantime nearly two thousand years have passed. The end of the world still has not come. Only some fundamentalist sects expect it in their own generation. Under such conditions an imminent expectation seemed senseless, and constant expectation, an offspring of imminent expectation, also seemed something no one could successfully maintain.

The book of Wisdom shows us the way out of this dilemma: it portrays the Israelites' waiting in connection with the Passover feast, that is, with the liturgy. So also the Christian liturgy, at every eucharistic celebration, is oriented to the coming of the Lord. As part of the Eucharistic Prayer the community prays:

> We proclaim your Death, O Lord,
> and profess your Resurrection
> until you come again.

Thus the liturgy keeps our waiting alive, making it a statement of the whole congregation. Above all, the church is convinced that the Lord's coming is already beginning, namely, in the celebration of the Eucharist. The Lord is already coming, entering into our midst—and because that is so, God's new world arises out of the celebration of the Eucharist: a world in which people are united in heart and mind, in which they share their goods, their lives, and their histories with one another, in which they hang their hearts on God's plan and their lamps burn and they are dressed for action.

This is a new kind of waiting, one that already experiences the liberating arrival of Christ in the here and now and that, precisely out of this already-present coming of the Risen One, constantly seeks a way by which Christ can take shape in the community's everyday life.

Caution: Luke is no dreamer. He portrays all that not only as present but equally as a warning, as hope and as burning expectation: this is what Christian community should be.

The Miracle at Cana

The narrative of the wine miracle at the wedding in Cana (John 2:1-12) is one of those stories in which there are always new things to discover because the narration is masterful and every sentence is theology. But how can we still hope to find something new in the text? As is true of every good story, there are a number of possibilities. Here is what I will do: first, I will simply list the characters who appear in the narrative.

Persons

If we follow the course of the narrative we find that the following characters appear, or at least are mentioned: the mother of Jesus, then Jesus himself, then his disciples; there are also servants, the steward, the bridegroom, and finally even Jesus' brothers. The bride and the wedding party do not appear. From that we can already see that this is not simply a description of the typical course of a wedding; at any rate, it could at that time have lasted a whole week or even longer (see Tob 8:19; 11:18). Here, rather, the narrator's interest is presented in the shortest possible snippets, with the aid of artful editing. But what was that interest, and what roles do the individual persons play in developing it?

The most important role belongs to *Jesus*. He is the crucial actor. He rescues the wedding and gives it the lavish abundance a great feast requires. Yet at the same time—as the dialogue with his mother is meant to show—he is moved not simply by the crisis situation but by the will of God. That is precisely what is expressed by the concept of the "hour" that plays such an important part in John's gospel and will be fulfilled on the cross (John 7:30; 8:20). When his mother tells him that the wine has run out, Jesus responds: "My hour has not yet come" (John 2:3-4). The hour of those who think only in terms of human preconceptions "is always here." That is underscored by the confrontation between Jesus and his brothers in John 7:1-9. Jesus, however, acts out of a profound understanding of his heavenly Father and in full harmony with the Father. For that very reason the over-flowing glory of the Father can illuminate his actions.

There is a second actor in the story, besides Jesus, who plays a similarly important role. The sphere of his actions occupies no less than a third of the whole narrative. In the Greek text he is called the *architríklinos*, and interpreters have long sought an adequate transla-tion for the word. Martin Luther, in his famed *Biblia Germanica*, settled on *Speisemeister*, "master of the feast," and many have followed him. Others chose terms such as "head waiter," "sommelier," or para-phrases such as "the one responsible for the feast." The most common English translation is "steward."

In Germany *Speisemeister* cannot be used as a translation any longer because every kind of lunch counter, canteen, and catering service uses the name. (The ad industry has long since recognized that bibli-cal language can be gloriously misused for advertising purposes.) The term "Festordner," equivalent to English "steward," is rising in popularity—and rightly so! The task of the *architríklinos* can best be compared with that of a "master of ceremonies" or "wedding plan-ner," something that exists in most world cultures. Such a person not only administers the formal invitations to the coming marriage (in some cultures by visiting every family individually) but is responsible for the whole course of the celebration. The steward or wedding planner supervises everything, thus taking the weight off the couple and their parents. She or he is the director of the whole affair.

It was thus characteristic of any steward to be deeply involved in the regular rhythm of the marriage feast. Stewards had to be all-seeing and stick their noses into everything. Above all, they had to keep the whole picture in view. So the steward in our story smells everything, tastes everything, sees everything—and yet is not aware of "where the wine came from" (John 2:9). This steward is one of those who hear but do not understand, who see but do not recognize.

But now the crucial moment arrives: although the steward hears and does not understand, sees and does not recognize—indeed, is really a tragic figure—he is important to the story because he has to attest to the outstanding quality of the wine that Jesus provides for the feasting guests: "But you have kept the good wine until now," he tells the bridegroom (John 2:10). He has not understood a thing, and yet he is indispensable in the dramatic course of what is happening here.

The *bridegroom*, too, remains ignorant. He plays a very minor role. Basically he is only needed on the surface of the story so that the steward can recite his portentous "rule for wine" to him. The steward reminds the bridegroom that the good wine is to be served *at the beginning of the feast*. Only when the guests are drunk does one bring ordinary wine from the cellar. Even so, in the deep structure of the narrative the bridegroom represents Christ himself since, according to the steward's assertion, the bridegroom has "kept" the good wine (John 2:10). That is to say: he knows the day and the hour.

Clearly present as counter-figures to the steward are *Jesus' disciples*. It is true that they really appear only at the end of the narrative. They populate the finale, but nothing is said about them except that they "believe." That is: in contrast to the steward, the disciples are those who grasp what is really going on. Thus they already stand, with their whole selves, within the *new existence* that is dawning in Jesus. Somehow or other the disciples thus meld with the *servants*, of whom it is said that they, who had drawn the water, "knew where the wine came from" (John 2:9).

The last sentence of the story also mentions "Jesus' brothers" (John 2:12). They go to Capernaum with Jesus, his mother, and the disciples—probably near the end of the wedding feast. This could be an indication that the bride or bridegroom are relatives of Jesus; that is why he, his mother, and his siblings are at the feast, but Jesus' brothers play no part in the real complex of the story.

And *Mary*, Jesus' mother: what is her role in the whole affair? It is not said of her, as of the disciples, that she "believes." Thus she does not have the same narrative function as the disciples but neither does she belong among those who are involved in the whole event and still do not understand what is really happening.

Her function, as we have already indicated, is different: she exemplifies the fact that Jesus' "hour" is not identical with human "hours," that God's plan does not coincide with our human plans. It is for that reason, and only for that reason, that Jesus rejects his mother's request so impersonally: "Woman, what concern is that to you and to me?" (John 2:4). What is unusual in his rebuff is not the address, "Woman." In the ancient Greek-speaking world a respected woman of high standing could be politely addressed that way—especially by her son (cf. Homer, *Od.* XIX 105, 165, 221, 262, 336). What is crucial, rather, is the dismissive "what concern is that to you and to me?" We would have to paraphrase it as "what do I have to do with you *in this situation*?"

The exchange serves to make clear, through the person of Mary, that the true Israel, the one Jesus is gathering around him, does not happen where family, clan, flesh and blood draw human beings together. No, Jesus' true Israel only happens where people let themselves be drawn into God's plan—without regard for family ties (see Mark 3:20-35).

What is significant is that within this narrative Mary is not like the disciples; she does not represent the eschatological Israel that is now coming into existence through Jesus; instead, she is the preliminary stage for it: those within Israel who have not yet taken the step to true understanding. She represents Israel "pre-Jesus," though certainly in its best form: she is fully present to it. She is ready to hear. Even after Jesus' harsh words she stays on track. She allows herself to be corrected, and then she tells the servants: "Do whatever he tells you" (John 2:5). She believes as faithful Israel believed before Jesus. We must even say that she alone, *within the course of the narrative as such*, is the one who expects her son to act. She alone has a premonition of the eschatological fullness that is dawning in Jesus, so she represents not only the old Israel but the Israel that looks forward in hope to the messianic era and that stands, full of expectancy, on the threshold of what is to come.

The Drama of Salvation History

Thus the drama of salvation history is condensed in the story of the wedding at Cana. First there is the wedding party: people who celebrate, who eat and drink, sing and dance, have all the time in the world, and tell each other all sorts of stories. The text does not say all that, but it is implied. After all, it speaks of six water jars, each of which contains at least twenty gallons. These expensive vessels were made of stone in order to correspond to priestly rules for purification (according to which stone, unlike clay, was not subject to contamination). Such large stone vessels would, of course, be owned only by a wealthy house, one that ranked high in the ritual order. We have to imagine that the wedding party here described were correspondingly numerous and of high standing.

The miracle happens, then, for the sake of this very wedding party. It is about them most of all. But this wedding party is Israel, the world community, the history of the world. The fact that I am not overinterpreting here is clear from the expansive Prologue of the Fourth Gospel, where we find the word "world" (*kosmos*) no fewer than four times.

Many are involved in this dramatic story in which the whole world is to find its happiness and its salvation: first and foremost Jesus, the messianic bridegroom who brings about the longed-for salvation, who in fact *is* himself that salvation. In addition the narrative speaks of Israel, the Israel that waits and hopes and, with the realism that is proper to it ("they have no wine"), longs for the messianic salvation and keeps watch for it. As we have already seen, in our narrative this waiting and hoping Israel is embodied in Mary.

Then there are the disciples. They have understood what is happening at this wedding; they know that everything has begun, and so they represent the Israel that already believes in Christ. But then there are all those who are involved in the story, who are immediately present and still do not understand—and yet are necessary to the story because they help it along. They are embodied in the steward.

And this comprehensive drama of our salvation, this arousing, all-deciding history of our world is concentrated in a brief narrative—in the story of a wedding that took place somewhere in a tiny Jewish village.

The Glory That Remains Hidden

The whole text is obviously directed to the statement at the end:

> *Jesus did this, the first of his signs, in Cana of Galilee, and [thus] revealed his glory; and his disciples believed in him.* (John 2:11)

Here we have an allusion to the Prologue of John's gospel where those who believe in Jesus recite in hymnic fashion: "and we have seen his glory" (John 1:14). Here, at the marriage in Cana, we are shown how people concretely began to believe in Jesus' "glory."

But why do we learn in the course of the narrative about the steward's lack of understanding? Why the broadly constructed motif of the hiddenness of the event? This is an important part of the narrative, and it reveals a crucial strategy that is connected to its final statement:

Jesus' glory is revealed, yet at the same time it remains hidden—and not only hidden, but misperceived by many.

This motif also refers to the Prologue at the point where it reads: ". . . yet the world did not know him" (John 1:10). It is not only this link to the Prologue that is established here; the steward's lack of understanding already sketches something that will become increasingly apparent in the course of the gospel: Jesus will encounter more and more people who see what he does and yet do not believe him—who, in fact, question his mission and reject him. In this regard the scene in John 7:25-30 is especially pertinent. It takes place in the temple during the Feast of Booths. Jesus has to argue with Jerusalemites who witness his appearance and say:

> ". . . *we know **where** this man is from; but when the Messiah comes, no one will know **where** he is from.*" (John 7:27)

The text continues immediately:

> *Then Jesus cried out as he was teaching in the temple, "You know me, and you know where I am from. I have not come on my own. But the one who sent me is true, and you do not know him. I know him, because I am from him, and he sent me." Then they tried to arrest him, but no one laid hands on him, because his hour had not yet come.* (John 7:28-30)

The link between this text and the story of the wine miracle is obvious: the steward "did not know **where** the wine came from," (John 2:9)—and here the Jerusalemites think they know exactly **where** Jesus comes from because the one whose glory was revealed in the wine miracle comes from Nazareth, an altogether insignificant village (John 1:46). The Jerusalemites are quite sure of that—and yet in reality they do not know **where** Jesus ultimately comes from because they do not believe in Jesus' messianic secret and his coming from God. They are mistaken about the true "where" of Jesus (cf. also John 8:14; 9:29-30; 19:9). Thus the keyword "where" in the Cana narrative prepares for later conflicts in John's gospel.

Then is the steward a purely negative figure, like some of the Jerusalemites later (cf. differently John 7:31)? We need to be cautious here, because we cannot draw that conclusion from the story. At this point things are not as critical as they will become in the course of the gospel. In a certain sense everything is still open: not everyone can see; not everyone is in a position to understand. Those who do not see and do not understand may yet come to believe, or they may come to be opponents of Jesus. But in any case they are important, perhaps even just as important as those who already understand.

In this connection let us consider Mary again. She, too, as we have seen, did not yet understand everything within the Cana story. She will appear only once more in the course of the narrative, at Jesus' execution, and it is only beneath the cross that she reaches full understanding. On the cross Jesus again takes up the address "woman" from the Cana narrative and says to her: "Woman, behold your son!" (John 19:26). In this way the dying Jesus links his mother with the disciple who embodies the believing, understanding church. The church comes into existence beneath the cross, made up of hopeful Israel and the already-believing disciples.

So, as we have said, within the Cana story Mary has not nearly understood everything, but she is *on the way* to understanding, and despite her lack of understanding she aids the success of the drama of God's wedding with the world. She helps with her sober nature and her Jewish realism. She helps by saying, "They have no wine" and requesting of the servants, "Do whatever he tells you." She trusts her son; indeed, she entrusts herself to him, even though she does not yet understand everything. Evidently that is something important; in fact, it is decisive.

But what about the steward? He understands nothing at all; he is incomprehension in person, and yet he also helps to make the wedding a success. He is indispensable to the narrative. He helps with his amazement; he helps by calling to mind, through his citation of the notorious "rule for wine," how things normally go in this world: deception and subtle trickery. He even helps by applying his talent for organization. He is indispensable.

Is it really so bad not to understand everything yet? *From a purely historical point of view* the Jesus movement was a colorful collage. There were the Twelve, then a larger number of disciples, then people who wanted to be healed and therefore joined Jesus' following; there were those already healed who had returned home and gratefully told others about their healing; there were friends, companions, supporters, occasional helpers, the curious, even profiteers. Not even the Twelve, who unconditionally followed Jesus, comprehended everything. Only after Easter did they gradually come to understand.

And What about Us?

Isn't the same true about us? All of us, without exception, have not understood everything—not by a long shot. Sometimes we believe with our whole existence, but often we are tempted and full of questions. We suffer from the church as it really exists, but we suffer even more from ourselves. We are lame, deaf, skeptical, distracted. In our midst Jesus constantly turns water into wine—and we don't even notice what is happening.

Nevertheless, we can take our parts in the great drama that began with the faith of Abraham, who left his paternal home and motherland simply to answer God's call. We can be participants in the thrilling drama in which Israel's prophets, even when they were ridiculed, persecuted, and killed, showed this people the true God. We can take part in that unbelievable story of Israel in which faith and hope are never destroyed: the story that, despite all resistance, led to Jesus, he who is now forever the way, the truth, and the life (John 14:6).

And Jesus is not dead. He lives and has become the unchangeable goal of this great drama that one day will transform the whole world. Each of us, in our own ways, can play our parts in this apparently confusing world drama that will prove to be a rapturously festive marriage feast, one on which the sun will never set. The best wine will be savored only at the end.

Acknowledgments

Every attentive reader will have noticed that this book was not composed in a single extended effort. It contains seventy interpretations of biblical texts that I have presented in a wide variety of situations in recent years.

The short pieces "The Treasure of 'Now'" (p. 71) and "Inattentive" (p. 320) fall somewhere out of the frame, but I hope they will interest my readers. Formally distinct is also the lecture "Spiritual Communities in Light of the Bible" (p. 78), which I presented on November 16, 2016, at the annual meeting of the Jesusbruderschaft in Gnadenthal and the family communities of the EKD (Evangelical Lutheran Church in Germany). I have included it in this book because it speaks of what I consider fundamentals for addressing current questions.

But let me come to the point! I thank my brother Norbert, who read the manuscript of this book and suggested some important improvements. Likewise helpful was my uninterrupted exchange with my friend Marius Reiser, who is much more familiar with ancient literature than I. Thank you, Marius, for all your suggestions!

As always, I should at this point mention my patient assistant Hans Pachner, who located the necessary literature for me; then Raphael Jaklitsch, my IT-specialist, who is always on the spot when I am battling with my computer; and, not least, Herr Dr. Bruno Steimer of Herder Publishing, who suggested this book and supported it from the outset with his experience and skill.

Once again I send special thanks to Freiburg, to Frau Francesca Bressan of Herder's foreign rights division. It is thanks to her courtesy and diligence that so many of my books have appeared in other languages. *Grazie mille*, Francesca!

A hearty handshake to my house community: Carmelita and Gerd Block and Elisabeth Weinzierl. They listened carefully to many of the new texts, pointed out inconsistencies, and with their knowledge and joy have lent life to my work.

And now finally to those whom I must by no means forget: I greet all my readers with much gratitude. Even in times of COVID-19 and despite the closing of bookshops they did not let themselves be prevented from acquiring my books and—most important of all—reading them.

Gerhard Lohfink

Locating the Individual Chapters
in the Church Year

Most of the chapters in this book explore texts that occur in the lectionary for Sundays and feast days. The following list should be an aid to locating them within the church year, or at least in the Roman Catholic lectionary. The letters A, B, and C represent the three years in the lectionary cycle.

Year(s)	Sunday or Feast Day	Title	Page
C	Third Sunday in Lent	Does God Have a Name?	31
C	Third Sunday of Easter	The Longest Easter Story	153
C	Sixth Sunday of Easter	Can Memory Save?	73
C	Trinity Sunday	The Self-Giving God	177
C	Second Sunday in Ordinary Time	The Miracle at Cana	343
C	Thirteenth Sunday in Ordinary Time	A Cloak Flies through the Air	272
C	Sixteenth Sunday in Ordinary Time	Mary and Martha	276
C	Seventeenth Sunday in Ordinary Time	The Strangeness of the Our Father	308
C	Nineteenth Sunday in Ordinary Time	Active Waiting	339
C	Twenty-second Sunday in Ordinary Time	Table Arrangements in the Reign of God	247
C	Twenty-third Sunday in Ordinary Time	Discipleship: Hard and Easy	232
C	Twenty-seventh Sunday in Ordinary Time	The Two Sides of Faith	35
C	Twenty-seventh Sunday in Ordinary Time	A World Transformed	41
C	Twenty-ninth Sunday in Ordinary Time	A Battle in the Wilderness	265
C	Thirty-first Sunday in Ordinary Time	Zacchaeus's Joy	211

Index of Scripture Passages